Undesirable but Unreturnable Migrants: The Challenges of Dealing with Criminal Migrants in Need of Protection

International Refugee Law Series

VOLUME 25

The titles published in this series are listed at *brill.com/irls*

Undesirable but Unreturnable Migrants: The Challenges of Dealing with Criminal Migrants in Need of Protection

A Comparative Analysis of Australia, Belgium and Canada

By

Júlia Zomignani Barboza

BRILL | NIJHOFF

LEIDEN | BOSTON

Library of Congress Cataloging-in-Publication Data

Names: Barboza, Júlia Zomignani author
Title: Undesirable but unreturnable migrants : the challenges of dealing with criminal migrants in need of protection : a comparative analysis of Australia, Belgium, and Canada / Júlia Zomignani Barboza.
Description: Leiden ; Boston : Brill Academic Publishers, Inc, 2026. | Series: International refugee law series ; volume 25 | Includes bibliographical references and index.
Identifiers: LCCN 2025029966 | ISBN 9789004719903 hardback | ISBN 9789004719910 epub
Subjects: LCSH: Emigration and immigration law--Australia--Criminal provisions | Emigration and immigration law--Belgium--Criminal provisions | Emigration and immigration law--Canada--Criminal provisions | Refoulement--Australia | Refoulement--Belgium | Refoulement--Canada | Illegal immigration--Australia | Illegal immigration--Belgium | Illegal immigration--Canada
Classification: LCC K3275 .B39 2026 | DDC 342.7108/2--DC23/ENG/20250711
LC record available at https://lccn.loc.gov/2025029966

Typeface for the Latin, Greek, and Cyrillic scripts: "Brill". See and download: brill.com/brill-typeface.

ISSN 2213–3836
ISBN 978-90-04-71990-3 (hardback)
ISBN 978-90-04-71991-0 (e-book)
DOI 10.1163/9789004719910

Contents

Acknowledgements

This book is based on my Ph.D. research, which was conducted between 2018 and 2024. Before sharing it would with you, I would thus like to thank the members of my Ph.D. advisory committee, my supervisor Paul de Hert and my former colleague (and current friend) Amy Weatherburn. They gave me the academic guidance (and often emotional support) necessary to complete my research. I would also like to thank Sarah Singer, who during my research stay in London gave me very accurate feedback and allowed me to unblock my case studies, which are the backbone of this book. Thank you as well to the two remaining members of my Ph.D. jury, Kristin Henrard and Stefaan Smis, whose feedback further allowed me to improve the research.

I conducted my Ph.D. research as part of the Fundamental Rights Research Centre of the Vrije Universiteit Brussel, where I was lucky to benefit from a welcoming and supportive environment, which helped me progress with the research, even during the hardest moments. I thus also want to thank my former colleagues from the research group for all the encouragement, guidance and patience throughout the years when the research was conducted.

Lastly, I would like to thank my family for their unconditional love and my partner for always being there for me.

Introduction

Migration and security are two topics that are frequently conflated in migration policies as States try to keep undesirable migrants – such as criminals or suspected terrorists – out of their territory. This is why States usually insert clauses in their national laws to ensure such migrants are deprived of the right to enter or stay within their borders. States' default response to these undesirable migrants, who are sometimes considered a threat to national security due to their acts, is to start procedures to return them to their country of origin. However, when there is a risk that undesirable migrants will be subjected to ill-treatment, such as torture or extrajudicial execution upon return, human rights law provides broad protection against their removal, as it sets an absolute prohibition (known as non-refoulement) on returning someone in these conditions.[1] This prohibition derives from the fundamental right to life, which accepts no derogation,[2] and the right to be free from torture (or the prohibition of torture), which is an absolute peremptory norm of international law.[3] Consequently, there are no exceptions that States can use to justify expulsions that would violate non-refoulement obligations. These migrants are thus und-

1 In this regard, the United Nations (UN) Special Rapporteur on the human rights of migrants stated that "[T]he prohibition of torture and ill-treatment is further developed by the absolute and non-derogable principle of non-refoulement, which prohibits States from deporting any person to another State's jurisdiction or any other territory where there are substantial grounds for believing that he or she would be in danger of being subjected to torture or ill-treatment or other serious human rights violations, or where there would be a real risk of such violations." (Human Rights Council (2018). Report of the Special Rapporteur on the human rights of migrants (A/HRC/38/41). United Nations, para. 20).

2 According to the UN Human Rights Committee, the right to life "(...) is the supreme right from which no derogation is permitted even in time of public emergency which threatens the life of the nation" (Human Rights Committee (1982). General comment No. 6: Article 6 (Right to life). Office of the High Commissioner for Human Rights, para. 1).

3 See, e.g. Chahal v. United Kingdom, 22414/93 (European Court of Human Right, 15 November 1996), paras. 79–81; Human Rights Committee (1992). CCPR General Comment No. 20: Article 7 (Prohibition of Torture, or Other Cruel, Inhuman or Degrading Treatment or Punishment); Human Rights Committee (2006). Consideration of Reports Submitted by States Parties under Article 40 of the Covenant (CCPR/C/CAN/CO/5), para. 15; Communication No. 39/1996, CAT/C/18/D/39/1996 (Committee Against Torture, 28 April 1997), para. 14.5; Committee Against Torture (2005). Summary Record of the Public Part of the 652nd Meeting (CAT/C/SR.652), para. 59; Committee Against Torture (2007). Consideration of Reports Submitted by States Parties under Article 19 of the Convention (CAT/C/NPL/CO/2), para. 17; and Committee Against Torture (2006). Consideration of Reports Submitted by States Parties under Article 19 of the Convention (CAT/C/FRA/CO/3), para. 6.

 | DOI:10.1163/9789004719910_002

esirable (due to their criminal acts or for being a threat to security) but also unreturnable (due to the non-refoulement obligations owed to them). From now on, they will be referred to as undesirable but unreturnable migrants. As returning them would violate international law, host States are thus forced to find a different solution to regulate their situation.

The challenge of identifying an alternative solution for these migrants has been the object of debate by scholars. Indeed, there is an emerging literature on the topic of undesirable but unreturnable migrants, which has found its most fertile period between 2014 and 2016 with the Refugee Law Initiative research project on the topic.[4] The project concluded with a conference in January 2016, during which numerous participants contributed to the existing literature on the topic. Some of the papers led to special editions of the Refugee Survey Quarterly[5] and the Journal of International Criminal Justice[6] in 2017.

Building on the work done by the scholars who participated in the conference as well as by others working on this topic, this book aims to study some of the different solutions used by States to regulate the situation of undesirable but unreturnable migrants. It does so by first presenting some of the solutions discussed in the literature and subsequently exploring in depth how three States – Australia, Belgium and Canada – regulate the situation of these migrants. These countries have diverse systems in place to address the issue, allowing different measures to be analysed, and also represent different legal systems and a geographical variety of destination countries, which allows the analyses to be transferable to other countries. In view of this, the guiding question for this book is: What lessons can be learned from the experiences of Australia, Belgium and Canada when regulating the situation of undesirable but unreturnable migrants?

Overall, it can be said that there has been a tendency to prioritise national security over the rights of migrants,[7] which is particularly relevant when regu-

4 Project website: https://rli.sas.ac.uk/projects-0/undesirable-unreturnable-migrants.

5 Refugee Survey Quarterly, 36(1) (2017).

6 Journal of International Criminal Justice, 15(1) (2017).

7 For example, it has been said that "many counter-terrorist regimes have made significant changes to deportation, immigration and asylum laws. In general, then, the approach of domestic legislatures in enacting new laws on the subject of terrorism after 11 September, 2001 has been to create new criminal sanctions and to increase police and security intelligence organization powers in the pursuit of national security. This has been achieved at a cost to traditional civil liberties and human rights principles in each of the nations and has placed some of the fundamental values and assumptions of each legal system under strain." Golder, B., & Williams, G. (2006). Balancing national security and human rights: assessing

lating the situation of undesirable but unreturnable migrants. In view of this, States sometimes impose very restrictive measures on these migrants, such as indefinite detention, that go against internationally recognised human rights. Taking this into account, when assessing the solutions used by States to regulate the situation of undesirable but unreturnable migrants, this book will evaluate whether the measures in place comply with international human rights law. In this regard, it is important to note that all three analysed States are signatories to most of the core international human rights instruments,[8] as well as to the 1951 Convention Relating to the Status of Refugees (hereafter Refugee Convention), an instrument that may serve to grant protection against return to some undesirable but unreturnable migrants.[9] They should thus all apply the same human rights standards when defining migration law and policy.

The analysis of the solutions applied in these countries to regulate the situation of undesirable but unreturnable migrants is based on the legislation in place in each country. To ensure the interpretation of such legislation is correctly reflected in this book, the Case Law of the courts responsible for assessing jurisdictional errors, which determine the correct interpretation of the applicable law, is relied upon. Thus, in each country, the court of cassation handling migration procedures was identified, and the relevant cases analysed. In Australia, the relevant court was the Federal Court of Australia (at both first instance and appeal level); in Belgium, the Aliens Litigation Council (for decisions other than asylum) and the Council of State; and, lastly, in Can-

---

the legal response of common law nations to the threat of terrorism. Journal of Comparative Policy Analysis: Research and Practice, 8(1), 43–62, p. 47.

8 According to the United Nation's Office of the High Commissioner for Human Rights, the core human rights instruments are as follows: International Convention on the Elimination of All Forms of Racial Discrimination (ICERD), International Covenant on Civil and Political Rights (ICCPR), International Covenant on Economic, Social and Cultural Rights (ICESCR), Convention on the Elimination of All Forms of Discrimination against Women (CEDAW), Convention against Torture and Other Cruel, Inhuman or Degrading Treatment or Punishment (CAT), International Convention on the Protection of the Rights of All Migrant Workers and Members of Their Families (ICMW), International Convention for the Protection of All Persons from Enforced Disappearance (CPED), Convention on the Rights of Persons with Disabilities (CRPD) as well as the optional protocols to these treaties, when applicable. (See United Nations Office of the High Commissioner for Human Rights, The Core International Human Rights Instruments and their monitoring bodies. Available at: https://www.ohchr.org/EN/ProfessionalInterest/Pages/CoreInstruments.aspx). Australia is a party to all treaties except the ICMW and the CPED; Belgium and Canada are a party to all except the ICMW.

9 As will be shown later in this book, unreturnable migrants are likely to turn to refugee law to seek protection from removal to a place where they fear harm.

ada, the Federal Court and Federal Court of Appeal. The research this book is based on focused on cases decided between 1 January 2015 and 31 December 2020, and thus most of the cases referred to in this book are from this period.[10] To ensure the book's relevance at the time of writing, however, where needed to reflect recent developments, landmark cases decided after 31 December 2020 are also presented. Literature on the situation of undesirable but unreturnable migrants in the countries under study is also relied upon. In this regard, it is important to note that Australia and Canada were studied in the context of the abovementioned Refugee Law Initiative research project,[11] and thus the current work builds on the findings made then. Australia, Belgium and Canada were also studied by Rikhof in his work on exclusion from refugee status.[12] As the topic of exclusion somewhat intersects with that of undesirable but unreturnable migrants, the case studies in this book also build on his work.

After studying the solutions applied in Australia, Belgium and Canada to regulate the situation of undesirable but unreturnable migrants, this book presents the common grounds in State practice regarding who States consider undesirable, who they consider unreturnable, how these conclusions are reached, and, finally, which measures are then applied to regulate the situation of these migrants. Building on these findings, this book also proposes a possible solution on how States can regulate the situation of undesirable but unreturnable migrants while complying with their international human rights obligations.

The international human rights framework against which measures applied to regulate the situation of undesirable but unreturnable migrants will be assessed in this book is defined by global international treaties and is not limited to any region or specific State. To interpret such instruments, however, the Case Law of international, regional and national judicial or quasi-judicial bodies is relied upon. It is thus relevant to note that while regional treaties or national laws may be analysed, such instruments will be looked at in as much as the rights prescribed in them are equivalent to the rights laid down by international treaties.

10 The initial research analysed 99 cases decided in this period Australia, 291 in Belgium and 208 in Canada.

11 The work on these countries resulted in the following articles: Juss, S. S. (2017). Detention and delusion in Australia's Kafkaesque Refugee Law. Refugee Survey Quarterly, 36(1), 146–167; and Bond, J. (2017). Unwanted but unremovable: Canada's treatment of "criminal" migrants who cannot be removed. Refugee Survey Quarterly, 36(1), 168–186.

12 See Rikhof, J. (2023). Exclusion and Refoulement: Criminality in International and Domestic Refugee Law. Irwin Law Inc.

The main instruments guiding the human rights analysis of this book, therefore, are the International Covenant on Civil and Political Rights (ICCPR), the International Covenant on Economic, Social and Cultural Rights (ICESCR), the Convention and Protocol Relating to the Status of Refugees (Refugee Convention) and the Convention against Torture and Other Cruel, Inhuman or Degrading Treatment or Punishment (Convention against Torture).

CHAPTER 1

The Challenge of Regulating the Situation of Undesirable but Unreturnable Migrants

1 Introduction

Migration and security are two topics that are frequently conflated in migration policies as States try to keep criminal or dangerous non-nationals[1] out of their territory. This is why States usually insert clauses in their national laws to ensure such migrants are deprived of the right to enter or stay within their borders. These migrants, who are banned for having engaged in criminal activities or who, due to their actions or behaviours, are considered a threat to national security or public order in their host State, are the undesirable migrants that are the focus of this book.[2]

Once a migrant is considered undesirable, States seem to have a unified way of handling them, that is, returning them to their country of origin. Return, however, will sometimes be halted by international law – more specifically by refugee law or human rights law.[3] This is because these bodies of law protect migrants from being sent back to a place where they may face gross human rights violations. Thus, some migrants will be undesirable but also unreturnable.

Regulating the situation of these migrants, hereafter referred to as undesirable but unreturnable migrants, can be challenging for host States, as they may be obliged to keep such migrants in their territory for long periods if the human rights concerns that prevent their return are not resolved. At the same

1 In this book, the words migrant, alien and non-national are used interchangeably to refer to a person who does not have the nationality of the country where they are. Although it is recognised that the term migrant can relate to both international and internal migrants, in this book, the word migrant will be applied exclusively to refer to third-country nationals, that is, international migrants.

2 As each country may have its own rules about who is undesirable, the laws applicable in each of the countries analysed in this book will be spelled out in the relevant chapters and any common ground between these definitions is mentioned in Chapter 5.

3 Return may also be halted by more practical impediments to return, for instance, lack of travel documents or unavailable means of travel. This book only focuses on cases of unreturnability due to human rights concerns, and thus other instances are not directly addressed in this work. Some of the conclusions, however, will be transferable to all cases of unreturnability.

 | DOI:10.1163/9789004719910_003

time, States may wish to protect their national security or community from criminal or dangerous individuals, as undesirable migrants may be. Numerous solutions have been proposed and applied to regulate the situation of these migrants, but they all pose challenges to the host State.

This chapter is thus dedicated to explaining who undesirable migrants are, the legal framework that can make undesirable migrants unreturnable, and presenting some of the solutions proposed to regulate their situation, positioning the topic of undesirable but unreturnable migrants in the literature.

2 Undesirable Migrants: Who Are They and What Is the Consequence of Undesirability?

Since the terrorist attacks of 11 September, 2001, in the United States, there has been a growing securitisation of migration and a consequent association between migrants and threats to security. As Kidane puts it:

> Although the link between national security and immigration is by no means contemporary, the existing level of intersection between antiterrorism laws and immigration is essentially a post-9/11 phenomenon. The reason for this phenomenon is that the 9/11 attacks were planned and executed by aliens.[4]

In view of this, States have been changing their laws and policies to strengthen their border controls. In some cases, States have been said to do so in violation of the rights of some of the most vulnerable migrants, that is, asylum seekers[5] and refugees.[6] For example, Top noted that the fight against terrorism has had

4 Kidane, W. (2009). The terrorism bar to asylum in Australia, Canada, the United Kingdom, and the United States: transporting best practices. Fordham International Law Journal, 33(2), 300–371, p. 301.

5 Refugee status is declaratory, not constitutive; "(…) usual practice, however, is to refer to someone seeking refugee status as an asylum seeker, while those successfully accorded refugee status are refugees" (Gilbert, G. (2017). Undesirable but unreturnable extradition and other forms of rendition. Journal of International Criminal Justice, 15(1), 55–74, p. 57). Therefore, throughout this book, asylum seekers are considered those seeking asylum and/or undergoing refugee status determination process, but not yet formally recognised as refugees.

6 This book considers as refugees those who fall within the refugee definition contained in article 1 of the Refugee Convention. That is, any person who "owing to well-founded fear of being persecuted for reasons of race, religion, nationality, membership of a particular social group or political opinion, is outside the country of his nationality and is unable or, owing to

important consequences on the protection of asylum seekers who face political persecution through prosecution – that is, those accused of political crimes. While migrants accused of political crimes would once find protection in other countries, Top notes that this protection:

> (…) has not only weakened, but even disappeared from some institutional settings, such as the European Union (EU). In a context where the war on terror is at the top of the agenda, this development has significant adverse consequences on the asylum possibilities for political activists, as there are ever fewer offences that are considered to be 'political' and thus eligible for protection.[7]

This securitisation of migration, however, has significant consequences not only for asylum seekers but also for the lives of migrants in general. Indeed, the trend to associate security and migration more broadly (that is, going beyond refugee protection) was mentioned by different scholars around the world throughout the years.[8] It has been marked by the creation of the term Crimmigration Law,[9] currently used in academic discourse in different countries as varied as the United States,[10] Poland[11] and Brazil.[12]

---

such fear, is unwilling to avail himself of the protection of that country; or who, not having a nationality and being outside the country of his former habitual residence as a result of such events, is unable or, owing to such fear, is unwilling to return to it" (article 1(A), Refugee Convention), and who does not fall under articles 1C, 1D, 1E or 1F of the same Convention. This definition is explained in more detail in Section 3.1 below.

7 Top, S. (2018). The collapse of the political offence exemption in EU extradition law: the end of political asylum? In E. Kuzelewska, A. Weatherburn, & D. Kloza (Eds.), Irregular Migration as a Challenge for Democracy (Vol. 5, pp. 165–177). Intersentia, p. 166.

8 See, e.g. Kodiyath, S. P., & Padathu Veettil, S. (2017). Invisible people: suspected LTTE members in the special refugee camps of Tamil Nadu. Refugee Survey Quarterly, 36(1), 126–145, p. 145; Golder, B., & Williams, G. (2006). Balancing national security and human rights: Assessing the legal response of common law nations to the threat of terrorism. Journal of Comparative Policy Analysis: Research and Practice, 8(1), 43–62, p. 47.

9 This term refers to the increasing conflation between immigration law and criminal law. This conflation was noted by different authors, including not only the ones referenced elsewhere in this section, but also Bigo (see, e.g. Bigo, D. (1998). Sécurité et immigration: Vers une gouvernementalité par linquiétude ? Cultures & Conflicts, 31–32, 1–19); Mitsilegas (see, e.g. G. L. Gatta, V. Mitsilegas, & S. Zirulia (Eds.). (2022). Controlling Immigration through Criminal Law: European and Comparative Perspectives on "Crimmigration" (1st ed.). Hart Publishing; Mitsilegas, V. (2018). European criminal law and the dangerous citizen. Maastricht Journal of European and Comparative Law, 25(6), 733–751; Mitsilegas, V. (2017). The Security Union as a paradigm of preventive justice: Challenges for citizenship, fundamental rights and the rule of law. In S. Carrera & V. Mitsilegas (Eds.), Constitutionalising the Security Union: Effectiveness, Rule of Law and Rights in Countering Terrorism and

In 2018, Chlebny noted that this could have important human rights consequences when she said:

> As a result of the threat of terror and mass immigration to Europe, the immigration law has become stricter. (...) In these circumstances more than ever before an administrative court judge is confronted with problems of human rights in the context of threat to public order and national security.[13]

The association between migration and security also has important policy consequences. For example, D'Appollonia noted that:

> The association between immigration and integration issues on one side, and insecurity on the other, are now deeply ingrained in public discourse and policy on both sides of the Atlantic. Collectively, they have produced what I have elsewhere characterized as the securitization of immigration governance. It is a process through which Western political elites – governments, leading political parties, and associated policy networks – rhetorically frame immigration as a security threat. This characterization produces a series of policies that justify an expansion of state powers, often at the expense of civil liberties.[14]

Crime (pp. 5–20). Centre for European Policy Studies (CEPS)) and Bello (Bello, V. (2022). The spiralling of the securitisation of migration in the EU: From the management of a 'crisis' to a governance of human mobility? Journal of Ethnic and Migration Studies, 48(6), 1327–1344).

10 See, e.g. Saad-Diniz, E. (2018). Crimmigration Law. International Journal of Refugee Law. 30(2), 401–403.

11 See, e.g. Perkowska, M. (2018). The impact of the migration crisis on Polish immigration and criminal law. In E. Kuzelewska, A. Weatherburn, & D. Kloza (Eds.), Irregular Migration as a Challenge for Democracy (Vol. 5, pp. 165–177). Intersentia.

12 See, e.g. Zago de Moraes, A. L. (2015). Crimigração: A Relação Entre Política Migratória e Polítical Criminal no Brasil (Ph.D. Thesis, Pontifícia Universidade Católica – RS).

13 Chlebny, J. (2018). Public order, national security and the rights of third-country nationals in immigration cases. European Journal of Migration and Law, 20(2), 115–134, p. 116.

14 d'Appollonia, A. C. (2015). Migrant Mobilization and Securitization in the US and Europe – How Does It Feel to Be a Threat? Palgrave Macmillan, p. 3.

Top also mentions that migrants may end up being the object of repressive policies and suffer from actual or symbolic violence in their country of residence.[15]

Apart from the hostility that can be directed towards migrants in view of these policies, another consequence may be that States apply stricter restrictions as to who is allowed in. In this regard, with a view towards protecting their national security or community, States usually insert clauses in their national laws to ensure migrants who have been involved in criminal activities or migrants who are considered a threat to security (such as suspected terrorists) are deprived of the right to enter or stay within their borders. This is the case in all three States that will be studied in the following chapters of this book. In Australia, for example, those who request international protection[16] will be denied a protection visa if they are deemed to be a risk to security or if they have been convicted of a serious crime.[17] Similarly, any third-country national may be refused a visa to enter Australia or have an existing visa cancelled if they have a substantial criminal record, have committed certain specified crimes or if there are reasonable suspicions that the concerned person has committed certain criminal acts or is involved with criminal groups.[18] In Belgium, residence permits can be rejected or cancelled for public order or national security reasons.[19] Similarly, in Canada, those who have been involved in criminality, serious criminality, organised criminality, human rights violations or are considered a threat to security will be deemed inadmissible to the country and will not be allowed to enter or stay in the country.[20]

---

15 Top, S. (2018), p. 177.

16 According to the United Nations High Commissioner for Refugees (UNHCR), "[T]he need for international protection arises when a person is outside their own country and unable to return home because they would be at risk there, and their country is unable or unwilling to protect them" (UNHCR (2018). Persons in need of international protection. International Journal of Refugee Law, 30(1), 134–139, p. 134). Thus, building on this concept, in this book, international protection is defined as the protection against return to a place where the concerned migrant would be at risk of human rights violations.

17 Section 36, Migration Act 1958: https://www.legislation.gov.au/C1958A00062/latest/text.

18 Section 501, Migration Act 1958: https://www.legislation.gov.au/C1958A00062/latest/text.

19 See, e.g. articles 21, 22, and 44bis, Loi du 15 décembre 1980 sur l'accès au territoire, le séjour, l'établissement et l'éloignement des étrangers / Wet van 15 December 1980 betreffende de toegang tot het grondgebied, het verblijf, de vestiging en de verwijdering van vreemdelingen: https://www.ejustice.just.fgov.be/eli/loi/1980/12/15/1980121550/justel.

20 Sections 34 to 37, Immigration and Refugee Protection Act of 2001: https://laws.justice.gc.ca/eng/acts/i-2.5/.

Provisions of this type can be found in multiple jurisdictions. Once they are triggered, States usually start return procedures, as the concerned migrant most likely does not have the right to stay in the country (either because this right was denied or because it was withdrawn). Indeed, in Poland, Perkowska noted that "[W]here a non-citizen violates immigration law that has been defined as criminal, or commits a crime that is a deportable offence, both incarceration and deportation may result."[21] A similar remark was made in international media about the United States. When noting that at least a thousand foreigners who served in the United States army are estimated to have been later removed from the country following a criminal conviction, it was said that these veterans suffer a double penalty: first the criminal conviction, then exile.[22]

In practice, migrants are often returned to their country of origin, where they (most likely) have a right to enter and reside. It should be noted, however, that returning third-country nationals may interfere with their rights. While preventing crime and protecting national security or public order may be valid reasons for such interference, there are instances in which such interference will not be acceptable and, therefore, may put a halt to return (making the concerned migrants unreturnable).

In this context, the next section will discuss the two main bodies of international law that protect migrants against return, namely refugee law and human rights law.

3 International Protection: How Can International Law Prevent Return to Harm (Thus Creating Unreturnable Migrants)?

3.1 *The Protection Stemming from Refugee Law*

Refugee law is the body of law that seeks to protect migrants from persecution in their country of origin. The main refugee law instrument is the 1951 Convention Relating to the Status of Refugees[23] (hereafter Refugee Convention).

21 Perkowska, M. (2018), p. 209.

22 Arratibel, A. J. (28 May 2023). Récit. "Les États-Unis sont ma patrie" : ces vétérans de l'armée américaine renvoyés au Mexique. Courrier International. Available at: https://www.courrierinternational.com/long-format/recit-les-etats-unis-sont-ma-patrie-ces-veterans-de-l-armee-americaine-renvoyes-au-mexique.

23 UN General Assembly, Convention Relating to the Status of Refugees, 28 July 1951, United Nations, Treaty Series, vol. 189, p. 137 (hereafter Refugee Convention).

According to the United Nations (hereafter UN) Refugee Agency, the Office of the High Commissioner for Refugees (hereafter UNHCR), this convention:

> (…) provides a universal code for the treatment of refugees uprooted from their countries as a result of persecution, including serious human rights violations or other forms of serious harm, as well as in the context of violence or armed conflict. Its key elements include: a definition of the term refugee (with provisions for inclusion, exclusion and cessation); a guarantee of protection against refoulement; and a set of minimum civil, political, economic, social and cultural rights.[24]

As this short description by UNHCR notes, the Refugee Convention contains inclusion clauses (which define who is a refugee), cessation clauses (which determine when a refugee is no longer in need of protection) and exclusion clauses (which exclude from refugee status those who are considered undeserving of it).

Regarding inclusion clauses, according to article 1A(2) of the Refugee Convention, a refugee is someone who "owing to well-founded fear of being persecuted for reasons of race, religion, nationality, membership of a particular social group or political opinion, is outside the country of his nationality and is unable or, owing to such fear, is unwilling to avail himself of the protection of that country." The main protection afforded to those who fall under this definition is (refugee law) non-refoulement, which is materialised in the Refugee Convention in article 33(1). This article states that "[N]o Contracting State shall expel or return ("refouler") a refugee in any manner whatsoever to the frontiers of territories where his life or freedom would be threatened on account of his race, religion, nationality, membership of a particular social group or political opinion."

Cessation clauses, defined in article 1C of the Refugee Convention, in turn, determine when this protection is no longer needed and thus when a migrant ceases to be a refugee. They include, among others, when the concerned refugee obtains the nationality of the country of asylum, re-avails themselves of the protection of their own country, or when they are no longer at risk (because the circumstances in connexion with which they have been recognised as a refugee have ceased to exist).

---

24 UNHCR (2019). Handbook on Procedures and Criteria for Determining Refugee Status under the 1951 Convention and the 1967 Protocol relating to the Status of Refugees (HCR/1P/4/ENG/REV. 4), p. 9.

Finally, regarding exclusion clauses, Rikhof noted that while the Refugee Convention was drafted primarily as:

> (…) a vehicle for the protection for people seeking asylum status, it was felt that persons who had been involved in criminal activity should not benefit from such generosity. With the memory of the Second World War still fresh in the mind of the drafters of the Refugee Convention, a clause denying asylum rights to criminals did not take long to become embedded in the text of this instrument.[25]

This clause is article 1F of the Refugee Convention, which denies refugee status to those who are considered undeserving of being granted asylum due to their past deeds. This article states that:

> The provisions of this Convention shall not apply to any person with respect to whom there are serious reasons for considering that:
> (a) he has committed a crime against peace, a war crime or a crime against humanity, as defined in the international instruments drawn up to make provision in respect of such crimes;
> (b) he has committed a serious non-political crime outside the country of refuge prior to his admission to that country as a refugee;
> (c) he has been guilty of acts contrary to the purposes and principles of the United Nations.

In a similar manner, the Refugee Convention, in article 33(2), creates an exception to the (refugee law) non-refoulement principle by allowing States to return a refugee to a country where they would face persecution if that person is considered a threat to the security or community of the country of asylum. This provision states that

> 2. The benefit of the present provision [protection from refoulement] may not, however, be claimed by a refugee whom there are reasonable grounds for regarding as a danger to the security of the country in which he is, or who, having been convicted by a final judgment of a particularly serious crime, constitutes a danger to the community of that country.

25 Rikhof, J. (2023). Exclusion and Refoulement: Criminality in International and Domestic Refugee Law. Irwin Law Inc., p. 124.

In refugee law, these provisions have different goals. As Gilbert explains, article 1F "(…) prevents someone even qualifying as a refugee"[26] while "Article 33.2, on the other hand, applies to persons who have refugee status in the state of refuge, but whose guarantee of non-refoulement is withdrawn; Article 33.2 does not challenge their refugee status."[27] He further notes, however, that "(…) some governments have fused Articles 1F and 33.2 into one provision when incorporating the Convention into domestic law."[28] Indeed, as will be exemplified in the case studies in the following chapters, articles 1F and 33(2) are often conflated in national law, which tends to unify both provisions into a list of exceptions to granting a visa or permit to migrants requesting protection. These exceptions, however, do not provide States with a carte blanche to return all undesirable migrants, as "[D]espite the potential breadth of the language of Article 33(2), international law indicates that the exceptions should be interpreted restrictively"[29] and the same can be said of Article 1F. Furthermore, as was mentioned above, refugee law is not the only body of international law that protects migrants against return to harm. Human rights law also contains provisions that protect migrants against being sent back to a place where they are at risk. The next section thus discusses the protection granted by this latter body of international law.

3.2 *The Protection Stemming from International Human Rights Law*

The right to life and the right to be free from torture are fundamental rights contained in most international human rights instruments. According to Rikhof, the prohibition of torture and of arbitrary killing have also obtained the status of *ius cogens*, that is, of customary international norms from which no derogation is permitted.[30] The International Covenant on Civil and Political Rights (hereafter ICCPR) prescribes the right to life in its article 6[31] and the

26 Gilbert, G. (2014). Exclusion under Article 1F since 2001: Two steps backwards, one step forward. In V. Chetail & C. Bauloz (Eds.), Research Handbook on International Law and Migration (pp. 519–540). Edward Elgar Publishing, pp. 520–521.

27 Ibid. idem.

28 Ibid. idem.

29 Farmer, A. (2008). Non-refoulement and Jus Cogens: Limiting anti-terror measures that threaten refugee protection. Georgetown Immigration Law Journal, 23, 1–38, p. 11.

30 Rikhof, J. (2023), pp. 9–10.

31 This articles states as follows:

"1. Every human being has the inherent right to life. This right shall be protected by law. No one shall be arbitrarily deprived of his life.

2. In countries which have not abolished the death penalty, sentence of death may be imposed only for the most serious crimes in accordance with the law in force at the time of the commission of the crime and not contrary to the provisions of the present Cove-

right to be free from torture in its article 7.[32] This latter right is further protected by a convention dedicated exclusively to the prohibition of torture – that is, the Convention against Torture and Other Cruel, Inhuman or Degrading Treatment or Punishment (hereafter Convention against Torture).

Both these rights are associated with a prohibition to expel an individual to a country in which they would be subjected to threats to their life or where they may suffer inhumane treatment (the human rights non-refoulement obligation). For example, regarding article 7, the UN Human Rights Committee states that "(...) States parties must not expose individuals to the danger of torture or cruel, inhuman or degrading treatment or punishment upon return to another country by way of their extradition, expulsion or refoulement."[33] Similarly, article 3 of the abovementioned Convention against Torture states that "[N]o State Party shall expel, return ('refouler') or extradite a person to another State where there are substantial grounds for believing that he would be in danger of being subjected to torture."

This prohibition of sending someone back to a place where their right to life or to be free from torture would be at risk is absolute, that is, comprising no exceptions. In this regard, concerning the right to be free from torture, the UN Human Rights Committee stated that:

> 3. The text of article 7 [ICCPR] allows of no limitation. The Committee also reaffirms that, even in situations of public emergency such as those

---

nant and to the Convention on the Prevention and Punishment of the Crime of Genocide. This penalty can only be carried out pursuant to a final judgement rendered by a competent court.

3. When deprivation of life constitutes the crime of genocide, it is understood that nothing in this article shall authorize any State Party to the present Covenant to derogate in any way from any obligation assumed under the provisions of the Convention on the Prevention and Punishment of the Crime of Genocide.

4. Anyone sentenced to death shall have the right to seek pardon or commutation of the sentence. Amnesty, pardon or commutation of the sentence of death may be granted in all cases.

5. Sentence of death shall not be imposed for crimes committed by persons below eighteen years of age and shall not be carried out on pregnant women."

6. Nothing in this article shall be invoked to delay or to prevent the abolition of capital punishment by any State Party to the present Covenant."

32 This article states as follows: "No one shall be subjected to torture or to cruel, inhuman or degrading treatment or punishment. In particular, no one shall be subjected without his free consent to medical or scientific experimentation."

33 Human Rights Committee (1992). General Comment No. 20: Article 7 (Prohibition of Torture, or Other Cruel, Inhuman or Degrading Treatment or Punishment). Office of the High Commissioner for Human Rights, para. 9.

> referred to in article 4 of the Covenant, no derogation from the provision of article 7 is allowed and its provisions must remain in force. The Committee likewise observes that no justification or extenuating circumstances may be invoked to excuse a violation of article 7 for any reasons, including those based on an order from a superior officer or public authority. (...)
>
> 9. In the view of the Committee, States parties must not expose individuals to the danger of torture or cruel, inhuman or degrading treatment or punishment upon return to another country by way of their extradition, expulsion or refoulement.[34]

The absolute prohibition of torture and its consequent non-refoulement obligation have also been expressed by the UN Committee against Torture, which assesses the compliance of State-parties with the Convention against Torture. According to the latter Committee:

> (...) the prohibition of torture, as defined in article 1 of the Convention [against Torture], is absolute. Article 2 (2) of the Convention provides that 'no exceptional circumstances whatsoever, whether a state of war or a threat of war, internal political instability or any other public emergency, may be invoked as a justification of torture'. The Committee further recalls that other acts of ill-treatment are equally prohibited and that the prohibition of ill-treatment is likewise non-derogable.
>
> 9. The principle of 'non-refoulement' of persons to another State where there are substantial grounds for believing that they would be in danger of being subjected to torture is similarly absolute.[35]

Thus, the protection given by human rights law is broader than the one given by refugee law, as it comprises no exception. Considering this difference in protection between these two bodies of law, the next section will look at the

---

34 Ibid., paras. 3 and 9. See also Human Rights Committee (2004). General Comment No. 31 [80] The Nature of the General Legal Obligation Imposed on States Parties to the Covenant (CCPR/C/21/Rev.1/Add. 13). Office of the High Commissioner for Human Rights, para. 12.

35 Committee against Torture (2018). General comment no. 4 (2017) on the implementation of article 3 of the Convention in the context of article 22 (CAT/C/GC/4). United Nations, paras. 8–9.

interaction between refugee law and human rights law with regards to the rights they afford to migrants fleeing harm.

3.3 *The Interactions between Human Rights and Refugee Law: Is Refugee Law Still Relevant?*

As noted in the previous sections, the non-refoulement obligation exists in both refugee law and human rights law. However, the range of this obligation differs within the two bodies of law. In refugee law, there is an exception to such obligation, as article 33(2) of the Refugee Convention provides that non-refoulement "(…) may not, however, be claimed by a refugee whom there are reasonable grounds for regarding as a danger to the security of the country in which he is, or who, having been convicted by a final judgment of a particularly serious crime, constitutes a danger to the community of that country."

In the realm of international human rights law, in turn, no such exception exists, as the protection offered by the right to life and by the prohibition of torture are non-derogable. In this regard, the UN Human Rights Committee said that "[T]he obligation not to extradite, deport or otherwise transfer pursuant to article 6 of the Covenant may be broader than the scope of the principle of non-refoulement under international refugee law, since it may also require the protection of aliens not entitled to refugee status."[36]

Chetail explains some of these differences between the two bodies of law when he notes that refugee law predates human rights law and thus inserts itself in a different historical context. According to him:

> The original design of the [Refugee] Convention and its historical context have heavily shaped the idiosyncratic features of refugee law and exacerbated its differences from subsequent human rights treaties. In schematic terms, refugee law is selective, contingent, and decentralized,

36 Human Rights Committee (2018). General comment no. 36 (2018) on article 6 of the International Covenant on Civil and Political Rights, on the right to life (CCPR/C/GC/36). Office of the High Commissioner for Human Rights, para. 31. Similarly, the UN Special Rapporteur on torture and other cruel, inhuman or degrading treatment or punishment noted that "[W]hile non-refoulement protection under refugee law extends only to persons entitled to refugee status and allows for exceptions based on considerations of national or public security, no such limitation or exception is permissible where deportation would expose a person to a real risk of torture or ill-treatment. As an intrinsic component of the peremptory prohibition of torture, the prohibition of refoulement overrides not only national immigration laws but also contradicting international obligations, such as those of extradition treaties" (Human Rights Council (2018). Report of the Special Rapporteur on torture and other cruel, inhuman or degrading treatment or punishment (A/HRC/37/50). United Nations, para. 37).

> whereas human rights law is inclusive, categorical, and control-oriented. Each of these characteristics unveils their distinctive legal nature but also the potential of their interaction.[37]

In this regard, he further states that "[T]he primary design of refugee protection has dramatically evolved as a result of the subsequent expansion of human rights law."[38]

Rikhof also discusses some of the interactions between refugee law and human rights law. Regarding the different application of the non-refoulement principle in the two bodies of law, he notes that States "(...) have moved beyond the concept contained in article 33 of the Refugee Convention and have recently added human rights *non-refoulement* notions borrowed from the CAT [Convention against Torture] and the ICCPR."[39] In this regard, he further notes that while refugee law protects those who fear persecution for specific reasons, "(...) not all issues arising out of situations of turmoil causing refugee movements are covered by the Refugee Convention,"[40] and that is why concepts such as subsidiary or complementary protection[41] came to "(...) fill the gap between new realities and the existing Convention's legal regime."[42]

Indeed, States often frame both refugee and human rights law protection under the larger umbrella term of international protection, which consists of both refugee protection (as defined by the Refugee Convention) and subsidiary or complementary protection (a status deriving from non-refoulement obligations stemming from human rights law). In practice, however, as will be shown in the case studies in the following chapters, States also extend exclusion clauses to subsidiary or complementary protection, which may lead to a broad range of different scenarios.

In view of the above, it may seem that refugee protection has somewhat lost its relevance, as human rights law provides greater protection against non-

37 Chetail, V. (2021). Moving towards an integrated approach of refugee law and human rights law. In C. Costello, M. Foster, & J. McAdam (Eds.), The Oxford Handbook of International Refugee Law (1st ed., pp. 202–C11.P64). Oxford University Press, p. 205.

38 Ibid., p. 207.

39 Rikhof, J. (2023), p. 25.

40 Ibid., p. 18.

41 In this book, the terms subsidiary and complementary protection are used interchangeably to refer to the protection status offered by States to those who cannot be returned to their country of origin due to human rights concerns but who fall outside the scope of refugee protection.

42 Rikhof, J. (2023), p. 18.

refoulement, and States also grant (subsidiary of complementary) protection status to those who do not meet the refugee definition yet cannot be returned due to human rights concerns. It is important to note, however, that, as mentioned above, the Refugee Convention also guarantees "(...) a set of minimum civil, political, economic, social and cultural rights"[43] to refugees, thus going beyond protection from refoulement. These rights may vary depending on the refugee's migration status in the host country. Chetail summarises Refugee Convention rights according to their level of applicability as follows: all refugees are entitled to:

> (...) the prohibition of discrimination (Article 3), acquisition of movable and immovable property and other rights pertaining thereto (Article 13), free access to domestic courts (Article 16(1)), rationing (Article 20), primary education (Article 22(1)), fiscal equality (Article 29), transfer of assets (Article 30), and protection against refoulement (Article 33(1)).[44]

Refugees in the territory of a State party to the Refugee Convention, regardless of their migration status, in turn, are entitled to "(...) freedom of religion (Article 4), the delivery of identity papers (Article 27), and the prohibition of penalties on account of illegal entry (Article 31(1))."[45] Other Convention rights, however, require regular migration status in the host State, such as lawful presence, lawful stay or habitual residence. These rights include the rights to engage in self-employment (article 18), freely move within the host territory (article 26), protection against expulsion (article 32), association and to form trade unions (article 15), access to wage-earning employment (article 17), practice liberal professions (article 19), housing (article 21), public relief (article 23), protection of labour legislation and social security (article 24), issuance of travel documents (article 28), access to legal assistance (article 16(2)) and the protection of artistic rights and industrial property (article 14).[46]

Besides some of these rights depending on migration status, the level of protection they offer also varies. In this regard, the Refugee Convention provides that refugees should enjoy the rights to freedom of religion, protection

---

43 UNHCR. (2019). Handbook on Procedures and Criteria for Determining Refugee Status under the 1951 Convention and the 1967 Protocol Relating to the Status of Refugees, p. 9.

44 Chetail, V. (2014). Are refugee rights human rights? An unorthodox questioning of the relations between refugee law and human rights law. In R. Rubio Marín, Human rights and immigration (pp. 19–72). Oxford University Press, p. 41.

45 Ibid. idem.

46 Ibid. idem.

of artistic rights and industrial property, access to courts, rationing, primary education, public relief, protection of labour legislation and social security, and fiscal equality in the same way as nationals of the host country do. The rights to acquisition of movable and immovable property, engage in self-employment, practice liberal professions, housing, freedom of movement, and education other than elementary education, in turn, should be accorded to refugees in not less favourable manner than they are granted to migrants generally in the same circumstances. Lastly, regarding the rights to association and access to wage-earning employment, refugees should receive the most favourable treatment accorded to migrants in the same circumstances.[47] Other rights prescribed in the Convention do not contain such qualifications.

As these rights are also prescribed more generally (instead of in relation to refugees) in human rights instruments, Chetail argues that even though these rights are explicitly afforded to refugees by the Refugee Convention, the protection of rights granted to refugees by international refugee law has been somewhat superseded by the protection granted by human rights instruments. According to him:

> Besides granting additional rights to refugees and asylum seekers, general human rights instruments prove to be more adequate and more protective even when the rights in question are already covered by the Geneva [Refugee] Convention. The minimum standards prescribed by refugee status have been increased – and in some instances superseded – by human rights law.[48]

He further notes that:

> (…) the general applicability of human rights to noncitizens coupled with the prohibition of discrimination based on nationality substantially erode the traditional distinction between nationals and aliens which conditions most of the benefits attached to refugee status. In other words, human rights law cogently requires the assimilation to nationals even for rights which are determined by reference to the treatment accorded to aliens under the Geneva [Refugee] Convention.[49]

47 See ibid., p. 42.
48 Ibid., p. 48.
49 Ibid., p. 49.

Hathaway, in turn, is of a different opinion, as he argues that "(…) it is decidedly not the case that general civil and political rights render cognate guarantees in the Refugee Convention superfluous."[50] This is because, among other reasons:

> (…) governments faced with genuine public emergencies are authorized to withdraw all but a few core civil rights from non-citizens, even if the measures taken would ordinarily amount to impermissible discrimination on grounds of national origin, birth, or other status. In contrast, once an individual's refugee status is affirmatively assessed, refugee rights must be honored at all times, including during "time of war or other grave and exceptional circumstances" [article 9 Refugee Convention].[51]

In practice, the Court of Justice of the European Union (hereafter CJEU) identified at least one instance in which the Refugee Convention offered greater protection to refugees in a case concerning the right to public relief.[52] In that case, the CJEU found that although social assistance could be limited to core benefits for beneficiaries of subsidiary protection, refugees were entitled to the same social assistance provided to nationals, regardless of the type of permit they had in the host country (whether temporary or permanent).[53] This is because "(…) both Article 29 of Directive 2011/95 [Qualification Directive, explained below] and Article 23 of the Geneva [Refugee] Convention cover all refugees and do not make the rights to which they are entitled depend on the length of their stay in the Member State concerned or the duration of the residence permit they have."[54] Thus, this case shows that non-discrimination clauses in human rights instruments may not have completely eroded the distinctions between nationals and migrants recognised in the Refugee Convention, at least when it comes to social and economic rights.[55] It further

---

50 Hathaway, J. C. (2021). The Rights of Refugees under International Law (2nd ed.). Cambridge University Press, p. 88.

51 Ibid., p. 89.

52 Case C-713/17 (Court of Justice of the European Union, 21 November 2018).

53 Ibid., paras. 19–20.

54 Ibid., para. 28.

55 In this regard, it is relevant to note that Chetail's abovementioned observation regarding the erosion of the distinctions between nationals and aliens concerned the application of the ICCPR, which sets civil and political rights. Regarding economic, social and cultural rights, Pijnenburg noted that "(…) when realising socio-economic rights, States have a sovereign right to differentiate between people on the move and their own nat-

demonstrates that, at least in some cases, the refugee law instrument may still serve to grant more rights to refugees than they would be entitled to should the Convention not prescribe them.

National efforts to reconcile the different obligations arising from refugee law and human rights law obligations at the national level will be presented in the following Chapters 2 to 4. Before delving into the application of these bodies of law at the national level, however, the next section will present how the European Union (hereafter EU) has tried to create regional consensus on international protection. This serves to provide an example of how the two bodies of law interact in practice.

3.4 *International Protection in the EU: A Practical Example of the Interactions between Refugee Law and Human Rights*

When it comes to refugee protection in the EU, the Charter of Fundamental Rights of the European Union (hereafter EU Charter) states that the right to asylum shall be guaranteed with due respect for the rules of the Refugee Convention (article 18). In this regard, a set of legislative texts has been put in place to harmonise the application of the Refugee Convention in EU Member States, such as the EU Qualification Directive,[56] which defines the qualification of someone as a refugee. It is important to note, however, that in 2026, this Directive will be replaced by the EU Qualification Regulation.[57] This sec-

ionals, provided such limitation is proportionate and serves a legitimate aim. Crucially, the principle of non-discrimination on the ground of nationality allows for more differentiation than on other grounds on account of States' sovereign right to control the entry and stay of foreigners on their territory" (Pijnenburg, A. (2021). At the Frontiers of State Responsibility: Socio-economic Rights and Cooperation on Migration (1st ed.). Intersentia, p. 101). Similarly, Di Pascale noted that "[T]he position of non-citizens under the International Covenant on Economic, Social and Cultural Rights (ICESCR) appears somewhat more limited than under the International Covenant on Civil and Political Rights (ICCPR)" Di Pascale, A. (2014). Italy and unauthorized migration: Between state sovereignty and human rights obligations. In R. Rubio Marín (Ed.), Human Rights and Immigration (pp. 278–310). Oxford University Press, p. 282.

56 Directive 2011/95/EU of the European Parliament and of the Council of 13 December 2011 on standards for the qualification of third-country nationals or stateless persons as beneficiaries of international protection, for a uniform status for refugees or for persons eligible for subsidiary protection, and for the content of the protection granted (hereafter Qualification Directive).

57 Regulation (EU) 2024/1347 of the European Parliament and of the Council of 14 May 2024 on standards for the qualification of third-country nationals or stateless persons as beneficiaries of international protection, for a uniform status for refugees or for persons eligible for subsidiary protection and for the content of the protection

tion will thus present the current framework as well as the changes that will be brought by the new legislation.

The EU is known for having a strong human rights protection system, based on the EU Charter and the European Convention on Human Rights (to which all EU countries are bound), as well as the oversight of these instruments, provided, respectively, by the CJEU and the European Court of Human Rights. Thus, human rights non-refoulement has greatly influenced the regional application of the asylum framework, which, as will be shown below, also includes subsidiary protection.

Regarding inclusion clauses for refugee protection, the Qualification Directive builds on the refugee definition contained in article 1A(2) of the Refugee Convention, further clarifying its interpretation in the EU, as the Refugee Convention does not provide practical guidance on its application. In this regard, the Qualification Directive defines acts of persecution (article 9) and provides the elements to be taken into account to establish the protective grounds prescribed in the Refugee Convention – namely race, religion, nationality, membership of a particular social group or political opinion (article 10). These articles remain largely unchanged in the upcoming Qualification Regulation.

While the Refugee Convention guides the recognition of those who are considered to be refugees, the Qualification Directive and the Qualification Regulation that will succeed it, influenced by human rights law, more broadly refer to international protection, including both refugees and those who qualify for subsidiary protection.[58] Thus, different from the refugee definition, under the Qualification Directive and the upcoming Qualification Regulation, for one to qualify for subsidiary protection, there is no specified reason for persecution, and indiscriminate violence, as opposed to targeted persecution (required in refugee protection), is also considered to constitute serious harm

granted, amending Council Directive 2003/109/EC and repealing Directive 2011/95/EU of the European Parliament and of the Council (hereafter Qualification Regulation).

58 As mentioned in the previous section, the latter are those who, despite not qualifying for refugee status, are deemed to be in need of protection as they risk being subjected to serious harm if returned to their country of origin. This is in line with Article 78 of the Consolidated versions of the Treaty on European Union and the Treaty on the Functioning of the European Union, which establishes that "[T]he Union shall develop a common policy on asylum, subsidiary protection and temporary protection with a view to offering appropriate status to any third-country national requiring international protection and ensuring compliance with the principle of non-refoulement."

(article 15, Qualification Directive and Qualification Regulation). In practice, the subsidiary protection status may enable States to comply with their non-refoulement obligations under human rights law, which, as explained earlier in this chapter, are broader than the non-refoulement principle under refugee law.[59]

Despite this expansion in protection, the EU also extends the exclusion clauses from the Refugee Convention for subsidiary protection, a status based on human rights law, thus potentially limiting the extent of this protection. In this regard, article 1F of the Refugee Convention is very closely mirrored in the Qualification Directive and in the upcoming Qualification Regulation in articles 12(2), regarding refugee status, and 17, regarding subsidiary protection. The latter, however, presents itself more strictly, as it only mentions serious crime, omitting the non-political reference contained in the former as well as in the Refugee Convention. In the upcoming Qualification Regulation, it is also specified that the commission of a serious crime will lead to exclusion from subsidiary protection, whether the crime is committed before or after arrival in the host country. Lastly, article 17(1) of both the Directive and the Regulation includes an extra ground for exclusion from subsidiary protection, which is that the concerned person constitutes a danger to the community or to the national security. Both articles 12 and 17 may also be used to justify the revocation of a previously granted status, a situation that is not regulated by the Refugee Convention.

As noted above, apart from the exclusion clauses of article 1F, article 33(2) of the Refugee Convention also includes an exception to the principle of non-refoulement, despite it being the cornerstone of refugee protection. The wording of article 33(2) is closely followed in article 21 of the Qualification Directive. The exception to non-refoulement in the EU context, however, has lost most of its power when a decision of the CJEU stated that, where returning a

59 The EU also has a third protection status, namely temporary protection, which applies in the event of a mass influx of displaced persons to EU Member States. It is regulated by Council Directive 2001/55/EC of 20 July 2001 on minimum standards for giving temporary protection in the event of a mass influx of displaced persons and on measures promoting a balance of efforts between Member States in receiving such persons and bearing the consequences thereof. At the time of writing, this status was only enacted once, in 2022, to grant status to Ukrainians fleeing the armed conflict in Ukraine. See Council implementing decision (EU) 2022/382 of 4 March 2022 establishing the existence of a mass influx of displaced persons from Ukraine within the meaning of Article 5 of Directive 2001/55/EC, and having the effect of introducing temporary protection. Temporary protection is not addressed in this chapter, as it does not involve an individualised non-refoulement assessment.

refugee would expose them to the risk of their fundamental rights being infringed, the EU member State concerned may not derogate from the principle of non-refoulement under article 33(2) of the Refugee Convention.[60] In view of this, the wording of the upcoming Regulation was changed, and article 21 in the Regulation simply states that "[T]he principle of non-refoulement shall be respected in accordance with Union and international law."

Apart from establishing the principle of non-refoulement and its (now toothless) exception, article 21 of the Qualification Directive also states that "Member States may revoke, end or refuse to renew or to grant the residence permit of (or to) a refugee" who is considered a danger to the security of the member State, or, having been convicted of a serious crime, constitutes a danger to the member State's community. The content of article 33(2) is also included in the Qualification Directive in article 14(4) on revocation of refugee status and in 14(5) as an optional ground for refusal of such status. There is no equivalent in relation to subsidiary protection; however, as explained above, article 17 is framed in stricter terms and thus very close to including both articles 1F and 33(2) of the Refugee Convention (apparently merging the two when it comes to subsidiary protection).

In the upcoming Regulation, the wording of article 14 has been changed to say that where a refugee constitutes a danger to national security or, after having been convicted by a final judgement of a particularly serious crime, constitutes a danger to the community, refugee status shall (instead of may) be revoked. If refugee status has not yet been granted, it may be refused on the same grounds.

The way the wording of article 33(2) was included in article 14 of the Qualification Directive and of the Qualification Regulation thus seems to bring it closer to an exclusion clause. In the Refugee Convention, however, article 33(2) does not serve to exclude someone from refugee status. In this regard, Singer noted that "[A]rticle 14(4) and (5) QD [Qualification Directive] appear to set out new grounds of exclusion from refugee status on the basis of host State security concerns which go beyond those exhaustively set out in the 1951 [Refugee] Convention."[61] In view of this, States have turned to the CJEU to ask

60 Joined Cases C-391/16, C-77/17 and C-78/17 (Court of Justice of the European Union, 14 May 2019), para. 95.

61 Singer, S. (2018). National security, criminality and exclusion from refugee protection under the EU qualification directive: expanding the grounds of exclusion by the back door. Immigration, Asylum and Nationality Law, 32(3), 284–300, p. 299.

whether article 14 of the Qualification Directive served to create a new ground for exclusion from refugee status and whether that was compatible with the Refugee Convention.[62]

When looking at the compatibility between the regional (EU) framework and the international (Refugee Convention) one, the CJEU made three findings that are noteworthy in the context of this chapter. First, the CJEU noted that article 33(2) of the Refugee Convention denies the benefit of the principle of non-refoulement to a refugee. A person who has their protection status revoked in view of articles 14(4) and (5) or 21(2) of the Qualification Directive, in turn, is still protected from return when that would expose the concerned refugee to a risk to their fundamental rights. This is because the Qualification Directive (as well as the other instruments composing the Common European Asylum Framework) must be interpreted and applied in a way that observes the rights guaranteed by the EU Charter. These rights include the absolute prohibition of removal to a State where there is a serious risk that the concerned person would be subjected to the death penalty, torture or other inhuman or degrading treatment or punishment (article 19(2) EU Charter). Thus, the CJEU concluded that EU law provides more extensive international protection than that guaranteed by the Refugee Convention.[63] This is reflected in the wording of article 21 of the Qualification Regulation, as noted above.

Second, regarding articles 14(4) and 14(5) of the Qualification Directive, the CJEU noted that revocation or denial of refugee status under these provisions cannot be interpreted as meaning that the concerned person is not (or is no longer) a refugee for the purposes of the Refugee Convention, if they fit the refugee definition. Thus, these provisions do not create an extra exclusion clause for the purposes of the Refugee Convention. Instead, the consequence of a revocation or denial of status under article 14 is that the concerned refugee will not or will no longer be entitled to all the rights and benefits set out in the Qualification Directive.[64] However, they will continue to be entitled to a certain number of rights laid down in the Refugee Con-

62 Joined Cases C-391/16, C-77/17 and C-78/17 (Court of Justice of the European Union, 14 May 2019).

63 Ibid., paras. 94–95.

64 For example, article 24 of the Qualification Directive provides that "[A]s soon as possible after international protection has been granted, Member States shall issue to beneficiaries of refugee status a residence permit." Article 24(2) of the Qualification Regulation reiterates this.

vention.[65] This reasoning also applies to the new wording of article 14 in the Regulation.[66]

Consequently, the third finding is that those who meet the refugee definition (as provided in the Refugee Convention) but have had their status revoked or denied under article 14(4) or (5) will still enjoy, at a minimum, the rights prescribed in article 14(6)[67] of the Directive (14(3) in the Regulation) and the rights set out in the Refugee Convention that are guaranteed for any refugee who is present in the territory of a contracting State and do not require a lawful stay.[68] The Court also stated that, beyond article 14(6) of the Qualification Directive, EU member States must:

> (…) comply with the relevant provisions of the [EU] Charter, such as those set out in Article 7 thereof, relating to respect for private and family life, Article 15 thereof, relating to the freedom to choose an occupation and the right to engage in work, Article 34 thereof, relating to social security and social assistance, and Article 35 thereof, relating to health protection.[69]

It should be noted, however, that the right to work and the right to social security and assistance, as prescribed in the EU Charter, are limited to those legally residing in the country (in the same way that the Refugee Convention limits these rights to those lawfully staying in the territory of a contracting State). Consequently, they may not apply to those who have lost status or

65 Joined Cases C-391/16, C-77/17 and C-78/17, paras. 97–100. Before the CJEU delivered its decision, Singer had already foreseen that the Court could adopt this approach to separate the European status from the international status. In this regard, she said the CJEU may "determine the existence of different European refugee statuses – one based on the full set of rights included in the QD [Qualification Directive], the other focusing only on the core rights set out in the 1951 [Refugee] Convention." Singer, S. (2018), p. 299.

66 In this regard, Steve Peers noted that it can "be argued that the case law [of the CJEU] is still relevant to the new Regulation, unless the relevant text has been amended; in some cases the Regulation (or the preamble to it) reflects some of that case law." Peers, S. (30 December 2023). The New EU Asylum Laws, part 1: the Qualification Regulation. EU Law Analysis. http://eulawanalysis.blogspot.com/2023/12/the-new-eu-asylum-laws-part-1.html.

67 These include the rights to non-discrimination, freedom of religion, access to courts, education, and non-refoulement.

68 Joined Cases C-391/16, C-77/17 and C-78/17, paras. 105–107. These rights are identified in Section 3.3 above.

69 Ibid., para. 109.

had their status denied, unless they are granted legal stay through other means (that are not international protection).

4 How to Regulate the Situation of Undesirable but Unreturnable Migrants?

The previous section showed that human rights law provides an absolute protection against removing someone to a place where they may face gross human rights violations (human rights non-refoulement). Before such protection was defined in international human rights law instruments, however, the Refugee Convention already granted protection against return to harm to certain migrants. The Refugee Convention, however, excluded from this protection those who were considered undeserving of it due to past actions. It also allowed return to a place of risk when the concerned refugee was considered a threat to the national security or the community of the host country. This gap in protection was somewhat filled by human rights law with the solidification of (human rights) non-refoulement obligations and their acceptance as absolute. In view of this, States created a human rights-based status, known as subsidiary or complementary protection. As this status is inspired by the Refugee Convention, however, it often excludes the same migrants who would be excluded from refugee status.

As human rights law protects those who may face harm upon return from removal regardless of their migration status, these migrants may find themselves in an unusual situation, in which they were refused status (or had an existing status revoked) yet are not subjected to return. This section will thus explore some of the solutions proposed to regulate the situation of these migrants. Some of these solutions and their shortcomings were explored during the Refugee Law Initiative research project on undesirable but unreturnable migrants (mentioned in this book's introduction)[70] and thus this section builds, among others, on the work done by the scholars involved in that project and in the subsequent conference[71] and special editions.[72]

70 Project website: https://rli.sas.ac.uk/projects-0/undesirable-unreturnable-migrants.

71 For the main findings of the conference, see: Refugee Law Initiative, Arts & Humanities Research Council and Center for International Criminal Justice (2016). Undesirable and Unreturnable? Policy challenges around excluded asylum seekers and other migrants suspected of serious criminality who cannot be removed (Policy brief).

72 The special editions are: Refugee Survey Quarterly, 36(1) (2017) and Journal of International Criminal Justice, 15(1) (2017).

4.1 *Diplomatic Assurances: A Way around Non-refoulement Obligations?*

The unreturnable migrants this book focuses on are those who cannot be returned to their country of origin because there is a risk that they would be subjected to gross human rights violations there. A proposed solution to eliminate this concern and, therefore, return such migrants to their countries of origin, is to obtain diplomatic assurances that they will not be subjected to human rights abuses upon return.

UNHCR has defined diplomatic assurances as "(...) an undertaking by the receiving State to the effect that the person concerned will be treated in accordance with conditions set by the sending State or, more generally, in keeping with its human rights obligations under international law."[73] With the increasing securitisation of migration since the terrorist attacks of 11 September, mentioned in Section 2 above, States have resorted more often to diplomatic assurances as a way to send undesirable migrants back to their country of origin without disrespecting their human rights obligations.

Diplomatic assurances, however, have been highly criticised by some, who consider them an unacceptable way to try and circumvent the absolute prohibition of torture and other forms of ill-treatment.[74] There are many reasons for such criticism. To start with, it can be said that diplomatic assurances carry an inherent paradox as they are frequently given by States that are known to disrespect human rights. Consequently, host States that seek diplomatic assurances by countries of origin "(...) effectively acknowledge the existence of a widespread practice of torture in the receiving State while asking for an exception to the practice in the individual case."[75] Furthermore, as diplomatic assurances are not always legally binding, nor do they always provide any mechanism for enforcement or legal remedy in case of non-compliance, questions can be raised about their validity and reliability.[76] It has also been claimed that concluding such assurances is very time and res-

73 UNHCR, Note on Diplomatic Assurances and International Refugee Protection (August 2006), p. 2.

74 See, e.g. Emmerson, B. (2016). Report of the Special Rapporteur on the promotion and protection of human rights and fundamental freedoms while countering terrorism (No. A/71/384), p. 13; and Amnesty International (April 2017). Diplomatic Assurances Against Torture – Inherently Wrong, Inherently Unreliable.

75 Larsaeus, N. (2006). The Use of Diplomatic Assurances in the Prevention of Prohibited Treatment. Refugee Studies Centre Working Paper No. 32. University of Oxford, p. 19.

76 UNHCR, Note on Diplomatic Assurances and International Refugee Protection (August 2006), p. 3

ource-consuming[77] and that monitoring compliance with them is a hard, if not impossible, endeavour (this last point will be further elaborated below).

Despite such criticism, international courts and human rights monitoring bodies do not entirely rule out the possibility of such assurances "(…) either eliminating the risk of torture altogether or reducing such a risk below the threshold required to avoid refoulement."[78] Not all diplomatic assurances, however, will be able to achieve this level of reliance. In fact, there are many criteria that must be met before such assurances can be considered reliable by international bodies. UNHCR, for example, argued that, when looking at assurances, States must consider the risk posed to the individual, the source of the danger feared and whether assurances in this setting can be effective. To conduct such an assessment, States need to verify whether the receiving country can ensure compliance with the assurances and whether assurances are binding on the State bodies that should refrain from conducting the illicit behaviour or that are in charge of the individual's protection when the risk emanates from non-State actors (for example, if the assurance comes from the executive power, but should be followed by prison authorities, which are not bound by the promise of the executive, such assurance is unlikely to be deemed satisfactory). Furthermore, such analysis must be made "(…) in light of the general human rights situation in the receiving State at the relevant time, and in particular, any practice with regard to diplomatic assurances or similar undertakings."[79] Another essential aspect of such assurances, often highlighted by the UN Human Rights Committee and the UN Committee against Torture, is the need to have monitoring mechanisms in place to ensure compliance.

---

77 Refugee Law Initiative, Arts & Humanities Research Council and Center for International Criminal Justice (2016). Undesirable and Unreturnable? Policy challenges around excluded asylum seekers and other migrants suspected of serious criminality who cannot be removed (Policy brief), p. 4.

78 Giuffré, M. (2015). Expelling undesirable foreigners: the challenge of human rights. Centre of International Criminal Justice, Free University Amsterdam, p. 5.

79 UNHCR, Note on Diplomatic Assurances and International Refugee Protection (August 2006), p. 9. At the European level, the European Court of Human Rights also emphasises the need to consider a State's human rights records and whether the authority issuing the assurance will be able to implement it (see, e.g. Salerno, M. E. (2017). Can diplomatic assurances, in their practical application, provide effective protection against the risk of torture and ill treatment? A focus on the evolution of the pragmatic approach of the European Court of Human Rights in removal cases of suspected terrorists. New Journal of European Criminal Law, 8(4), 453–475; Giuffré, M. (2015); and Larsaeus, N. (2006). In all three papers the authors analyse the Case Law of the European Court of Human Rights to spell out the requirements set out by the Court to consider assurances reliable).

Without such mechanisms, diplomatic assurances by themselves are not considered enough by these human rights bodies. The case of Régent Boily, who was extradited from Canada to Mexico, where he claimed he risked being subjected to torture in detention, serves to exemplify this. In that case, the UN Committee against Torture noted that when evaluating whether diplomatic assurances could eliminate the risk of torture it "(…) must take into account whether the obtained diplomatic assurances include follow-up procedures that would guarantee their effectiveness."[80] For Régent Boily, the Committee assessed that diplomatic assurances were insufficient as:

> (…) the agreed system of diplomatic assurances was not carefully enough designed to effectively prevent torture. The diplomatic and consular authorities of the State party were not given due notice of the complainant's extradition and not informed of the need to stay in close and continuous contact with him from the moment he was handed over. In this case the diplomatic assurances and the foreseen consular visits failed to anticipate the likelihood that the complainant had the highest risk of being tortured during the initial days of his detention.[81]

Such monitoring mechanisms serve both purposes of preventing torture from happening and functioning as a system to detect violations.[82] They can include a variety of actions conducted by different actors. For example, it has been suggested that private interviews with the person concerned without advanced notice and independent medical examinations are some of the key activities to be conducted when assessing compliance with diplomatic assurances.[83] Monitoring is frequently conducted by diplomats of the sending State, but it has been argued that independent organisations, preferably international organisations, may be more effective due to their expertise. Furthermore, the sending State may have little interest in revealing a possible breach, as breaches can put it at fault for sending the concerned individual back.[84]

Even when such mechanisms are in place, however, their ability to ensure compliance with diplomatic assurances has been questioned. Amnesty Inter-

---

80 Communication No. 327/2007, CAT/C/47/D/327/2007 (Committee against Torture, 1 July 1996), para. 14.4.

81 Ibid., para. 14.5.

82 See Salerno, M. E. (2017), p. 471; and Larsaeus, N. (2006), pp. 18–19.

83 Larsaeus, N. (2006), p. 18.

84 Salerno, M. E. (2017), p. 473.

national, for example, claims that "[T]hose subjected to torture or other ill-treatment are also often afraid to recount their abuse to their lawyers, family members and any person attempting to conduct post-return monitoring for fear of reprisals against themselves or their families."[85] Furthermore, it has been argued that such mechanisms can be inefficient because torture is hard to detect and, consequently, there are not many cases in which oversight can satisfactorily ensure that torture will not be practiced.[86]

In light of the above, it is possible to conclude that diplomatic assurances can, in some specific cases, be deemed to reduce the risk of human rights violations sufficiently in the receiving State to the point that it would not put the sending State in breach of human rights by returning the concerned migrant. However, the situations in which this would be the case are rather limited due to the constraints associated with such measures. This is because assurances alone are insufficient to remove the human rights concerns that make them unreturnable, and, therefore, only a limited number of undesirable but unreturnable migrants could be sent back in this way.

4.2 *Prosecuting Undesirable Migrants for Crimes Committed before Arrival in the Host State*

As mentioned above, migrants may be considered undesirable because of crimes (or suspicion of criminal activity) committed before their arrival in host countries. This is especially the case for those denied refugee status (or subsidiary or complementary protection) on the basis of article 1F of the Refugee Convention.[87] Consequently, it seems logical that these alleged criminal acts should be investigated and, if necessary, the individuals concerned should be prosecuted for their actions. In fact, States have an obligation to prosecute some of the crimes that give rise to a 1F exclusion, such as the international

85 Amnesty International (April 2017).

86 Salerno, M. E. (2017), p. 473.

87 Art. 1F of the Refugee Convention states that: "The provisions of this Convention shall not apply to any person with respect to whom there are serious reasons for considering that:

(a) he has committed a crime against peace, a war crime, or a crime against humanity, as defined in the international instruments drawn up to make provision in respect of such crimes;

(b) he has committed a serious non-political crime outside the country of refuge prior to his admission to that country as a refugee;

(c) he has been guilty of acts contrary to the purposes and principles of the United Nations."

crimes of genocide,[88] crimes against humanity and war crimes,[89] as well as other crimes they may be bound to prosecute by the ratification of international treaties.[90] Many of the treaties that impose an obligation on States to prosecute a crime also include (or have been interpreted to include[91]) the obligation to establish jurisdiction allowing States to conduct such prosecution regardless of where the crime has occurred or the nationality of those involved. As one of the main legal principles to fight impunity, such jurisdiction is known as universal jurisdiction and is frequently prescribed as an obligation to extradite or prosecute (*aut dedere aut judicare*). This means that when faced with certain crimes, States may have to opt between either prosecuting the suspected perpetrators themselves or extraditing them to a country that has an interest in conducting the criminal proceedings.[92]

Consequently, in the case of undesirable but unreturnable migrants excluded from refugee status (or subsidiary or complementary protection) under article 1F of the Refugee Convention, host States are likely to be obliged either to investigate[93] the alleged crimes or to extradite the concerned

88 See articles III to V of the UN Convention on the Prevention and Punishment of the Crime of Genocide (UN General Assembly, Convention on the Prevention and Punishment of the Crime of Genocide, 9 December 1948, United Nations, Treaty Series, vol. 78, p. 277).

89 See 1949 Geneva Conventions: first convention, articles 49 and 50; second convention, articles 50 and 51; third convention, articles 129 and 130; fourth convention, articles 146 and 147.

90 See, e.g. article 7 of the Convention Against Torture.

91 See, e.g. Adanan, A. (16 May 2019). Symposium on the Genocide Convention: Reflecting on the Genocide Convention at 70: How genocide became a crime subject to universal jurisdiction. EJIL: Talk! Available at: https://www.ejiltalk.org/symposium-on-the-genocide-convention-reflecting-on-the-genocide-convention-at-70-how-genocide-became-a-crime-subject-to-universal-jurisdiction/.

92 It should be noted that in the context of the Council of Europe, extradition is said to take preference over prosecution. See Bribosia, E., & Weyembergh, A. (1997). Extradition et asile: Vers un espace judiciaire européen ?. Revue belge de droit international, 1, 69–98, p. 79.

93 As was noted by the International Law Commission's Working Group on the obligation to extradite or prosecute, "[T]he effective fulfilment of the obligation to extradite or prosecute requires undertaking necessary national measures to criminalize the relevant offences, establish jurisdiction over the offences and the person present in the territory of the State, investigate or undertake primary inquiry, apprehend the suspect, and submit the case to the prosecuting authorities (which may or may not result in the institution of proceedings)." The Working Group goes on to say that "[T]he obligation to prosecute is actually an obligation to submit the case to the prosecuting authorities; it does not involve an obligation to initiate a prosecution. Indeed, in light of the evidence, fulfillment of the obligation may or may not result in the institution of proceedings. The competent author-

migrants to a country that will do so. It should be noted, however, that "[E]xtradition shall not be granted, if, in the view of the [competent authority of country adopting the law],[94] the person sought [has been or] would be subjected in the requesting State to torture or cruel, inhuman or degrading treatment or punishment."[95] As crimes that give rise to exclusion from refugee status are frequently committed in the country of origin, however, extradition in such cases is unlikely, since the migrants this book focuses on are at risk of human rights violations in their country of origin. It follows that sending them back to their countries for prosecution will, in most cases, not be a suitable option. Furthermore, countries of origin may not be willing to receive these migrants, as they may not wish to see the return of those who committed atrocities in their territories, which will further limit the possibilities of extradition.

Extradition, therefore, will almost always only be possible when a country other than the country of origin has an interest in the prosecution of the alleged crime. Even if extradition to a third State is possible, however, the host State is still under the obligation to ensure that the third country will not subsequently extradite or deport the concerned migrant to their country of origin. This is because the principle of non-refoulement protects individuals not only from direct return to a country where they would face torture or other forms of inhumane treatment, but also from indirect return.[96] This obligation, therefore, further limits the possibility of sending concerned migrants to another country to stand trial.

Short of a third State to extradite the concerned migrant to, "(…) another option may be transfer to face prosecution before an international criminal

---

ities decide whether to initiate proceedings, in the same manner as they would for any alleged offence of a serious nature under the law of the State concerned." International Law Commission (2013). Report of the working group on the obligation to extradite or prosecute (aut dedere aut judicare) (No. A/CN.4/L.829). United Nations.

94 The extraditing country.

95 Model Law on Extradition (2004), Chapter 2, Section 6: Torture, cruel, inhuman or degrading treatment or punishment. United Nations Office on Drugs and Crime. Considering that for the purposes of this book the unreturnability of migrants is due to human rights concerns, it is assumed that there is a risk of torture or other form of degrading treatment in the country of origin.

96 See, e.g. Committee against Torture (2018). General comment no. 4 (2017) on the implementation of article 3 of the Convention in the context of article 22 (CAT/C/GC/4). United Nations, p. 2: "(…) the person at risk should never be deported to another State from which the person may subsequently face deportation to a third State in which there are substantial grounds for believing that the person would be in danger of being subjected to torture."

tribunal."[97] This alternative has been accepted by the UN International Law Commission as a means to satisfy a State's obligation to extradite or prosecute.[98] When making this statement, however, the Commission "(...) did not address the obstacles faced by international criminal tribunals and how these might impact states' efforts to fulfil their obligation to extradite."[99] To start with, international tribunals have fixed mandates, sometimes limited to specific events, timeframes and/or geographical locations. This restricts the number of persons that may be tried by such tribunals. Furthermore, in practice, due to their finite resources, international tribunals usually only prosecute a limited number of people within those that fall under their mandate, typically focusing on the individuals that are deemed to be the 'most responsible' for the commission of atrocities.[100] As rejected asylum seekers may not be regarded as such high-ranking persons of interest, the possibility of transferring them to an international tribunal are rather limited.

When under a duty to extradite or prosecute and unable to extradite or transfer the concerned individual, States are left with the obligation to investigate the alleged crime nationally. Such an alternative, however, presents multiple challenges to the host State. For example, the cost of investigating and collecting evidence about a crime committed abroad can be very high. In the Belgium v. Senegal case before the International Court of Justice, debating questions relating to the obligation to prosecute or extradite, Senegal mentioned that it sought financial support to prepare the trial being discussed during the case due to the distance to witnesses and the difficulty in gathering evidence.[101] In that case, neither Senegal nor the Court accepted that financial difficulties can justify failure to initiate investigative procedures arising from an international obligation.[102] However, the fact remains that conducting an investigation that gathers a sufficient amount of evidence for prosecution and, potentially, conviction, when the investigative authority is physically far and

97 Singer, S. (2017). "Undesirable and Unreturnable" in the United Kingdom. Refugee Survey Quarterly, 36(1), 9–34, p. 27.

98 See International Law Commission (2014). Final report – Working Group on the obligation to extradite or prosecute (aut dedere aut judicare) (A/CN.4/L.844). United Nations, p. 7.

99 Moyo, M. P. (2015). Final report on the obligation to extradite or prosecute (Aut Dedere Aut Judicare). International Legal Materials, 54(4), 758–779, p. 759.

100 Refugee Law Initiative, Arts & Humanities Research Council and Center for International Criminal Justice. (2016), p. 4.

101 Questions relating to the obligation to prosecute or extradite (Belgium v. Senegal) (International Court of Justice, 20 July 2012), para. 109.

102 Ibid., paras. 109 and 112.

does not have jurisdiction over the persons or objects located at the place of the crime, is very challenging. In these situations, the United Kingdom (hereafter UK), for example, when choosing whether to investigate a certain crime committed outside its territory, places considerable emphasis on whether the State in which the crime was committed will cooperate with the investigations.[103] Considering, however, that it is likely that the crime has taken place in the migrant's country of origin and, in the case of unreturnable migrants, it has been deemed that the concerned migrant faces a real risk of being subjected to human rights violations in that country, it is unlikely that meaningful cooperation is achieved.[104] Such practical obstacles to domestic prosecution have been said to explain the small number of criminal investigations started under universal jurisdiction.[105]

In light of the above, it can be said that despite the interest in prosecuting alleged serious crimes, very few undesirable but unreturnable migrants will, in practice, be subjected to prosecution, either nationally in the host country, in a third State or by an international tribunal. While this creates many challenges (such as impunity and lack of reparations for victims) that are not the object of this book, it also shows that prosecution is unlikely to provide a solution for the undesirability of undesirable but unreturnable migrants. This not only relates to the challenges associated with extradition, transfer and domestic prosecution, but also to the fact that not all undesirable but unreturnable migrants can be prosecuted for the reasons they are deemed undesirable. For example, they may be considered undesirable because they are suspected of having committed crimes for which universal jurisdiction is not prescribed and, therefore, the host State does not have jurisdiction to prosecute.[106] The undesirability may also arise from the fact that they are involved with certain groups that are planning crimes or attacks against the

103 Singer, S. (2017), p. 28.

104 In the United Kingdom, for example, cooperation will not be established with countries that are involved in armed conflict or are politically unstable or where there is a risk of harm to victims or witnesses (ibid. idem). Considering that such situations are often present in countries of origin of migrants in need of international protection, it is likely that countries of origin where international crimes have been committed will not meet this cooperation threshold. Similarly, if the threat of harm faced by the undesirable migrant themselves comes from the authorities of the state of origin (or is condoned by them), it is questionable whether any cooperation coming from such state would be legitimate or reliable.

105 See, e.g. Rikhof, J. (2017). Prosecuting asylum seekers who cannot be removed. Journal of International Criminal Justice, 15(1), 97–113, p. 109.

106 It is debated whether a general obligation to extradite or prosecute has arose or is arising in international customary law. See, e.g. International Law Commission (2014), p. 4; and

host State, but have not yet committed these crimes and, therefore, there are no acts to prosecute. Lastly, even for those who can be prosecuted, either for crimes committed abroad or for those who are deemed undesirable due to crimes committed in the host country, the question of what happens after prosecution continues. Indeed, return proceedings for undesirable migrants sometimes start after they have been convicted and served their sentences. In Belgium, for example, an order to leave the territory was issued against a man from Rwanda, who was convicted for war crimes in Belgium, after he was released from prison and despite the fact that he may be at risk in Rwanda.[107]

In this regard, it is worth noting that according to the Refugee Convention, those who fall under the exclusion clauses of article 1F will not be deemed refugees even if they have already served a sentence for the crimes they committed. In this situation, if host States do not provide status to these migrants after prosecution and serving their sentence, they will be left in legal limbo (discussed in Section 4.4 below). Prosecution alone, therefore, is not a solution, even for undesirable but unreturnable migrants who may be subjected to it. Some States thus opt instead to place them in detention. This alternative is analysed in the next section.

4.3 *Immigration Detention: Another Form of Human Rights Abuse?*

As was mentioned earlier in this chapter, following the terrorist attacks of September 11, States have increasingly associated migration with criminal activity and terrorism, implementing laws and policies that limit the rights of migrants in the name of national security. In this context, the use of immigration detention has been a frequent measure used by States against migrants. While the right to liberty is guaranteed in human rights, it is not an absolute right and thus may be interfered with in certain circumstances. In the migration context, the UN Human Rights Committee noted that "[D]etention in the course of proceedings for the control of immigration is not per se arbitrary, but the detention must be justified as reasonable, necessary and proportionate in the light of the circumstances and reassessed as it extends in time."[108] More

---

Kelly, M. J. (2004). Aut Dedere Aut Judicare and the Death Penalty Extradition Prohibition. International Legal Theory, 10, 53–82, pp. 57–59.

107 See, e.g. Arrêt n° 205 280 (Conseil du Contentieux des Etrangers, 13 June 2018); Arrêt n° 213 120 (Conseil du Contentieux des Etrangers, 29 November 2018).

108 Human Rights Committee (2014). General comment no. 35: Article 9 (Liberty and security of person) (CCPR/C/GC/35). Office of the High Commissioner for Human Rights, para. 18.

specifically, the UN Human Rights Committee stated that for detention not to be arbitrary, it:

> (…) must be justified as being reasonable, necessary and proportionate in the light of the circumstances and reassessed as it extends in time. To detain immigrants further while their claims are being resolved would be arbitrary in the absence of particular reasons specific to the individual, such as an individualized likelihood of absconding, a danger of crimes against others, or a risk of acts against national security. The decision must consider relevant factors case by case, and not be based on a mandatory rule for a broad category; must take into account less invasive means of achieving the same ends, such as reporting obligations, sureties or other conditions to prevent absconding; and must be subject to periodic re-evaluation and judicial review.[109]

In the European context, the European Convention on Human Rights explicitly allows, in article 5, "the lawful arrest or detention of a person to prevent his effecting an unauthorised entry into the country or of a person against whom action is being taken with a view to deportation or extradition." Furthermore, EU member States are also limited by the EU Return Directive,[110] which only allows the use of detention when the measure is needed to facilitate the removal of an alien where there is a reasonable prospect of removal (which is frequently not the case for unreturnable migrants).

Despite such human rights limitations to the use of immigration detention, scholars still point to the growing use of detention in migration cases.[111] This increased use of detention, especially in national security cases, has also been recognised by a former UN Special Rapporteur on the promotion and protection of human rights and fundamental freedoms while countering terrorism, who stated that "States have repeatedly attempted to use administrative detention as a means of dealing with foreign nationals considered to be a security threat."[112]

---

109 Communication No. 1875/2009, CCPR/C/113/D/1875/2009 (Human Rights Committee, 26 March 2015).

110 Directive 2008/115/EC of the European Parliament and of the Council of 16 December 2008 on common standards and procedures in Member States for returning illegally staying third-country nationals.

111 Hiemstra, N. (2016). Deportation and detention: Interdisciplinary perspectives, multiscalar approaches, and new methodological tools. Migration Studies, 4(3), 433–446, p. 435.

112 Emmerson, B. (2016), p. 18.

In fact, there are states, such as Australia and India, that still resort to the indefinite detention of migrants.[113] This practice is heavily criticised by judicial and semi-judicial bodies. For instance, indefinite detention has been considered incompatible with the European human rights framework by the UK House of Lords in 2004.[114] The UN Human Rights Committee[115] and a former UN Special Rapporteur on the promotion and protection of human rights and fundamental freedoms while countering terrorism are of the same opinion, the latter having said that "(…) indefinite or mandatory detention should be prohibited."[116]

Although such extreme practice is limited to a small number of States, detention of varied lengths is applied worldwide for undesirable but unreturnable migrants. In Canada, for example, "[A]lthough the Supreme Court of Canada has criticised indefinite detention where removal is not possible, lengthy detention with regular detention reviews is permissible in Canadian law."[117]

In the EU, the EU Return Directive limits detention to a maximum period of 18 months.[118] The Directive, however, does not limit the number of times a person can be placed in detention, only limiting the cumulative amount of time in detention to 18 months. Some States, therefore, restrict detention to

113 For example, both countries are known to have kept migrants coming from Sri Lanka in indefinite detention, possibly for alleged association with the Liberation Tigers of Tamil Eelam (LTTE), although the reasons for considering such migrants as a threat to national security are not always disclosed. See, e.g. Juss, S. S. (2017). Detention and delusion in Australia's Kafkaesque refugee law. Refugee Survey Quarterly, 36(1), 146–167; and Kodiyath, S. P., & Padathu Veettil, S. (2017). Invisible people: Suspected LTTE members in the special refugee camps of Tamil Nadu. Refugee Survey Quarterly, 36(1), 126–145.

114 Giuffré, M. (2015), p. 3.

115 In its Case Law, the Committee has in many occasions deemed indefinite detention to be arbitrary, as administrative detention can only be applied when it is justified on an individual basis and when it has been shown that less intrusive measures cannot achieve the same aim (e.g. compliance with the State's need to respond to a security risk). Automatic indefinite detention, consequently, is never acceptable. See, e.g. Communication No. 2233/2013, CCPR/C/116/D/2233/2013 (Human Rights Committee, 22 March 2016); Communication No. 2136/2012, CCPR/C/108/D/2136/2012 (Human Rights Committee, 25 July 2013); Communication No. 2094/2011, CCPR/C/108/D/2094/2011 (Human Rights Committee, 26 July 2013).

116 Emmerson, B. (2016), p. 17.

117 Bond, J. (2017). Unwanted but unremovable: Canada's treatment of "criminal" migrants who cannot be removed, p. 184. Refugee Survey Quarterly, 36(1), 168–186.

118 Article 15, Directive 2008/115/EC of the European Parliament and of the Council of 16 Dec-ember 2008 on common standards and procedures in Member States for returning illegally staying third-country nationals.

time periods shorter than 18 months, but resort to multiple repeated detention periods until the time limit imposed by the EU legislation is reached. For example, it was reported that France, in 2014, had a maximum detention period of 45 days, but placed no limit on the number of times an individual could be detained, leading to cycles of repeated arrest-detention-release, which have been claimed to develop mental disorders in those subjected to them.[119] While the country presently has a maximum detention period of 6 months, after said period expires, undesirable migrants can be placed under home custody for an undetermined amount of time, which ultimately leads to *de facto* unlimited restrictions on the individual's liberty.[120] Similarly, in Belgium, an Iraqi national claimed that the detrimental effects of prolonged periods of detention and designated residence in a specific location were the reason that forced him to accept to return to Iraq, where he knew he might be subjected to torture.[121] In the latter case, the European Court of Human Rights found that Belgium violated the European Convention on Human Rights by applying different legal provisions to detain the concerned migrant for longer than the maximum period of 8 months prescribed by the Belgian law on foreigners.[122]

These last paragraphs have shown that prolonged or indefinite detention is still, in some cases, resorted to as a way to deal with undesirable but unreturnable migrants. Such measures, however, are often applied in violation of international human rights law.[123] Indefinite detention, more specifically, is always considered a human rights violation. Consequently, detention does not pro-

---

119 Gosme, C. (2014). Limbo spaces between illegal and legal stay: Resulting from EU management of non-removable third country nationals (Ph.D. thesis, Sciences Po), p. 200.

120 Peyronnet, C. (2017). Undesirable and unreturnable migrants under French law: Between legal uncertainty and legal limbo. Refugee Survey Quarterly, 36(1), 35–60, pp. 53–56.

121 Before the European Court of Human Rights, his case was presented as follows: "Après avoir tenté pendant des mois de convaincre les autorités belges qu'il ne présentait plus de danger pour celles-ci, mais qu'il courait un grave danger en cas de retour en Irak, et avoir épuisé toutes les voies de recours internes à cette fin, il a perdu tout espoir se rendant compte qu'il se trouvait en Belgique dans une situation inextricable et ne pouvait continuer à vivre enfermé de manière définitive sans avenir et loin de sa famille. Déjà fragilisé psychologiquement par de longues périodes de détention et d'assignation à résidence, les pressions exercées par le service d'immigration et le directeur du centre fermé durant les semaines ayant précédé son départ, à l'abri de tout observateur, ont été telles qu'il en est arrivé à ne plus rien envisager d'autre comme possibilité qu'un retour en Irak où il savait pourtant pertinemment risquer sa vie et son intégrité physique." M.S. v. Belgium, 50012/08 (European Court of Human Rights, 31 January, 2012), para. 117.

122 Ibid., para. 179.

123 See, e.g. Communication No. 2233/2013, para. 10.4; and Communication No. 2136/2012, para. 10.4.

vide a long-term solution to the situation of undesirable but unreturnable migrants.

In view of the limitations imposed on the use of detention by national and international legislation (for example, the EU Return Directive) as well as of the oversight of their application by human rights bodies, some States do opt to release or not to detain these migrants. In some cases, however, they are released into an unregulated situation, in which they are not granted any residence status to stay in their host country, leaving them in a situation of limbo. This option is addressed in the next section.

4.4 *Limbo: A State of Indefinite Suspension and Neglect*

In view of the limitations of the abovementioned alternatives, some States opt not to take steps to find a solution and simply do not regulate the situation of undesirable but unreturnable migrants. Such States do not return these migrants but also do not grant them any residence status to remain in their territory. In these cases, therefore, the individual truly remains in 'legal limbo' as a *persona non grata.*

In Europe, the European Court of Human Rights accepted this approach in 2005 in the Bonger v. the Netherlands case.[124] In that case, the Court stated that the European Convention on Human Rights did not guarantee to non-nationals the right to enter, reside or remain in a member State. More specifically, the Court stated that a right to a residence permit could not be derived from the prohibition of torture and its consequent prohibition of refoulement.

For States, limbo has been said to curb public expenditure, as those who do not have a residence status in the country are usually not entitled to most socio-economic rights and, therefore, States have less socio-economic obligations towards them, making limbo a cheaper option than detention or regularisation.[125] It is worth noting, however, that regardless of their status in the host country, all migrants are entitled to certain social, economic and cultural rights.[126] According to international and regional human rights bodies, these

---

124 Teshome Goraga Bonger v. the Netherlands, 10154/04 (European Court of Human Rights, 15 September 2005).

125 Gosme, C. (2014), p. 301.

126 These rights are prescribed in human rights instruments that generally apply to all and have been interpreted to apply to migrants in an irregular situation due to their human dignity. It should be mentioned, however, that in the EU context some of these rights have been explicitly prescribed in the EU Return Directive for migrants who cannot be removed, regardless of their status. For discussions on the application of these rights in the context of the Return Directive, see, e.g. Return Handbook (Commission Recommendation (EU) 2017/2338). (2017). European Commission; Peers, S. (2015). Irregular mig-

include, at a minimum, the right to essential and emergency healthcare;[127] the right to an adequate standard of living, including shelter,[128] food and

rants: Can humane treatment be balanced against efficient removal? European Journal of Migration and Law, 17(4), 289–304; Lutz, F. (2018). Non-removable returnees under union law: Status quo and possible developments. European Journal of Migration and Law, 20(1), 28–52; and Farcy, J.-B. (2020). Unremovability under the return directive: An empty protection? In M. Moraru, G. Cornelisse, & P. De Bruycker (Eds.), Law and Judicial Dialogue on the Return of Irregular Migrants from the European Union (pp. 437–453). Hart Publishing.

127 See, e.g. Committee on Economic, Social and Cultural Rights (2000). General Comment No. 14 (2000): The right to the highest attainable standard of health (article 12 of the International Covenant on Economic, Social and Cultural Rights) [E/C.12/2000/4], para. 34; Committee on Economic, Social and Cultural Rights (2017). Duties of States towards refugees and migrants under the International Covenant on Economic, Social and Cultural Rights (E/C.12/2017/1). United Nations Economic and Social Council, para. 12; Committee on Economic, Social and Cultural Rights (1990). General comment no. 3: The nature of States parties' obligations (art. 2, para. 1, of the Covenant). United Nations Economic and Social Council, para. 10; Office of the High Commissioner for Human Rights (2014). The Economic, Social and Cultural Rights of Migrants in an Irregular Situation (HR/PUB/14/1). United Nations, p. 59; International Federation of Human Rights Leagues (FIDH) v. France, Complaint No. 14/2003 (European Committee of Social Rights, 8 September 2004), para. 32; European Union Agency for Fundamental Rights (2011). Fundamental rights of migrants in an irregular situation in the European Union., p. 71; Parliamentary Assembly (2006). Human rights of irregular migrants (Resolution 1509 (2006)). Council of Europe. Available at: https://pace.coe.int/en/files/17456/html; Pijnenburg, A. (2021). At the Frontiers of State Responsibility: Socio-economic Rights and Cooperation on Migration (1st ed.). Intersentia, pp. 130–132; Di Pascale, A. (2014). Italy and Unauthorized Migration: Between State Sovereignty and Human Rights Obligations. In R. Rubio Marín, Human rights and immigration (pp. 278–310). Oxford University Press, p. 284; and Wessels, J. (17 March 2023). Planned destitution as a policy tool to control migration in the EU: Socio-economic deprivation and international human rights law. EU Immigration and Asylum Law and Policy. Available at: https://eumigrationlawblog.eu/planned-destitution-as-a-policy-tool-to-control-migration-in-the-eu-socio-economic-deprivation-and-international-human-rights-law/.

128 See, e.g. Committee on Economic, Social and Cultural Rights (1991). General comment no. 4: The right to adequate housing (art. 11 (1) of the Covenant) (E/1992/23). United Nations Economic and Social Council, para. 6; Committee on Economic, Social and Cultural Rights (1990). General comment no. 3, para. 10; Office of the High Commissioner for Human Rights (2014). The Economic, Social and Cultural Rights of Migrants in an Irregular Situation, pp. 70–72; Conference of European Churches (CEC) v. the Netherlands, Complaint No. 90/2013 (European Committee of Social Rights, 1 July 2014), para. 144; Defence for Children International (DCI) v. Belgium, Complaint No. 69/2011 (European Committee of Social Rights, 23 October 2012), para. 82; Defence for Children International (DCI) v. the Netherlands, Complaint No. 47/2008 (European Committee of Social Rights, 20 October 2009), para. 64; European Union Agency for Fundamental

water;[129] education for children;[130] and, when migrants in an irregular situation engage in work (regardless of whether they work irregularly), they are entitled to just and favourable conditions,[131] equal treatment[132] and fair remuneration,[133] and should also be able to benefit from social security contributions made or be reimbursed for such contributions if expelled from the host country.[134] Not granting migrants access to these rights may constitute not only a violation of these specific rights, but also of other rights, such as the right to life.[135]

Rights (2011), p. 59; Parliamentary Assembly (2006). Human rights of irregular migrants (Resolution 1509 (2006)). Council of Europe; Pijnenburg, A. (2021), p. 127; Di Pascale, A. (2014), p. 284; and Wessels, J. (17 March 2023).

129 See, e.g. Committee on Economic, Social and Cultural Rights (1990). General comment no. 3, para. 10; Office of the High Commissioner for Human Rights (2014). The Economic, Social and Cultural Rights of Migrants in an Irregular Situation, p. 61; Pijnenburg, A. (2021), pp. 128–129; and Wessels, J. (17 March 2023).

130 See, e.g. Committee on Economic, Social and Cultural Rights (1990). General comment no. 3, para. 10; Committee on Economic, Social and Cultural Rights (2017). Duties of States towards refugees and migrants under the International Covenant on Economic, Social and Cultural Rights, para. 9; Office of the High Commissioner for Human Rights (2014). The Economic, Social and Cultural Rights of Migrants in an Irregular Situation, p. 95; Parliamentary Assembly (2006). Human rights of irregular migrants (Resolution 1509 (2006)). Council of Europe; Pijnenburg, A. (2021), p. 134; Di Pascale, A. (2014), p. 284; and Wessels, J. (17 March 2023).

131 See, e.g. Committee on Economic, Social and Cultural Rights (2016). General comment no. 23 (2016) on the right to just and favourable conditions of work (article 7 of the International Covenant on Economic, Social and Cultural Rights) [E/C.12/GC/23]. United Nations Economic and Social Council, para. 5; Parliamentary Assembly (2006). Human rights of irregular migrants (Resolution 1509 (2006)). Council of Europe; Pijnenburg, A. (2021), pp. 135–136; and Di Pascale, A. (2014), p. 284.

132 See, e.g. Committee on Economic, Social and Cultural Rights (2016). General comment no. 23, para. 47; Committee on Economic, Social and Cultural Rights (2017). Duties of States towards refugees and migrants under the International Covenant on Economic, Social and Cultural Rights, para. 13; Office of the High Commissioner for Human Rights (2014). The Economic, Social and Cultural Rights of Migrants in an Irregular Situation, pp. 117–118

133 See, e.g. Committee on Economic, Social and Cultural Rights (2016). General comment no. 23, para. 11; and European Union Agency for Fundamental Rights (2011), p. 48.

134 This last right, however, has been established at the Council of Europe level and not internationally. See Parliamentary Assembly (2006). Human rights of irregular migrants (Resolution 1509 (2006)). Council of Europe, para. 13.4; Office of the High Commissioner for Human Rights (2014). The Economic, Social and Cultural Rights of Migrants in an Irregular Situation, p. 107.

135 In this regard, Pijnburg said that: "(…) there is a certain degree of overlap between civil and political rights and socio-economic rights, notably as regards the right to life and the prohibition of torture and other forms of ill-treatment. (…) to the extent that the right to

In this regard, the UN Human Rights Committee addressed the overlap between the right to healthcare and the right to life in a case concerning an irregular migrant who was denied access to Canada's Federal Government programme of healthcare for immigrants (the Interim Federal Health Benefit Program or IFHP) for several years. The Committee considered that, in that case, the concerned migrant "(…) had been exposed to a serious threat to her life and health because she had been excluded from the benefits of IFHP."[136] The Committee thus found that Canada violated her right to life, stating that "(…) the distinction drawn by the State party for the purpose of admission to the Programme between those with legal status in the country and those who had not been fully admitted to Canada was not based on a reasonable and objective criterion and therefore constituted discrimination."[137] The Committee further noted that:

> While the Covenant [ICCPR] does not recognize the right of aliens to enter and reside in the territory of a State party, the Committee also stated that aliens had an 'inherent right to life'. States therefore cannot make a distinction, for the purposes of respecting and protecting the right to life, between regular and irregular migrants.[138]

Despite being entitled to the abovementioned socio-economic rights, whether migrants in limbo can actually enjoy them has been questioned, as:

> (…) migrants, and especially irregular migrants, are in practice often prevented from effectively enjoying their rights by many legal and practical barriers. One prominent barrier is the duty of public service providers to report the presence of irregular migrants.[139] Others are admin-

life and the prohibition of torture and other forms of ill-treatment overlap with socio-economic rights, they require States to realise these rights at all times, including for people on the move [migrants]." Pijnenburg, A. (2021), p. 93.

136 Communication No. 2348/2014, CCPR/C/123/D/2348/2014 (Human Rights Committee, 24 July 2018), para. 11.4.

137 Ibid., para. 11.8.

138 Ibid., para. 11.7.

139 For example, this is the case in Greece, where "(…) a wide spectrum of public actors is prohibited from providing services to undocumented migrants, and the majority of service providers (doctors, landlords, etc.) are obliged to report them to the authorities." Carrera, S., Vosyliute, L., Allsopp, J., Smialowski, S., & Sanchez, G. (2018). Fit for purpose? The Facilitation Directive and the criminalisation of humanitarian assistance to irregular migrants: 2018 update. European Parliament, p. 37.

> istrative obstacles (such as requirements for identity documents, social security numbers and proof of address that irregular migrants cannot obtain), complex administrative, judicial and other systems, lack of information and training (both for service providers and irregular migrants), financial barriers, linguistic hurdles, and fears that accessing services will result in detention or deportation or more generalized fear of making contact with the authorities.[140]

Lack of regulation can thus have very perverse consequences for the concerned migrants. For example, there is a risk that migrants in limbo will find themselves in situations of homelessness, without access to healthcare for lack of means or for fear of detention or return when seeking assistance or contacting service providers.[141] Other issues that are said to be associated with limbo states include migrants having no means of survival[142] and consequently resorting to begging or even stealing, especially as having no status can have detrimental effects on a person's mental health and further stimulate the commission of crimes, either for survival or out of frustration. They may also resort to sex-related work or be subjected to abusive employment relationships in the informal market.

In this context, some propose the erection of firewalls between immigration status and access to basic rights as a way to reduce some of the above-mentioned barriers to the enjoyment of such rights, which are the main negative consequence of limbo. In this case:

> (…) the goal and function of firewalls is to create an environment in which migrants can feel safe in accessing and enjoying their basic rights and entitlements, and in approaching and using the existing services in that regard, without fear of denunciation to immigration enforcement

140 Office of the High Commissioner for Human Rights (2014). The Economic, Social and Cultural Rights of Migrants in an Irregular Situation, p. 126.

141 See, e.g. Gosme, C. (2014), p. 152; and Hastie, B., & Crépeau, F. (2015). The case for 'firewall' protections for irregular migrants: Safeguarding fundamental rights. European Journal of Migration and Law, 17(2–3), 157–183, pp. 158–159.

142 In the context of the European Union, for example, Directive 2009/52/EC prohibits the employment of illegally staying third-country nationals and allows European Union member States to impose financial sanctions on those who employ irregular migrants. See Directive 2009/52/EC of the European Parliament and of the Council of 18 June 2009 providing for minimum standards on sanctions and measures against employers of illegally staying third-country nationals.

> authorities or perceived risks of detection or identification of their irregular status.[143]

Separating services from immigration status allows undesirable but unreturnable migrants in limbo to have access to some of the rights they are entitled to, such as healthcare and education, without fear. Without any legal status, however, there are rights that are unlikely ever to be enjoyed by these migrants, such as the right to work. Not having means to earn a living, these migrants are not able to settle and, therefore, even with firewalls (which are not always present[144]), they remain in limbo, with no certainty about their future. As time passes, this situation may get harder to endure and the chances that the rights of migrants in limbo are violated increases, as prolonged deprivation of social, economic and cultural rights can lead, for example, to a violation of the prohibition on inhuman and degrading treatment.[145] Thus, migrants in this situation are left in a position of indefinite suspension and neglect, with very limited access to important socio-economic rights and benefits.

5 Conclusions on the Literature Regarding Solutions for Undesirable but Unreturnable Migrants

Since the terrorist attacks of 11 September, 2001, in the United Sates, countries have further strengthened the association between security and migration. Some of the consequences of this include limiting refugee protection and enacting anti-migration policies, which may lead States to place further restrictions on who they allow in. Ultimately, this may lead to an increase in the number of undesirable migrants. Once a migrant is identified as undesirable, the default State response is to return them to their country of origin. In some cases, however, return will not be possible as it would constitute a human rights violation.

143 Hastie, B., & Crépeau, F. (2015), p. 166.

144 Indeed, the UN special rapporteur on the human rights of migrants noted that "(…) the current global context – characterized primarily by a security-centred approach and the criminalization of irregular immigration – is largely at odds with the existence of "firewalls" between public services and immigration authorities" (Report of the Special Rapporteur on the human rights of migrants (A/73/178/Rev.1) (2018). United Nations General Assembly, para. 38).

145 Pijnenburg, A. (2021), p. 78.

In this regard, human rights law provides an absolute protection against removing someone to a place where they may face gross human rights violations (non-refoulement). Before such protection was defined in international human rights law instruments, however, the Refugee Convention already granted protection against return to harm to certain migrants. The Refugee Convention, however, excluded from this protection those who were considered undeserving of it due to past actions. It also allowed return to a place of risk when the concerned refugee was considered a threat to the national security or the community of the host country. This gap in protection was somewhat filled by human rights law with the solidification of non-refoulement obligations and their acceptance as absolute.

As human rights law protects those who may face harm upon return from removal regardless of their migration status, these migrants may find themselves in an unusual situation, in which they were refused status (or had an existed status revoked) yet are not subjected to return. Regulating the situation of undesirable but unreturnable migrants can be challenging to host States, as they may be obliged to keep such migrants in their territory for long periods if the human rights concerns that prevent their return are not resolved. At the same time, States may wish to protect their national security or community from criminal or dangerous individuals, as undesirable migrants may be. This chapter thus introduced different measures identified by scholars that may be available for States to regulate (or not) the situation of undesirable but unreturnable migrants. It analysed the possibilities of returning such migrants with diplomatic assurances; extraditing such migrants for the purpose of prosecution or prosecuting them in the host country; subjecting them to immigration detention; and leaving them in a state of 'limbo'. It also presented some of the shortcomings associated with each of these options.

Against this background, the next chapters of this book will explore how three States regulate the situation of undesirable but unreturnable migrants, while critically assessing the human rights compliance and sustainability of the measures in place in each country to identify challenges and best practices.

CHAPTER 2

Australia: The Country Where Undesirable but Unreturnable Migrants Are Indefinitely Detained?

1 Introduction[1]

The previous chapter introduced the topic of undesirable but unreturnable migrants and presented some of the measures States may resort to in order to regulate their situation. This chapter and the two ones that follow it, in turn, look at specific countries to provide an in-depth analysis of how three States, located in different continents and following different legal systems, regulate the situation of these migrants in practice. The first State to be analysed in this context is Australia, widely known for its infamous detention system. In this regard, it is important to note that Australia is currently undergoing changes in the way it regulates the situation of undesirable but unreturnable migrants. This is because, in November 2023, the country's High Court declared indefinite detention to be unlawful in a case concerning an undesirable but unreturnable migrant.[2] The consequences of this Court decision are still developing and so this chapter will reflect the situation as it is at the time of writing.

Finally, as this chapter assesses whether the measures used in Australia to regulate the situation of undesirable but unreturnable migrants comply with human rights, it is also important to note that the country is a party to the Refugee Convention and many other human rights treaties, including the International Covenant on Civil and Political Rights (hereafter ICCPR) and the Convention against Torture and Other Cruel, Inhuman or Degrading Treatment or Punishment (hereafter Convention against Torture). Consequently, migrants in the country should be treated in accordance with the provisions of

1 The main findings of this chapter were published in Zomignani Barboza, J. (2022). Between a rock and a hard place: A human rights assessment of the fate of excluded asylum-seekers and criminal refugees in Australia. Refugee Survey Quarterly, 41(4), 725–745; and in Zomignani Barboza, J. (16 January 2024). Indefinite detention is finally declared unlawful in Australia: what next? RLI Blog on Refugee Law and Forced Migration. Available at: https://rli.blogs.sas.ac.uk/2024/01/16/indefinite-detention-is-finally-declared-unlawful-in-australia-what-next/.

2 NZYQ v Minister for Immigration, Citizenship and Multicultural Affairs [2023] HCA 37 (High Court of Australia, 28 November 2023).

 | DOI:10.1163/9789004719910_004

these international instruments, even though they are not directly applicable in Australia.[3]

2 Who Is Making the Decisions? The Law and the Authorities in Charge of Migration

Legislation wise, Australia has a complex migration system in place, which is regulated by the Migration Act.[4] To understand the application of this Act, this chapter will focus on court decisions adopted between 1 January 2015 and 31 December 2020, which marks the period between two important amendments[5] made to the Migration Act affecting undesirable but unreturnable migrants, one from 2014[6] and one from 2021.[7] These amendments are discussed in more detail below. As noted in the introduction to this chapter, more recent developments with a significant impact on undesirable but unreturnable migrants are also highlighted.

Institution wise, the Department of Home Affairs (hereafter Department) is the government body responsible for immigration decisions. Within the Department, the Minister for Immigration, Citizenship, Migrant Services and Multicultural Affairs (hereafter Minister) is the person in charge of immigration affairs.

In this regard, visa applications may be decided by a delegate of the Minister, working for the Department, or by the Minister themselves. Decisions by delegates may be appealed to the Administrative Review Tribunal (ART), which replaced the former Administrative Appeals Tribunal (AAT).[8] Decisions

---

3 In this regard, Australia's High Court has said: "[I]t is well established that the provisions of an international treaty to which Australia is a party do not form part of Australian law unless those provisions have been validly incorporated into our municipal law by statute." Minister for Immigration and ethnic Affairs v Ah Hin Teoh, [1995] 183 CLR 273 (High Court of Australia, 7 April 1995), para. 25.

4 Migration Act 1958 (hereafter Migration Act): https://www.legislation.gov.au/C1958A00062/latest/text.

5 While other amendments have been made to the Migration Act in the meantime, the two amendments mentioned here are directly relevant to undesirable but unreturnable migrants and thus only these two will be discussed in the chapter.

6 Migration and Maritime Powers Legislation Amendment (Resolving the Asylum Legacy Caseload) Act 2014 (hereafter 2014 Amendment): https://www.legislation.gov.au/C2014A00135/latest/text.

7 Migration Amendment (Clarifying International Obligations for Removal) Regulations 2021 (hereafter 2021 Amendment): https://www.legislation.gov.au/C2021A00035/asmade/text.

8 See Volume 2, Part 5, Migration Act.

made by the Minister personally are often not subject to appeal on the merits. All decisions taken by the Department (including those made by the Minister personally), however, are subject to judicial review.[9] The Federal Court of Australia has original jurisdiction to decide cases of undesirable migrants – that is, migrants who were refused a visa or had a visa cancelled on character grounds, which are most often related to criminal activities.[10] The decisions of this Court thus play an important role in shaping the application of the Migration Act to undesirable migrants. For this reason, decisions of this Court are referred to in this chapter to clarify the correct interpretation of the Migration Act to undesirable but unreturnable migrants.[11] Decisions by the Federal Court of Australia are made by a single (primary) judge[12] and may be appealed to the Full Court.[13] The decisions mentioned in this chapter specify whether the decision was made by a primary judge or the Full Court.

Decisions of the Federal Court of Australia may only exceptionally be appealed to the High Court.[14] As this is an exceptional case, decisions of the High Court were not included in this chapter, except where these have led to major changes for undesirable but unreturnable migrants.

3 Who Are the Undesirables?

This section identifies who the Migration Act considers as undesirable migrants. While specific provisions regarding undesirability may apply exclusively to certain categories of visas (for example, exclusion clauses mirroring the Refugee Convention will apply only to those applying for a protection visa), overall, undesirables in Australia are those who do not pass the so-called character test. In this regard, s 501 of the Migration Act regulates the different situations in which any visa[15] may be refused or cancelled (some-

9 See Volume 2, Part 8, Migration Act.

10 S 476A Migration Act. See also: Federal Court of Australia, Migration Guide: Migration Matters in the Federal Court. Available at: https://www.fedcourt.gov.au/law-and-practice/guides/migration.

11 See the introduction to this book for the case selection and reference period of the research on which the book is based.

12 S 20 Federal Court of Australia Act 1976 (hereafter Federal Court of Australia Act): https://www.legislation.gov.au/C2004A01586/latest/text.

13 S 25 Federal Court of Australia Act.

14 S 33 Federal Court of Australia Act.

15 It is worth mentioning that, as the Refugee Convention (and the equivalent national criteria to grant refugee status) already contains exclusion clauses, it has been ques-

times mandatorily so[16]) due to certain aspects of the concerned migrant's character (the character test). Most of these aspects are related to involvement in criminal activities. In sum, it can be said that there are five main reasons why a migrant would be considered undesirable in Australia: committing an international crime; committing a serious crime; being a threat to national security; committing a migration offence; or being a common criminal. These reasons are explained in the following subsections.

3.1 *Those Who Committed International Crimes*

As noted in Section 3.1 of Chapter 1, the Refugee Convention excludes from refugee protection those who engage in international crimes – that is, those who commit a crime against peace, a war crime, or a crime against humanity. The Migration Act mirrors these exclusion criteria listed in article 1F of the Refugee Convention in s 5H(2)(a) and thus denies a protection visa[17] to those who engaged in such crimes.

---

tioned whether this 'extra' possibility of exclusion (that is, the character test) would apply to the grant of protection visas. In 2019 and 2020, a series of decisions of primary judges of the Federal Court of Australia concluded that, in view of the specific exclusion clauses that applied to protection visas, the character test should not be applied in protection cases (see, e.g. BAL19 v Minister for Home Affairs, [2019] FCA 2189 (Federal Court of Australia, 24 December 2019); BFW20 by his Litigation Representative BFW20A v Minister for Immigration, Citizenship, Migrant Services and Multicultural Affairs, [2020] FCA 562 (Federal Court of Australia, 30 April 2020); AEM20 v Minister for Home Affairs, [2020] FCA 623 (Federal Court of Australia, 12 May 2020)). When the matter reached the Full Court of the Federal Court, however, the Full Court made the opposite finding, concluding that the character test does, in fact, apply to protection visa applications. In this regard, the Full Court's decision said: "[I]t is somewhat surprising that a statute should provide two paths for dealing with the same subject matter in the one process under a single duty and do so differentially by requiring that subject to be addressed by different considerations. However, that is what I consider the Act does. That is done, in my view, because the Act intends to provide a path by which Australia's protection obligations may be discharged by the grant of a protection visa and a separate path in which the Minister is given the capacity not to discharge those obligations by the grant of a protection visa despite the visa applicant being a person in respect of whom Australia owes protection obligations." KDSP v Minister for Immigration, Citizenship, Migrant Services and Multicultural Affairs, [2020] FCAFC 108 (Federal Court of Australia, 23 June 2020), para. 100.

16 In this regard, s 501(3A) of the Migration Act stipulates that a visa must be cancelled when the person has a substantial criminal record; has committed a sexual offence involving a child; or the person is serving a sentence of imprisonment, on a full-time basis in a custodial institution, for an offence against an Australian law.

17 As will be explained below, protection visas in Australia can be granted based on both refugee and complementary protection.

Outside the international protection context, the Migration Act further excludes those who engage in international crimes from being granted any visa in the country. In this regard, s 501(6)(ba)(iii) of the Act deems that those who commit the crime of genocide, a crime against humanity, a war crime, a crime involving torture or slavery or a crime that is otherwise of serious international concern may not be granted a visa in Australia or may have an existing visa cancelled. Similarly, those who were charged with or indicted for such crimes are also considered undesirable according to s 501(6)(f) of the Migration Act.

In practice, a primary judge of the Federal Court made two important remarks regarding the application of this ground of undesirability, more specifically regarding war crimes and crimes against humanity.[18] First, the primary judge affirmed that the Minister could use his power to reject a protection visa on such grounds even when the concerned person is owed non-refoulement obligations and the Minister considers that they pose no threat to the Australian community. This is because, according to the primary judge, it is within the Minister's discretion to assign more weight to the expectation so the Australian community (in this case, that a war criminal or someone who commits a crime against humanity is denied a visa) than to the fact that the concerned migrant poses no harm to this community. Second, the primary judge found that, when the concerned migrant claims to have acted under duress (or, by analogy, another possible defence that applies to such crimes), this fact needs to be taken into account by the decision-maker before reaching a decision.[19]

---

18 These remarks were provided in the case CMA19 v Minister for Home Affairs, [2020] FCA 736 (Federal Court of Australia, 29 May 2020). This case concerned a citizen of Sri Lanka (pseudonymised CMA19), who was involved in the Liberation Tigers of Tamil Eelam (hereafter LTTE), an armed group involved in the Sri Lankan civil war, for 5 years, occupying different positions within the group. In Australia, he applied for a safe haven enterprise (protection) visa. The officer assessing his visa application deemed that his acts within the LTTE were committed under duress and that he thus complied with the visa requirements and should be granted a visa. The Minister, however, decided that they, personally, believed the applicant had voluntarily committed the acts and thus should be refused a visa under s 501. In their assessment, the Minister deemed the applicant was not a risk to the Australian community and was owed non-refoulement obligations; however, as the Minister believed the applicant had committed or facilitated war crimes or crimes against humanity, the Australian community expected him to be denied a visa and thus decided to refuse to grant the visa. The Minister's decision is the one under review in the case.

19 Another error derived from the claim of duress in this case. In the Minister's notice of intention to refuse the visa, the Minister mentioned that he would consider the nature and extent of CMA19's involvement in the LTTE. However, it was not clear that the Minister would, as they did, claim in the decision that they believed the applicant's involvement with the group was voluntary. As the Minister did not make it clear that

Lastly, Rikhof also noted that, overall, membership to an organisation that commits international crimes alone is not sufficient to exclude an asylum seeker under article 1F(a) in Australia.[20]

3.2 *Those Who Committed Serious Crimes*

As was mentioned in Section 3.1 of Chapter 1, not only those who commit international crimes are excluded from refugee protection. The Refugee Convention also excludes those who committed a serious non-political crime before entering the country of asylum (article 1F(b) Refugee Convention) and those who committed acts contrary to the purpose and principles of the United Nations (hereafter UN) (article 1F(c) Refugee Convention). Australia mirrors these provisions in sections 5H(2)(b) and (c) of the Migration Act, barring those involved in these acts from being granted a protection visa.

Regarding the practical application of this provision, Rikhof noted that serious non-political crimes include murder, abduction and rape, drug trafficking, people smuggling, extortion, and arson and malicious damage to property.[21]

People smuggling (s 501(6)(ba)(i) Migration Act), together with human trafficking (s 501(6)(ba)(ii) Migration Act) and sexual crimes against children (s 501(6)(e) Migration Act) have also been singled out as crimes that would lead to the denial or cancellation of any visa in the character test, regardless of when they were committed (that is, before or after arrival in Australia).

In this regard, the Federal Court clarified that these crimes would only lead to the rejection of a visa when they were committed after their inclusion in the Migration Act. More specifically, the Federal Court found a legal error in the Minister refusing a visa to someone owed protection because they reasonably suspected that the concerned migrant had been involved in people smuggling, when the ground according to which a visa could be rejected upon suspicion that the applicant was involved in people smuggling did not exist when the acts took place.[22]

As for the acts contrary to the purposes and principles of the UN, Rikhof observed that this provision was applied in at least three cases. In the first one, the killing of civilians during a non-international armed conflict was found to amount to a crime against humanity, a serious non-political crime and an act

---

duress was central to their assessment, the primary judge deemed that the applicant was denied procedural fairness.

20 Rikhof, J. (2023). Exclusion and Refoulement: Criminality in International and Domestic Refugee Law. Irwin Law Inc., pp. 310–312.

21 Ibid., p. 465.

22 AEM20 v Minister for Home Affairs, [2020] FCA 623.

contrary to the purposes and principles of the UN. In the second, it was used to exclude someone involved in terrorist activities. In the third one, it was applied in reference to a person involved in hostage-taking in the United States embassy.[23]

Crimes against humanity, as noted in the previous section, are singled out in the character test. Terrorism and hostage-taking, in turn, are not. The character test does exclude, however, those who are (or have been) associated with a group that is involved in criminal conduct (s 501(6)(b) Migration Act). Thus, those involved in terrorist acts as part of a terrorist group may fall under this provision of the character test.

3.3 *Those Who Are a Threat to National Security*

Section 3.1 of Chapter 1 noted that, apart from the exclusion clauses, the Refugee Convention also contains a provision providing an exception to the (refugee law) non-refoulement principle. That section also mentioned that, in practice, many States add that exception as an extra exclusion clause, instead of an exception to non-refoulement. This is the case in Australia, which prescribes, in s 36(1B) and (1C) of the Migration Act, two criteria that need to be fulfilled by applicants to be granted a protection visa. These criteria are, first, that the applicant is not assessed by the Australian Security Intelligence Organisation (hereafter ASIO) to be directly or indirectly a risk to security and, second, that the applicant is not a person whom the Minister considers, on reasonable grounds, is a danger to Australia's security or, having been convicted by a final judgement of a particularly serious crime, is a danger to the Australian community. The concept of danger, however, is not defined in the Migration Act. The Federal Court indicated, however, that elements such as the nature of the crime and reoffending are taken into account to determine whether someone would fall into the exclusion clause prescribed by s 36(1C), Australia's equivalent to article 33(2) of the Refugee Convention.[24]

---

23 Rikhof, J. (2023), p. 544–545.

24 In the concerned case, the Federal Court of Australia assessed the application of this provision in a case in which a man who fell under the exclusion clause of s 36(1C) – namely, after being convicted of a serious crime, he was considered to be a danger to the Australian community – questioned the AAT's conclusion that he was a 'danger', arguing that he was only a 'conventional' criminal. A primary judge of the Court, however, deemed that it was not necessary to consider the meaning of the word 'danger' in this case since the Tribunal reached its decision based on reasonable grounds. According to the primary judge "[T]he Tribunal had regard, in particular, to the serious nature of the applicant's offending – which included domestic violence, assaults (including with a weapon) and many instances of trafficking heroin – the fact of repeat offending over a

Outside international protection applications, the character test also serves to deny or cancel a visa on security grounds. More specifically, the character test has three provisions addressing the issue of national security or danger to the Australian community. The first is s 501(6)(d), which deems undesirable a person who, if allowed to enter or remain in Australia, risks engaging in criminal conduct; harassing, molesting,[25] intimidating or stalking another person; vilifying a segment of the Australian community; inciting discord in the Australian community or in a segment of that community; or representing a danger to the Australian community or to a segment of that community.

The second is s 501(6)(g), which considers undesirable those who have been assessed by ASIO to be directly or indirectly a risk to security. ASIO's practices, however, have been questioned regarding their human rights compliance. ASIO is not bound by conventional standards of proof (such as 'beyond reasonable doubt' or 'balance of probabilities')[26] or procedure, which means that many migrants with an adverse security assessment are not given a copy of their assessment or even a summary of the reasons for it,[27] limiting their possibility of challenging such decisions. The Australian Human Rights Commission expressed concern over this possibility, noting that "(…) a failure to provide sufficient details about the information relied upon by ASIO could amount to a lack of procedural fairness."[28] The UN Human Rights Committee was of a similar opinion when it decided the case of Mansour Leghaei. Leghaei had settled in Australia with his wife and children for some years on temporary permits when he applied for a permanent visa. This request, however, was denied, as Leghaei was assessed by ASIO as being a threat to national security

significant period of years, and the applicant's submission that he would not continue to re-offend (about which the Tribunal was not satisfied for the well-articulated and comprehensive reasons given)." (WGKS v Minister for Immigration, Citizenship, Migrant Services and Multicultural Affairs, [2020] FCA 1060 (Federal Court of Australia, 24 July 2020), para. 26).

25 Harassment and molestation are further defined in s 501(11) of the Migration Act, which states that: "For the purposes of the character test, conduct may amount to harassment or molestation of a person even though:
(a) it does not involve violence, or threatened violence, to the person; or
(b) it consists only of damage, or threatened damage, to property belonging to, in the possession of, or used by, the person."

26 Juss, S. S. (2017). Detention and delusion in Australia's Kafkaesque refugee law. Refugee Survey Quarterly, 36(1), 146–167, p. 161.

27 Ibid. idem.

28 Australian Human Rights Commission (2013). Tell Me About: Refugees with Adverse Security Assessments, p. 3.

without, however, being informed of the reasons for such assessment. In the Committee's decision, it is concluded that in view of "(…) the absence of any explanation from the State party as to the reasons for terminating his right to remain, except for the general assertion that it was done for 'compelling reasons of national security', the Committee finds that the State party's procedure lacked due process of law."[29] Thus, in some situations, finding a migrant to be undesirable under s 501(6)(g) or s 36(1B) of the Migration Act may be done in violation of their human rights.

The third reference to national security or danger to the community in the character test is s 501(6)(h), which considers undesirable a migrant who has an Interpol notice in relation to them, from which it is reasonable to infer that the person would present a risk to the Australian community or a segment of that community. A primary judge of the Federal Court noted, however, that this provision should not be applied blindly. Instead, the underlying facts of the notice must be assessed. More specifically, the primary judge found a legal error in the Minister refusing a protection visa due to an Interpol Red Notice, as it was considered that the criminal justice system in China (the country at the source of the Red Notice) has multiple flaws, including that torture is widespread to obtain false confessions and that approximately 95% of the criminal cases rely on confessions to convict.[30]

3.4 *Those Who Commit a Migration Offence*

The character test includes provisions considering undesirable migrants who engage in criminal acts directly linked to their migration situation. These are the crime of escaping migration detention (s 501(6)(ab) Migration Act); crimes committed while the person was in immigration detention (s 501(6)(aa)(i) Migration Act); crimes committed during an escape by the person from immigration detention (s 501(6)(aa)(ii) Migration Act); and crimes committed after the person escaped from immigration detention but before the person was taken into immigration detention again (s 501(6)(aa)(iii) Migration Act).

3.5 *Common Criminals*

Lastly, the character test considers undesirable those who, due to their past and present general or criminal conduct are not considered to be of good character (s 501(6)(c) Migration Act) as well as those who have a substantial

29 Communication No. 1937/2010. CCPR/C/113/D/1937/2010 (Human Rights Committee, 26 March 2015), para. 10.5.

30 ERY19 v Minister for Immigration, Citizenship, Migrant Services and Multicultural Affairs, [2020] FCA 569 (Federal Court of Australia, 4 May 2020).

criminal record (s 501(6)(a) Migration Act). In this regard, someone is considered to have a substantial criminal record when, among others, the person has been sentenced to a term of imprisonment of 12 months or more (s 501(7)(c) Migration Act); or the person has been sentenced to two or more terms of imprisonment, where the total of those terms is 12 months or more (s 501(7)(d) Migration Act). These provisions seem to be a catch-all that could lead to the denial or cancellation of a visa to anyone who engages in criminal activities that are not specified in the other provisions of s 501.

These provisions are particularly relevant as it is estimated that the greatest population of undesirables is composed of those who have had a residence permit revoked for crimes committed in the host State.[31] Thus, catchall provisions such as the ones above may increase the pool of undesirables. The character test, however, grants decision-makers some flexibility in its application. This flexibility allows decision-makers to balance a migrant's undesirability with factors that would favour their continued stay in the country, as will be explained in the next section.

3.6 *Discretion in Applying the Character Test: Not as Many Undesirables as Initially Foreseen?*

Despite the abovementioned strict character test that is provided in the Migration Act, it is important to note that before a visa is refused or cancelled on character grounds, the concerned migrant is invited to make submissions. These submissions can show that either they pass the character test or that there is another reason why they should be granted a visa, or why their visa should not be cancelled. When considering whether there is 'another reason', the Minister has issued guidance to the Department, in the form of Directions, on what should be taken into account by their delegates when exercising such discretionary power to refuse or cancel a visa. However, when the Minister personally makes a decision, this guidance does not need to be followed.

According to this guidance – more specifically, Direction 65 and its very similar successor, Direction 79,[32] the primary considerations for decision-

31 See Refugee Law Initiative, Arts & Humanities Research Council and Center for International Criminal Justice (2016). Undesirable and Unreturnable? Policy challenges around excluded asylum seekers and other migrants suspected of serious criminality who cannot be removed (Policy brief), pp. 3–4 and 31.

32 The similarities between both Directions led Direction No. 79 to be called the near-identical successor of Direction No. 65 in Honnery, C. (29 April 2020). The confused construction of 'non-refoulement' in the Ministerial Directions for visa cancellations. AUSPUBLAW. Available at: https://auspublaw.org/2020/04/the-confused-construction-of-non-refoulement-in-the-ministerial-directions-for-visa-cancellations/.

makers are the protection of the Australian community from criminal or other serious conduct; the best interests of minor children in Australia; and the expectations of the Australian community. Other considerations that should be taken into account are international non-refoulement obligations; the strength, nature and duration of the person's ties to Australia; the impact on Australian business interests; and the impact on victims. These considerations are the same for visa holders and visa applicants, however, when it comes to visa holders (who are in the process of having their visa cancelled or asking for the cancellation to be revoked), the extent of impediments if removed is also to be considered.

These considerations require decision-makers to take into account not only the possible danger the person represents but also their life in Australia and the consequences of return. This may allow migrants who do not pass the character test to be granted a chance to remain in the country when their actions will not overall constitute a threat or when stripping them of the right to stay in Australia would be a disproportionate measure. This can help diminish the pool of undesirable migrants.

Not all those who do not *a priori* pass the character test will find relief in this way though, as the decision-maker may not find that the balance weighs in their favour. Despite being undesirable, some of these migrants will also be unreturnable, as they may be owed non-refoulement obligations. The next sections will thus be dedicated to exploring how a migrant can claim their fear of harm upon return and thus be considered unreturnable in Australia.

4 Who Are the Unreturnable Migrants?

4.1 *Asking for Protection through a Protection Visa Application*

In Australia, those who fear harm in their country of origin may apply for one of the visas under the 'refugee and humanitarian visas'[33] category. The main visa in this category is the protection visa, defined in s 35A of the Migration Act. The requirements prescribed for someone to be granted a protection visa seek to implement the Refugee Convention, as interpreted by Australia, in national law, since, as mentioned above, international treaties do not directly apply in Australia.[34] The provisions of the Migration Act, however, do not

33 Visa categories: https://immi.homeaffairs.gov.au/visas/getting-a-visa/visa-listing.

34 It is relevant to note here that significant changes were made to the Migration Act with the 2014 Amendment to that Act. Before the Amendment, the definition of refugee applied in Australia was the Refugee Convention definition, since Australian law ref-

strictly follow the Refugee Convention, sometimes prescribing requirements that differ from the international treaty but that need to be fulfilled by a visa applicant to be granted a protection visa.

For example, ss 5H and 5J of the Migration Act closely mirror the refugee definition prescribed in the Refugee Convention (mentioned in Section 3.1 of Chapter 1), but further specify that there must be a real chance that the feared persecution will materialise if the person is returned to their country of nationality or habitual residence; and that the real chance of persecution must relate to all areas of the concerned country. This last requirement introduces in Australian law the notion of an internal flight alternative, that is, the possibility to deny a person refugee status if they could have moved to a different part of their own country to find safety. While this concept is not explicitly included in the Refugee Convention, it has been applied by decision-makers worldwide as well as by the United Nations High Commissioner for Refugees (hereafter UNHCR).[35] However, UNHCR limits its application to when the area of relocation is practically, safely, and legally accessible to the individual;[36] a requirement that is lacking in the Australian provision.

S 5J(3) adds another specification that is not included in the Refugee Convention, which is that the person does not have a well-founded fear of persecution if they could take reasonable steps to modify their behaviour so as to avoid a real chance of persecution, as long as the modification would not conflict with a characteristic that is fundamental to the person's identity or conscience; or conceal an innate or immutable characteristic of the person. S 5J(6) further determines that "any conduct engaged in by the person in Australia is to be disregarded unless the person satisfies the Minister that the person engaged in the conduct otherwise than for the purpose of strengthening the person's claim to be a refugee." This is, again, a provision that has no equivalent in the Refugee Convention.

These provisions point to the fact that the Australian legislator took a restrictive approach to the Refugee Convention by limiting its application at the national level. At the same time, however, the Migration Act also expands

erred directly to the Convention. After the Amendment, however, the reference to the Convention was removed and the interpretation of the Convention requirements was added to national law to define the refugee criteria as it is currently applied. See more on Administrative Appeals Tribunal, Guide to Refugee Law in Australia (2020), Chapter 1: Protection Visas.

35 See UNHCR (2003). Guidelines on International Protection: "Internal Flight or Relocation Alternative" within the Context of Article 1A(2) of the 1951 Convention and/or 1967 Protocol relating to the Status of Refugees (HCR/GIP/03/04).

36 Ibid.

complementary protection visas to those who, despite not meeting the refugee definition, are persons in respect of whom Australia has protection obligations because it is believed that they will suffer significant harm if returned to their country of origin (s 36(2)(aa) Migration Act). Significant harm in this case includes arbitrary deprivation of life, death penalty, torture and inhumane and degrading treatment or punishment (s 36(2A) Migration Act). Additionally, the real risk of being subjected to such harm must be faced by the non-citizen personally and not one faced by the population of the country generally (s 36(2B)(c) Migration Act). This complementary protection is thus applied to those who, despite not meeting the refugee criteria, may not be returned due to non-refoulement obligations arising from international human rights treaties protecting the right to life and the right to be free from torture (human rights non-refoulement).

Apart from these visa requirements, Australia has also included provisions on safe third countries, which work to prevent those in relation to whom there is a safe third country from applying for a protection visa (ss 91A to 91D Migration Act). The Migration Act also bars unlawful maritime arrivals (that is, those who arrive irregularly by boat) from applying to any visa in the country, unless the Minister exceptionally allows them to do so (s 46A Migration Act).

Lastly, as noted in Section 3 above, undesirable migrants will have their visa application rejected when they fall under exclusion clauses (which are listed as visa requirements for this particular type of visa). They may also be denied a protection visa (or have an existing visa cancelled) when they do not (or no longer) meet the character test.

Indeed, this has led undesirable but unreturnable migrants to question whether their non-refoulement claims would be assessed in a protection visa application, since they could simply be deemed excluded and denied a visa, without a decision-maker looking at the harm they would face upon return. The next section thus clarifies what is and what is not assessed in protection visa applications, according to the jurisprudence of the Federal Court.

4.2 *What a Protection Visa Application Actually Assesses: An Overview of the Case Law of the Federal Court Surrounding the* BCR16 *and Omar Cases*

The Federal Court of Australia mainly dealt with two issues related to what is assessed during a protection visa application. The first one is whether an undesirable migrant would have their protection claims assessed during a protection visa application or whether they could be found to be excluded and thus denied a visa before the decision-maker analysed their fear of harm upon return. The case at the centre of this issue is the BCR16 case decided by the

Full Court of the Federal Court of Australia. The second is whether a protection visa application will assess non-refoulement obligations as prescribed in international treaties. The case at the centre of this issue is the Omar case decided by a primary judge of the Federal Court.

Regarding the first issue, at the start of 2015, the Federal Court's position seemed to be that protection claims would be addressed in the protection visa procedure.[37] This position, however, changed in 2017, when the Full Court, in view of the arguments presented during the appeal of the BCR16 case,[38] adopted a different position. On that occasion, the Full Court noted that the protection visa criteria include not only non-refoulement issues, but also other conditions such as health and character requirements. Thus, a protection visa could be refused if the applicant did not meet these other requirements even before any protection claim was assessed. The appeal decision in BCR16 thus marked a change in the position of the Federal Court of Australia. This reasoning (that is, that a protection visa could be rejected without a non-refoulement assessment) was followed in multiple other cases brought before the Federal Court.[39] In response to the BCR16 appeal and the following cases, on 6 September 2017, the Minister issued Ministerial Direction No 75 – Refusal of Protection visas relying on ss 36(1C) and 36(2C)(b), which establishes that claims of persecution and/or fear of harm must be assessed before character and security concerns on protection visa applications.[40] In 2018, a primary judge of the Federal Court discussed the consideration of protection claims in view of the recent Direction 75 (requiring that protection claims be assessed

37 See, e.g. Ayoub v Minister for Immigration and Border Protection, [2015] FCAFC 83 (Federal Court of Australia, 12 June 2015); BCR16 v Minister for Immigration and Border Protection, [2016] FCA 965 (Federal Court of Australia, 17 August 2016); Minister for Immigration and Border Protection v Le, [2016] FCAFC 120 (Federal Court of Australia, 9 September 2016).

38 BCR16 v Minister for Immigration and Border Protection, [2017] FCAFC 96 (Federal Court of Australia, 13 June 2017).

39 See, e.g. ALN17 v Minister for Immigration and Border Protection, [2017] FCA 726 (Federal Court of Australia, 5 June 2017); Steyn v Minister for Immigration and Border Protection, [2017] FCA 1131 (Federal Court of Australia, 25 September 2017); BHA17 v Minister for Immigration and Border Protection, [2017] FCA 1288 (Federal Court of Australia, 7 November 2017); Minister for Immigration and Border Protection v BHA17, [2018] FCAFC 68 (Federal Court of Australia, 4 May 2018); FKP18 v Minister for Immigration and Border Protection, [2018] FCA 1555 (Federal Court of Australia, 18 October 2018); Hamidy v Minister for Immigration and Border Protection, [2019] FCA 221 (Federal Court of Australia, 27 February 2019).

40 As mentioned above, Directions issued by the Minister are binding on all their delegates, but not on the Minister themselves.

before character requirements).[41] In that occasion, the primary judge found that, in view of the Direction, it was the likely course of decision-making that protection claims would be considered in a protection visa application. Following decisions came to the same conclusion.[42]

After the Federal Court seemed to have settled the issue that protection claims would be assessed during a protection visa application, the second issue mentioned above arose before the Court. That is, whether a protection visa application would assess non-refoulement obligations as prescribed in international treaties. This issue gained relevance with the Omar case, decided by a primary judge of the Federal Court.[43] In that case, Omar argued that his non-refoulement claims would not be analysed in a protection visa application as the content of non-refoulement obligations differs from the protection visa criteria and a protection visa application would only look at

---

41 Ali v Minister for Immigration and Border Protection, [2018] FCA 650 (Federal Court of Australia, 10 May 2018).

42 See, e.g. Greene v Assistant Minister for Home Affairs, [2018] FCA 919 (Federal Court of Australia, 31 May 2018); Turay v Assistant Minister for Home Affairs, [2018] FCA 1487 (Federal Court of Australia, 3 October 2018); DOB18 v Minister for Home Affairs, [2018] FCA 1523 (Federal Court of Australia, 17 October 2018); Ibrahim v Minister for Home Affairs, [2018] FCA 1592 (Federal Court of Australia, 24 October 2018); BKS18 v Minister for Home Affairs, [2018] FCA 1731 (Federal Court of Australia, 13 November 2018); Sowa v Minister for Home Affairs, [2018] FCA 1999 (Federal Court of Australia, 14 December 2018); Ezegbe v Minister for Immigration and Border Protection, [2019] FCA 216 (Federal Court of Australia, 27 February 2019); GBV18 v Minister for Home Affairs, [2019] FCA 1132 (Federal Court of Australia, 29 July 2019); DGI19 v Minister for Home Affairs, [2019] FCA 1867 (Federal Court of Australia, 14 November 2019); FBW18 v Minister for Home Affairs, [2019] FCA 1878 (Federal Court of Australia, 15 November 2019); Ali v Minister for Home Affairs, [2019] FCA 1900 (Federal Court of Australia, 18 November 2019); Uolilo v Minister for Home Affairs, [2020] FCA 1135 (Federal Court of Australia, 7 August 2020). It is worth noting, however, that in one case from 2020 (CZW20 v Minister for Immigration, Citizenship, Migrant Services and Multicultural Affairs, [2020] FCA 1380 (Federal Court of Australia, 24 September 2020)), a primary judge considered that even if Direction 75 demanded that protection grounds be assessed before the ineligibility criteria in protection visa applications, it did not require all non-protection criteria (e.g. health or public interest criteria) to be considered beforehand. Thus, it was still possible that a protection visa be refused without the decision-maker assessing the protection claims. In response to these issues, however, the 2021 Amendment (mentioned below) works to settle similar disputes, as it inserted s 36A in the Migration Act, requiring that protection criteria be assessed before any other criteria in protection visa applications, thus more fully addressing the error identified in BCR16.

43 Omar v Minister for Home Affairs, [2019] FCA 279 (Federal Court of Australia, 7 March 2019).

the latter and not the former. The primary judge decided in Omar's favour. In his reasoning, the primary judge states that:

> (...) the relevant issue in the visa context is not whether non-refoulement obligations will be considered. They will not be. (...) At most, in determining whether the refugee and complementary protection criteria are satisfied, assessments of a not dissimilar kind may arise, but subject to statutory modifications of the content of the protection criteria. However, this relates only to the determination of one of the many criteria for the grant of a different kind of visa. There is no direct consideration of Art 33 of the Refugees Convention or the equivalent articles in the ICCPR and CAT [Convention against Torture].[44]

The decision, however, was appealed to the Full Court. Before the appeal was decided, decisions of primary judges differed, with some following the reasoning in Omar (that is, finding that the protection visa criteria differed from non-refoulement obligations),[45] with others calling Omar "(...) an outlier on the jurisprudential spectrum."[46] When the matter came to the Full Court during the appeal of Omar, the Full Court decided the issue on other grounds and thus refrained from clarifying the matter (that is, whether a protection visa application would sufficiently assess non-refoulement obligations).[47]

In sum, the Case Law of the Federal Court shows that, according to the Australian administration, protection claims should be assessed before char-

---

44 Ibid., paras. 57–58.

45 See, e.g. FQM18 v Minister for Home Affairs, [2019] FCA 1263 (Federal Court of Australia, 14 August 2019); EKC19 v Minister for Home Affairs, [2019] FCA 1823 (Federal Court of Australia, 8 November 2019); DGI19 v Minister for Home Affairs, [2019] FCA 1867; Hernandez v Minister for Home Affairs, [2020] FCA 415 (Federal Court of Australia, 31 March 2020); DP20 v Minister for Home Affairs, [2020] FCA 1055 (Federal Court of Australia, 24 July 2020).

46 GBV18 v Minister for Home Affairs, [2019] FCA 1132, para. 81. In 2020, a primary judge of the Federal Court tried to reconcile Omar with apparently opposing decisions through the lenses of materiality in the individual case. In that occasion, the primary judge considered that to be successful in an argument that the protection visa criteria differed from a non-refoulement assessment, an applicant had to point to differences between the assessments (such as the internal relocation principle, which applies to the former and not the latter) that could have led to material differences in the decision. See Ahmed v Minister for Immigration, Citizenship and Multicultural Affairs, [2020] FCA 557 (Federal Court of Australia, 29 April 2020).

47 Minister for Home Affairs v Omar, [2019] FCAFC 188 (Federal Court of Australia, 29 October 2019). See also Honnery, C. (2020, April 29).

acter issues in a protection visa application. The Full Court does not clarify, however, its stance on whether the protection criteria correspond to Australia's non-refoulement obligations, although some primary judges of that Court are of the opinion that it does not.

As noted in Section 3.6 above, however, decision-makers are also guided by the Minister to take non-refoulement into account when deciding on a visa refusal or cancellation on character grounds. Some findings on how a non-refoulement assessment takes place in that situation are thus presented in the next section.

4.3 *Assessing Non-refoulement Claims during a Visa Refusal or Cancellation on Character Grounds*

As mentioned in Section 3.6 above, ministerial guidance calls on decision-makers to consider non-refoulement before refusing or cancelling a visa on character grounds. Before the Federal Court, however, decision-makers often argued that this assessment did not have to be made during a visa rejection or cancellation when the concerned undesirable migrant could still apply for a protection visa.[48] The Federal Court, in turn, accepted (although not unanimously) four arguments[49] made by migrants that would point to a different interpretation, that is, that a non-refoulement assessment should take place during a visa rejection or cancellation regardless of whether the migrant could still apply for a protection visa.

The first is the argument made in Omar, mentioned above, that is, that the protection visa criteria differ from a non-refoulement assessment. As was noted in the previous section, however, this argument has not been unanimously accepted by Court judges.

The second is that the nature and scope of a non-refoulement assessment under the discretionary power to cancel a visa is different than an assessment

48 Here, it is important to note that a migrant who had a protection visa cancelled will not be allowed to re-apply for a protection visa (s 48A Migration Act) unless the Minister exceptionally allows them to (s 48B Migration Act). This may be a reason why unreturnable migrants would prefer to first apply for a different visa, if they can, instead of a protection visa (to ensure they can still apply for a protection visa even if their initial visa is cancelled).

49 Before the enaction of Direction 75, the Federal Court also accepted as a fifth argument the fact that protection claims would not necessarily be assessed before character aspects in a protection visa application. As noted in the previous section, however, this was resolved by the Direction and the 2021 Amendment (see footnote 42).

of whether the applicant fulfils or not visa conditions, in which the non-fulfilment will demand that the visa be denied.[50]

The third is that decision-makers need to consider claims made by concerned migrants, regardless of whether they relate to non-refoulement or not.[51] Thus, when claims related to non-refoulement are made, the decision-

---

50 See BCR16 v Minister for Immigration and Border Protection, [2017] FCAFC 96; Turay v Assistant Minister for Home Affairs, [2018] FCA 1487; Omar v Minister for Home Affairs, [2019] FCA 279; Sowa v Minister for Home Affairs, [2019] FCAFC 111 (Federal Court of Australia, 28 June 2019); Minister for Home Affairs v Omar, [2019] FCAFC 188; DGI19 v Minister for Home Affairs, [2019] FCA 1867; Ali v Minister for Home Affairs, [2020] FCAFC 109 (Federal Court of Australia, 29 June 2020). In this regard, in a case from 2020, a primary judge also noted that it was an error to defer a non-refoulement assessment to a future protection visa application because such application would have to be rejected if the applicant did not pass the character test and it was difficult to understand how s 501 would not prevent the grant of a protection visa when it was deemed that the criminality with which the concerned migrant in that case had been involved required his visa to be mandatorily cancelled (see FAK19 v Minister for Immigration, Citizenship, Migrant Services and Multicultural Affairs, [2020] FCA 1124 (Federal Court of Australia, 7 August 2020)). This is an interesting observation, as it applies to most of the cases regarding a visa cancellation on character grounds, but never seems to be brought up by the judges of the Federal Court. Indeed, while the discussion on deferring non-refoulement assessments to a future protection visa application, the Court's Case Law seems to avoid 'speculating' the result of that procedure, even if it seems quite clear that the chances of success for someone who's visa is being cancelled are slim.

51 See, e.g. Flores v Minister for Home Affairs, [2019] FCA 1043 (Federal Court of Australia, 5 July 2019); CHJK v Minister for Home Affairs, [2019] FCA 1330 (Federal Court of Australia, 23 August 2019); RZSN v Minister for Home Affairs, [2019] FCA 1731 (Federal Court of Australia, 24 October 2019); Minister for Home Affairs v Omar, [2019] FCAFC 188; CWGF v Minister for Home Affairs, [2019] FCA 1802 (Federal Court of Australia, 7 November 2019); EKC19 v Minister for Home Affairs, [2019] FCA 1823; DGI19 v Minister for Home Affairs, [2019] FCA 1867; FBW18 v Minister for Home Affairs, [2019] FCA 1878; Ali v Minister for Home Affairs, [2019] FCA 1900; DYY18 v Minister for Home Affairs, [2019] FCA 1901 (Federal Court of Australia, 18 November 2019); CTB19 v Minister for Immigration, Citizenship, Migrant Services and Multicultural Affairs, [2019] FCA 2128 (Federal Court of Australia, 18 December 2019); Hernandez v Minister for Home Affairs, [2020] FCA 415; Ahmed v Minister for Immigration, Citizenship and Multicultural Affairs, [2020] FCA 557; CCF20 v Minister for Home Affairs, [2020] FCA 676 (Federal Court of Australia, 20 May 2020); GCRM v Minister for Immigration, Citizenship, Migrant Services and Multicultural Affairs, [2020] FCA 678 (Federal Court of Australia, 20 May 2020); BRO18 v Minister for Home Affairs, [2020] FCA 688 (Federal Court of Australia, 22 May 2020); MNLR v Minister of Home Affairs, [2020] FCA 948 (Federal Court of Australia, 8 July 2020); KYMM v Minister for Immigration, Citizenship, Migrant Services and Multicultural Affairs, [2020] FCA 1069 (Federal Court of Australia, 28 July 2020); BPL20 v Minister for Home Affairs, [2020] FCA 1207 (Federal Court of Australia, 20 August 2020); Guclukol v Minister for Home Affairs, [2020] FCAFC 148 (Federal Court of Australia, 4 September 2020); Minister for Immigration, Citizenship, Migrant Services and Multi-

maker needs to engage with them fully and meaningfully. In some cases, the Court seems to have used this argument as a way to avoid making a strong stance on consideration of non-refoulement in these cases.[52]

The fourth is that non-refoulement should be assessed as a standalone reason to decide on the grant or cancellation of a visa on character grounds because Australia's compliance with its non-refoulement obligations affects the country's reputation and international standing. Thus, it can be considered as a matter of national interest that needs to be taken into account.[53]

In sum, the Case Law of the Federal Court of Australia seems to have evolved to consider that clearly stated non-refoulement claims need to be considered, at least in their facts, and that decision-makers need to take into account the differences between the discretionary cancellation or refusal of a visa and the mandatory refusal of another. Furthermore, in recent decisions, non-refoulement as a stand-alone matter of national interest affecting Australia's international reputation has been hinted at as another reason to take such claims into account. Together, these considerations seem to strengthen the case for non-refoulement claims being assessed before cancelling a visa of any undesirable migrant, even those who can still avail themselves of the right to apply for a protection visa. Thus, undesirable migrants may also have this alternative way (apart from a protection visa application) to bring their non-refoulement claims forward.

Lastly, it is worth noting that the Federal Court also briefly assessed the weight that should be given to non-refoulement in such cases. In this regard, in 2018, a primary judge of the Court addressed the issue of assessing non-refoulement in the context of Direction 65[54] (which defined what considerations should be taken into account to refuse or cancel a visa or revoke a visa cancellation).[55] That case concerned a decision by the AAT in which the Tri-

cultural Affairs v CTB19, [2020] FCAFC 166 (Federal Court of Australia, 1 October 2020); DPZ v Minister for Immigration, Citizenship, Migrant Services and Multicultural Affairs, [2020] FCA 1569 (Federal Court of Australia, 30 October 2020).

52 See Honnery, C. (2020).

53 See, e.g. Ali v Minister for Home Affairs, [2020] FCAFC 109; FAK19 v Minister for Immigration, Citizenship, Migrant Services and Multicultural Affairs, [2020] FCA 1124. See also the dissenting opinion on DOB18 v Minister for Home Affairs, [2019] FCAFC 63 (Federal Court of Australia, 18 April 2019).

54 As noted above, Direction 79, the successor of Direction 65, is very similar to Direction 65 and thus this interpretation can be applied to Direction 79 in the same way.

55 Suleiman v Minister for Immigration and Border Protection, [2018] FCA 594 (Federal Court of Australia, 2 May 2018).

bunal considered that, as non-refoulement is included in the Direction as an 'other' consideration to be taken into account – as opposed to a primary consideration – it should be treated as a secondary consideration of lesser importance than the primary ones and consequently one that did not outweigh the primary considerations. According to the primary judge, considering that other considerations were to be necessarily deemed as secondary was an error, as even though "Direction 65 does provide that, generally, primary considerations should be given greater weight,"[56] the Direction also "(…) makes clear that an evaluation is required in each case as to the weight to be given to the 'other considerations' (including non-refoulement obligations)."[57] This decision thus makes it explicit that non-refoulement can in certain situations outweigh primary considerations, including the protection of the Australian community from criminal or other serious conduct.

As noted in Section 3.6, however, non-refoulement is but one of the matters that need to be considered and consequently it may be that decision-makers still deem that a person's visa should be denied or cancelled despite the fact that they are *prima facie* unreturnable. The next sections thus discuss the consequences of a visa refusal or cancellation for undesirable but unreturnable migrants, while critically evaluating whether the measures applied in Australia comply with the applicable international human rights framework.

5 Solutions for Undesirable but Unreturnable Migrants

As noted above, *a priori* undesirable but unreturnable migrants may still be granted or allowed to keep a visa when, after balancing different elements, a decision-maker considers that the circumstances favour the concerned migrant's stay in Australia. In that case, their undesirability is not confirmed, and they can start or continue their migration paths. When that is not the case, however, undesirable but unreturnable migrants may face different fates in Australia, which are discussed in this section.

5.1 *Indefinite Detention: Australia as a Human Rights Violator*

The Migration Act prescribes the mandatory detention of migrants without a visa (s 189(1)) and only allows migrants to leave detention if they leave Australia or are granted a permit (s 196(1)). This strict detention regime was first confirmed by the High Court of Australia in the infamous Al-Kateb decision,

56 Ibid., para. 23.

57 Ibid. idem.

taken in 2004.[58] In that case, the Court affirmed that the correct interpretation of the applicable provisions of the Migration Act was that migrants would remain in detention until one of the abovementioned outcomes occurred (even if they were unlikely to occur), which, for some migrants, meant indefinite detention.

After Al-Kateb, the High Court of Australia continued to follow this reasoning for many years. Indeed, in a decision from 2021, the Court said that "[T]he duty imposed upon officers of the Executive by ss 189(1) and 196(1) of the [Migration] Act is to detain the unlawful non-citizen until the occurrence of one of the events referred to in s 196 [that is, removal or grant of a visa]."[59] The High Court continued to say that "[B]ecause the evident intention of the Act is that an unlawful non-citizen may not, in any circumstances, be at liberty in the Australian community, no question of release on *habeas* [*corpus*] can arise."[60] In saying so, the High Court indicated that *habeas corpus* is not available to those who are detained under Australia's mandatory detention regime. In this regard, the Australian Human Rights Commission affirmed that "Australia has one of the strictest immigration detention regimes in the world. It is mandatory, is not time-limited and people are not able to challenge their detention in court."[61] Indeed, the country's detention system is notorious worldwide to the point that it has been dramatised as a TV series (Stateless) in 2020 and called Kafkaesque by scholars.[62] Although important changes to this detention regime were brought by a 2023 decision of the High Court of Australia (which overruled Al-Kateb and is discussed in Section 5.5 below), indefinite detention was the most likely fate of undesirable but unreturnable migrants for over 19 years, and thus some remarks about this solution are warranted.

As was noted in Section 4.3 of Chapter 1, indefinite detention is considered arbitrary and thus in violation of human rights. In this regard, Australia's detention regime was deemed to be in violation of the human rights instruments the country is a party to by international human rights bodies. For example, article 9 ICCPR protects the right to liberty, prohibiting arbitrary detention and prescribing that everyone detained shall have the right to question the

58 Al-Kateb v Godwin, [2004] HCA 37 (High Court of Australia, 6 August 2004).

59 Commonwealth of Australia v AJL20, [2021] HCA 21 (High Court of Australia, 23 June 2021), para. 51.

60 Ibid., para. 61.

61 Australian Human Rights Commission (24 April 2023), Immigration detention and human rights. Available at: https://humanrights.gov.au/our-work/asylum-seekers-and-refugees/projects/immigration-detention-and-human-rights.

62 See S Juss, S. S. (2017).

legality of their detention in court. Concerning the practical application of article 9, when assessing Australia's compliance with the ICCPR in 2017, the UN Human Rights Committee noted that:

> (…) the rigid mandatory detention scheme under the Migration Act 1958 does not meet the legal standards under article 9 of the Covenant due to the lengthy periods of migrant detention it allows and the indefinite detention of refugees and asylum seekers who have received adverse security assessments from the Australian Security Intelligence Organisation, without adequate procedural safeguards to meaningfully challenge their detention.[63]

Indeed, in 2016, the UN Human Rights Committee decided a case concerning five undesirable but unreturnable migrants who were held in detention as their applications for protection visas were rejected since they all received an adverse security assessment by ASIO.[64] All concerned migrants had been recognised *prima facie* as refugees but had their applications rejected due to ASIO's assessment. They were not explained the reasons for the assessment and were not allowed to challenge it. While all five were later released from detention (after several years detained), the UN Human Rights Committee concluded that they had been arbitrarily detained (in violation of Article 9 ICCPR) during the period they spent in detention. The Committee reached this conclusion because Australia did not show that alternatives to detention were not sufficient to address possible security concerns posed by the concerned migrants, did not inform them of the reasons for the security assessments and did not give them the chance to challenge their detention.[65]

As shown above, not only those with an adverse security assessment but undesirable migrants more generally were likely to be subjected to indefinite detention when they were denied a visa or had an existing visa cancelled. In this regard, the UN Working Group on Arbitrary Detention has also found, in a

63 Human Rights Committee (2017). Concluding observations on the sixth periodic report of Australia (CCPR/C/AUS/CO/6). United Nations, para. 37.

64 Communication No. 2233/2013, CCPR/C/116/D/2233/2013 (Human Rights Committee, 22 March 2016).

65 More generally, the Committee has deemed, in its general comment no. 35 on the right to liberty, that "[T]he inability of a State party to carry out the expulsion of an individual because of statelessness or other obstacles does not justify indefinite detention." Human Rights Committee (2014). General comment No. 35: Article 9 (Liberty and security of person) (CCPR/C/GC/35). United Nations, para. 18.

case related to an undesirable but unreturnable migrant,[66] that the mandatory detention system applied in Australia lead to arbitrary detention as it did not allow detainees to challenge their detention. Furthermore, "[T]he Working Group has repeatedly pointed out that detention of asylum seekers must never be unlimited or of excessive length, that a maximum period should be imperatively provided by law and that indefinite detention is arbitrary."[67]

In view of the above, it is clear that indefinite detention is not a human rights-compliant solution to regulate the situation of undesirable but unreturnable migrants, as it violates these individuals' right to liberty.

In this regard, the Australian Human Rights Commission notes that:

> While the Commission acknowledges the use of immigration detention may be legitimate in certain circumstances, a person should only be held in an immigration facility for a strictly limited period of time if they are individually assessed as posing an unacceptable risk to the Australian community and that risk cannot be managed in a less restrictive way.[68]

The option of residing in the community is a less restrictive way available in Australian law in the form of assigned residence or the discretionary grant of a

66 Opinion No. 20/2018 concerning William Yekrop, A/HRC/WGAD/2018/20 (Working Group on Arbitrary Detention, 20 April 2018).

67 Ibid., para. 69. In this regard, the Working Group adopted multiple opinions in cases not concerning undesirable but unreturnable migrants in which it found that detainees were arbitrarily detained in Australia due to the country's immigration detention system. See, for example, Opinion No. 50/2018 concerning Edris Cheraghi, A/HRC/WGAD/2018/50 (Working Group on Arbitrary Detention, 22 August 2018); Opinion No. 21/2018 concerning Ghasem Hamedani, A/HRC/WGAD/2018/21 (Working Group on Arbitrary Detention, 20 April 2018); Opinion No. 71/2017 concerning Said Imasi, A/HRC/WGAD/2017/71 (Working Group on Arbitrary Detention, 21 November 2017); Opinion No. 42/2017 concerning Mohammad Naim Amiri, A/HRC/WGAD/2017/42 (Working Group on Arbitrary Detention, 21 August 2017); Opinion No. 28/2017 concerning Abdalrahman Hussein, A/HRC/WGAD/2017/28 (Working Group on Arbitrary Detention, 25 April 2017); and Opinion No. 8/2015 concerning Sayed Abdellatif, Ms. A and their six children, whose names are known to the Working Group on Arbitrary Detention, A/HRC/WGAD/2015/8 (Working Group on Arbitrary Detention, 24 April 2015). Similarly, in 2016, the UN Human Rights Committee found a violation of article 9 ICCPR as it deemed that a migrant was detained without justification and without the chance to challenge his detention. See Communication No. 2229/2012, CCPR/C/116/D/2229/2012 (Human Rights Committee, 29 March 2016).

68 Australian Human Rights Commission (24 April 2023).

visa by the Minister (known as alternative management options) and is thus analysed in the next subsection.

5.2 *Life in the Community. An Impossible Dream?*

As mentioned above, s 196 of the Migration Act provides that a migrant without a visa will remain in detention until they are removed from Australia or granted a visa. Regarding the latter option, the Migration Act grants discretionary powers to the Minister to grant visas in exceptional circumstances. For example, sections 46A, 195A, 351 and 501J of the Migration Act grant, respectively, discretionary powers to the Minister to accept, exceptionally, visa applications that would normally be barred; grant a detainee a visa when that is deemed to be in the public interest (whether they applied for it or not); and substitute a decision made by the ART with another that is more favourable to the concerned migrant – in the case of s 501J, the provision refers specifically to a protection visa decision (regarding the rejection or cancellation of such a visa).

There are, however, limitations to these provisions. S 46A, for example, only applies to unlawful maritime arrivals (that is, those who arrived irregularly in Australia by sea) and only serves to allow them to apply, exceptionally, for a visa they would not normally be allowed to apply for. It does not, however, offer the possibility to grant a visa to an undesirable but unreturnable migrant who, for example, had their visa cancelled or refused due to involvement in criminal activity.

Regarding ss 351 and 501J, the Minister provided guidance exemplifying some of the unique or exceptional circumstances that could justify the use of such discretionary powers.[69] These include "[C]ircumstances not anticipated by relevant legislation; or clearly unintended consequences of legislation; or the application of relevant legislation leads to unfair or unreasonable results in your case" and situations in which a migrant "(...) cannot be returned to your [their] country/countries of citizenship or usual residence due to circumstances outside your [their] control."[70] While these situations do not directly point to non-refoulement obligations, they do hint at similar situations and the list is said to be non-exhaustive. It is thus likely that unreturnability due to non-refoulement could be included in such circumstan-

69 See Australian Government Department of Home Affairs, Immigration and Citizenship, Status Resolution Service, Unique or exceptional circumstances. Available at: https://immi.homeaffairs.gov.au/what-we-do/status-resolution-service/ministerial-intervention.

70 Ibid.

ces. However, the Minister has also indicated cases in which it would be inappropriate to consider these powers, which include when "(…) the person has been refused a visa or has had a visa cancelled on character grounds" or "(…) the Australian Security Intelligence Organisation (ASIO) has determined that the person is a direct or indirect risk to national security through issuing the person with an Adverse Security Assessment (ASA) which remains in effect."[71] Consequently, it is unlikely that undesirable but unreturnable migrants could benefit from such provisions.

In this regard, it seems that s 195A would be the most fit solution for undesirable but unreturnable migrants. This provision allows the Minister to grant a migrant in detention a visa, regardless of whether they applied for it, when that is deemed to be in the public interest. Indeed, as was hinted by some decisions of the Federal Court of Australia (mentioned in Section 4.3 above), the fact that Australia owes the concerned person non-refoulement obligations can be considered in itself a matter of public interest, which may justify the use of this power. Furthermore, should there be security concerns about a migrant, Australia has a list of visa conditions that may be attached to the grant of a visa[72] in these cases. These include, among others, periodic reporting requirements (conditions 8401 and 8402); the requirement to continue to live in a specified address (condition 8505); the need to report any change of address (condition 8506); the requirement to obtain permission before undertaking certain jobs, such as those involving security-sensitive biological agents (condition 8551); a ban on weapons acquisition (condition 8554), on working in occupations that may give access to weapons (condition 8562), and on any use, access or training with weapons (condition 8563); the requirement not to communicate with certain people or organisations (such as those considered terrorist) (condition 8556); as well as the requirement not to engage in criminal conduct (condition 8564). Consequently, appropriate conditions could be imposed to undesirable but unreturnable migrants that could allow them to be in the Australian community but that, at the same time, would limit any threat they may pose to that community. This has also been proposed by the Australian Human Rights Commission, which said that:

> (…) alternatives to indefinite detention in closed facilities should be contemplated wherever possible. Where security or character concerns

---

71 Ibid.

72 S 41 Migration Act. See also Australian Department for Home Affairs, Check visa details and conditions, visa conditions. Available at: https://immi.homeaffairs.gov.au/visas/already-have-a-visa/check-visa-details-and-conditions/conditions-list#.

exist, conditions could be applied to mitigate any identified risks (such as a requirement to reside at a specified location, curfews, travel restrictions, regular reporting and, possibly, electronic monitoring).[73]

The practical use of this power, however, is hard to assess, as the statistics published by the Department of Home Affairs do not disclose all the information that would be needed for this analysis. What is clear, however, is that the number of visa refusals or cancellations on character grounds is much higher than the number of cases in which a Minister intervenes through their discretionary powers.[74] Furthermore, the Minister has no obligation to consider whether to exercise this power or not, regardless of the situation in which the migrant finds themselves. Thus, it is possible that this option is not even envisaged for some undesirable but unreturnable migrants. For example, in a

73 Australian Human Rights Commission. (2017). Asylum seekers, refugees and human rights – Snapshot report (2nd edition), p. 19.

74 For example, between 1 July 2019 and 30 June 2020, 1015 visas were cancelled and 355 were refused on character grounds.[1] Between 1 July 2020 and 30 June 2021, in turn, 939 were cancelled and 798 rejected.[2] On 30 June 2020, 703 persons were held in detention facilities after having lost their visa on character grounds (out of 1523 detainees in total).[3] On 30 June 2021, that number amounted to 798 (out of 1492 detainees in total).[4] It is, however, impossible to know how many of these undesirable migrants are also unreturnable and thus could benefit from being granted a status under s 195A to remedy that situation. The total number of Ministerial Interventions between July 2019 and June 2020, however, was only 81;[5] 54 between July 2020 and June 2021.[6] It is also impossible to know how many of these were based on s 195A and how many were based on the other provisions allowing Ministerial Intervention.

[1] Australian Department of Home Affairs, Character (s501) and general cancellation statistics (as at 31 December 2023). Available at: https://www.homeaffairs.gov.au/research-and-stats/files/character-and-general-cancellation-stats-31-dec-2023.pdf.

[2] Ibid.

[3] Australian Department of Home Affairs and Australian Border Force (2020), Immigration Detention and Community Statistics Summary – 30 June 2020. Available at: https://www.homeaffairs.gov.au/research-and-stats/files/immigration-detention-statistics-30-june-2020.pdf.

[4] Australian Department of Home Affairs and Australian Border Force (2021), Immigration Detention and Community Statistics Summary – 30 June 2021. Available at: https://www.homeaffairs.gov.au/research-and-stats/files/immigration-detention-statistics-30-june-2021.pdf.

[5] Australian Department of Home Affairs (2020), 2019 – 20 Migration Program Report: Program year to 30 June 2020. Available at: https://www.homeaffairs.gov.au/research-and-stats/files/report-migration-program-2019-20.pdf.

[6] Australian Department of Home Affairs (2021), 2020–21 Migration Program Report: Program year to 30 June 2021. Available at: https://www.homeaffairs.gov.au/research-and-stats/files/report-migration-program-2020-21.pdf.

case before the UN Working Group on Arbitrary Detention, the Australian Government seemed to indicate that it would also find it inappropriate for the power of s 195A to be used for the benefit of certain undesirable migrants. In that case, it was said that:

> On 28 February 2017, the Department of Home Affairs commenced an assessment of Mr. Yekrop's case against the section 195A ministerial intervention guidelines for possible referral to the Minister. On 24 October 2017, his case was found not to meet the guidelines for referral due to his criminal history, a visa cancelled under section 501 of the Australian Migration Act and another visa refused under section 501 of the Act.[75]

In this regard, in a decision from 2020, the Federal Court made the following observation regarding the use of this power in the case of an undesirable but unreturnable migrant:

> The Minister's opinion that Australia's non refoulement obligation to the applicant could be addressed by the use of his non-compellable power to grant him a visa in the public interest was infected by jurisdictional error. Having regard to his findings as to the risk the applicant represents to the Australian community, it is inconceivable that he gave the matter any genuine consideration. If he did, then his opinion was legally unreasonable.[76]

Indeed, when the Minister finds that a person is undesirable because they represent a risk to the Australian community, it cannot be expected that the same Minister would find it to be in the national interest to grant that person a visa. Thus, it is unlikely that many undesirable migrants could be considered to receive a visa under the Minister's discretionary power.

Short of granting undesirable but unreturnable migrants a visa, the Minister also has the option of placing them in assigned residence so they can reside in the community and not stay in closed immigration detention. This option is prescribed by s 197AB of the Migration Act. While assigned residence is still considered as a form of detention and may have strict conditions attached to it, it allows undesirable but unreturnable migrants to be in the community and have more freedom than when placed in closed detention. Regarding

75 Opinion No. 20/2018 concerning William Yekrop, para. 41.

76 AEM20 v Minister for Home Affairs, [2020] FCA 623, para. 117.

the practical use of these measures, in June 2020, there were 838 people detained under the assigned residence regime against 1523 in closed detention.[77] In June 2021, these numbers were, respectively, 526 and 1,492.[78] As explained above, it is not possible to know the exact profile of these detainees and, consequently, not possible to identify which ones, if any, are undesirable but unreturnable migrants. However, the Australian Human Rights Commission has noted that:

> (...) persons subject to an adverse security assessment issued by the Australian Security Intelligence Organisation (ASIO) or who present character issues that may indicate they fail the character test, are generally not considered for alternative, less restrictive forms of detention such as community detention as a matter of Government policy.[79]

It thus seems unlikely that undesirable migrants benefit from this measure in practice.

As will be shown in Subsection 5.5 below, after the 2023 decision of the High Court of Australia overruling Al-Kateb, undesirable but unreturnable migrants may, however, have the possibility of being granted a visa on conditions. Before discussing this new development, however, the next subsection will address another possibility, which is removal from Australia.

5.3 *Return. Australia as a Human Rights Violator (Again)*

Australia is a party to the ICCPR and the Convention against Torture and is thus bound by the non-refoulement obligations stemming from these instruments. Return should consequently not be envisaged for migrants who may face gross human rights violations in their country of origin. The 2014 Amendment to the Migration Act (which came into force in December 2014), however, seemed to go against Australia's international obligations. This is because the amendment inserted s 197C in the Act, which prescribes that for the

77 Australian Department of Home Affairs and Australian Border Force (2020), Immigration Detention and Community Statistics Summary – 30 June 2020. Available at: https://www.homeaffairs.gov.au/research-and-stats/files/immigration-detention-statistics-30-june-2020.pdf.

78 Australian Department of Home Affairs and Australian Border Force (2021), Immigration Detention and Community Statistics Summary – 30 June 2021. Available at: https://www.homeaffairs.gov.au/research-and-stats/files/immigration-detention-statistics-30-june-2021.pdf.

79 Australian Human Rights Commission. (2020). Inspections of Australia's immigration detention facilities 2019 – Report – December 2020, p. 136.

purpose of removal of unlawful non-citizens (that is, migrants without a visa), non-refoulement obligations are irrelevant. Thus, after the enactment of s 197C, it seemed that undesirable migrants could be returned to their country of origin even if that breached Australia's non-refoulement obligations. This raised many concerns, especially as between the enactment of the 2014 Amendment and the end of 2020 "[T]he number of visa cancellations on character grounds has increased by over 1100 per cent."[80] The Australian government, however, declared that, as a matter of policy, it would not remove migrants in violation of international law.[81] This conflict between law and policy was the source of much debate in the national Case Law, which influenced the enactment of the 2021 Amendment. This amendment aimed at putting an end to this contradiction by limiting the application of s 197C so that it is not applied against undesirable migrants in respect of whom Australia has protection obligations. The next paragraphs will thus briefly explain the judicial disputes and human rights concerns that arose between the two amendments.

In view of s 197C, undesirable but unreturnable migrants started turning to the Federal Court to argue that, should their visa be denied or cancelled, they would be returned to harm and that should be taken into account by the decision-maker. The Australian administration, in turn, argued that, in view of Australia's non-return policy, these migrants would not be returned but, instead, might face indefinite detention. Two cases decided by the Federal

80 Honnery, C. (2020, April 29); see also: Australian Department of Home Affairs, Visa Statistics, Visa Cancellation. Available at: https://www.homeaffairs.gov.au/research-and-statistics/statistics/visa-statistics/visa-cancellation.

81 Section 4.1 above presented the protection visa procedure, prescribed by the Migration Act to be the main procedure to assess international protection claims. Thus, the findings of the application for a protection visa can base the government's assessment that a person is owed non-refoulement obligations. It is worth noting, however, that when a failed asylum seeker requests the judicial review of a negative asylum decision, an administrative procedure – an international treaty obligations assessment –, not regulated by the Migration Act, is triggered to inform the policy-based decision of whether to return the concerned migrant or not. There is very little public information about this assessment, which prevents an analysis of its functioning. However, since, as shown below, the 2021 Amendment provides that protection claims must be assessed before any other protection visa criteria, it is unlikely that such an assessment would lead to entirely new claims and thus it is only a marginal tool to discover the unreturnability of migrants. On the assessment, see: Parliament of Australia, Chapter 6 – The Assessment Process. Available at: https://www.aph.gov.au/Parliamentary_Business/Committees/Joint/Former_Committees/immigrationdetention/report/c06#c06f25, paras. 6.38–6.40. On the lack of public information about the assessment, see: Right to Know, International Treaty Obligations Assessment (ITOA). Available at: https://www.righttoknow.org.au/request/international_treaty_obligations.

Court are particularly relevant in this regard. They are DMH16[82] and AJL20.[83] These cases, which concern the same person, will be explored in more detail in the next section, as they serve to exemplify in practice the challenges associated with regulating the situation of undesirable but unreturnable migrants. Their main findings, however, will be presented in this section to explain the developments between the two amendments to the Migration Act.

In DMH16, decided in 2017, the Minister refused to grant DMH16, a Syrian national, a protection visa due to his criminal history, despite the fact that non-refoulement applied to him. In his reasons for refusal, the Minister said that:

> In making my decision I am aware that while [DMH16] will not be removed from Australia if his visa application is refused (notwithstanding s197C of the Act), he may face the prospect of indefinite immigration detention because of the operation of s189 and s 196 of the Migration Act.[84]

DMH16, however, questioned whether that was the correct reading of s 197C. In this regard, the primary judge deemed that:

> (...) by the operation of s 197C, if the protection visa was refused the applicant would either be removed to Syria immediately, or, if the Minister decided to consider alternative management options, be detained for a definite period, namely, until the Minster considered whether to exercise the power under s 195A.[85]

Further stating that:

> Had the Minister properly understood the consequence of the refusal of the protection visa at the time he made the decision there is a possibility that he would have granted the protection visa in order to avoid the consequence that the applicant would be returned to Syria in contra-

82 DMH16 v Minister for Immigration and Border Protection, [2017] FCA 448 (Federal Court of Australia, 3 May 2017).

83 AJL20 v Commonwealth of Australia, [2020] FCA 1305 (Federal Court of Australia, 11 September 2020).

84 DMH16 v Minister for Immigration and Border Protection, [2017] FCA 448, para. 12.

85 Ibid., para. 26.

vention of Australia's non-refoulement obligations in respect of the applicant.[86]

Decisions of primary judges[87] and of the Full Court[88] following DMH16 continued to affirm that the consequence of s 197C was that undesirable but unreturnable migrants would be returned to their country of origin despite non-refoulement, and thus indefinite detention was not the expected fate they faced.[89]

In this regard, the UN Human Rights Committee, when assessing Australia's compliance with the ICCPR in 2017, called on Australia to ensure that the non-refoulement principle was secured in law and strictly adhered to in practice by repealing s 197C of the Migration Act and introducing a legal obligation to ensure that the removal of an individual is always consistent with Australia's non-refoulement obligations.[90] Indeed, as explained in Chapter 1, the obligation not to return someone to a place where their right to be free from torture or their right to life would be violated is a mandatory one, comprising no exceptions. Australian law, by allowing the disrespect of non-refoulement, created an exception that is not allowed and thus contravenes a peremptory norm of international law.

Ultimately, however, the clashes between Australia's law and policy regarding non-refoulement were resolved with the enactment of the 2021 Amend-

86 Ibid., para. 30.

87 See, e.g. AQM18 v Minister for Immigration and Border Protection, [2018] FCA 944 (Federal Court of Australia, 21 June 2018).

88 See, e.g. AQM18 v Minister for Immigration and Border Protection, [2019] FCAFC 27 (Federal Court of Australia, 22 February 2019).

89 See, e.g. CWGF v Minister for Home Affairs, [2019] FCA 1802. In view of Australia's non-return policy, however, some undesirable but unreturnable migrants seized the Federal Court to inquire whether the applicable policy, even though it seemed to go against the letter of the law, should be taken into account by decision-makers (see e.g. DFTD v Minister for Home Affairs, [2020] FCA 859 (Federal Court of Australia, 23 June 2020); WKMZ v Minister for Home Affairs, [2020] FCA 1127 (Federal Court of Australia, 7 August 2020); DFTD v Minister for Home Affairs, [2020] FCAFC 207 (Federal Court of Australia, 26 November 2020)). In one of these cases, a primary judge of the Federal Court concluded that the AAT "made no material error by relying on the policy statement against refoulement in the Direction [79] to conclude that the applicant faced a low risk of refoulement" (WKMZ v Minister for Home Affairs, [2020] FCA 1127, para. 32). This conclusion seems to be at odds with previous ones, which affirmed that the fate of undesirable but unreturnable migrants, in light of s 197C of the Migration Act, would be return.

90 Human Rights Committee (2017). Concluding observations on the sixth periodic report of Australia, paras. 33–34.

ment. This amendment was triggered by the decision of the AJL20 case by a primary judge of the Federal Court on 11 September 2020.[91] As noted above, AJL20 concerns the same person as DMH16.[92] In view of DMH16's visa refusal,[93] he was kept in detention, despite s 197C of the Migration Act. He thus turned to the Federal Court arguing that his detention was unlawful. According to him, the Migration Act prescribed that detention might only be used for specific purposes – in his case, removal from Australia – and that, according to the Act, removal of an unlawful non-citizen from Australia must be pursued or carried into effect "as soon as reasonably practicable."[94] He thus claimed that his detention was unlawful as his removal had not been pursued or carried out as soon as reasonably practicable. The primary judge concurred with this argument, as the return of AJL20 had not been pursued. According to the primary judge:

> [T]hat inaction was likely based on Commonwealth officers following Commonwealth policy. A policy of non-refoulement is morally justifiable. However, in relation to removal required by s 198 of the Act and in the light of s 197C, the pursuance of such a policy is not legally justifiable. As the applicant contended, by a submission to which the Commonwealth did not respond, the Commonwealth cannot act as though s 197C does not exist. If the policy was an obstacle to the applicant's removal from Australia as soon as reasonably practicable, that obstacle was self-imposed by the Commonwealth, is contrary to the Act's requirements, and cannot justify the inactivity in question.[95]

As the primary judge concluded that AJL20's detention was unlawful, they ordered his release. Considering Australia's strict detention policy, however, AJL20's release without a visa seemed at odds with the Migration Act. These contradictions between law and policy thus led to the enactment of the 2021 Amendment. This amendment modified s 197C to clarify that it would not apply to those who had been deemed to be owed protection obligations by Australia. Indeed, in the revised explanatory memorandum of the 2021

91 AJL20 v Commonwealth of Australia, [2020] FCA 1305.

92 Surprisingly, this fact is only mentioned in paragraph 97 of the AJL20 decision.

93 As will be explained in more detail in the next subsection, after DMH16 was decided, AJL20's case was sent back to the Minister for revision. A delegate of the Minister then decided, once more, not to grant AJL20 a visa.

94 Article 198 Migration Act.

95 AJL20 v Commonwealth of Australia, [2020] FCA 1305, para. 123.

Amendment, it is said that DMH16 and AJL20 "(...) altered the intended effect of this provision on persons who have been found to engage protection obligations."[96] Thus, since the 2021 Amendment, it is no longer the case that the Migration Act prescribes that those to whom non-refoulement applies are to be returned regardless of these international obligations.

Lastly, it is worth noting that the 2021 Amendment provides another possibility for undesirable but unreturnable migrants to leave detention, that is, voluntary return. This seems to present a catch 22 situation[97] (that is, a situation in which a successful outcome is impossible), as migrants are put in a position in which they can either remain in indefinite detention or choose to return to a place where they may be subjected to gross human rights violations. In practice, it is hard to see the voluntariness of such a decision. When faced with this question, the European Court of Human Rights deemed that the choice to return in a situation like this cannot be considered voluntary and that the returning country still violated non-refoulement by returning the concerned person.[98] Thus, despite the fact that, after the 2021 Amendment, the wording of the Migration Act no longer requires the forced return of undesirables to harm, Australia may still violate its international obligations through voluntary return.

5.4 *Solutions for Undesirable but Unreturnable Migrants in Practice: The Case of AJL20*

The above subsections presented the complex system in place in Australia to regulate the situation of undesirable but unreturnable migrants as well as the great importance of the DMH16 and AJL20 cases decided by the Federal Court. This section will thus present the facts and legal consequences of these cases in more detail to illustrate the impact of Australia's law and policy on the lives

---

96 Parliament of Australia (2021), Migration Amendment (Clarifying International Obligations for Removal) Bill 2021 – Revised Explanatory Memorandum. Available at: https://parlinfo.aph.gov.au/parlInfo/download/legislation/ems/r6696_ems_b5bd7c14-8a16-4782-8418-21f2a0c27b3d/upload_pdf/21040rem.pdf;fileType=application%2Fpdf#search=%22legislation/ems/r6696_ems_b5bd7c14-8a16-4782-8418-21f2a0c27b3d%22.

97 This expression originates from the novel of the same name, authored by Joseph Keller and published in 1961.

98 M.S. v. Belgium, No. 50012/08 (European Court of Human Rights, 31 January 2012). Similarly, the UN Special Rapporteur on the human rights of migrants noted that "States and other stakeholders who carry out returns under an assisted voluntary return programme to States that are not safe and in which migrants may face violations of their fundamental human rights may be in violation of the principle of non-refoulement" (Human Rights Council (2018). Report of the Special Rapporteur on the human rights of migrants (A/HRC/38/41). United Nations, para. 30).

of undesirable but unreturnable migrants. It will also briefly explain AJL20's case before the High Court of Australia, which overturned the decision of the Federal Court. Since DMH16 and AJL20 are the same person, the pseudonym AJL20 will be used throughout this section.

AJL20 is a Syrian national. He was born in 1991 and moved to Australia in 2005 holding a child visa. In 2011, he was sentenced to three years imprisonment for intentionally causing serious injury. His conviction led to the cancellation of his visa in 2014 as he no longer passed the character test. After this cancellation, he applied for a protection visa. During his protection visa procedure, it was found that Australia owed protection obligations to AJL20. Despite this fact, the Minister refused to grant him a visa because he had a significant criminal record and thus did not pass the character test.[99]

As was noted in the previous section, however, the protection visa rejection was quashed by the Federal Court because, according to the Court, the Minister made his decision based on a wrong interpretation of the law. That is, the Minister mentioned that he was aware that his decision could lead to the indefinite detention of AJL20 but would not lead to his return. Since the decision was made before the 2021 Amendment, however, the Court found that this was the wrong interpretation of the law, as s 197C of the Migration Act required that AJL20 be removed despite the non-refoulement obligations he was owed.[100]

After DMH16 was decided, AJL20's case was sent back to the Minister for revision. A delegate of the Minister then decided not to grant AJL20 a visa. Following this decision, in July 2019, the Minister chose not to apply alternative measures – that is, to make a residence determination or discretionarily

99 DMH16 v Minister for Immigration and Border Protection, [2017] FCA 448, paras. 3–6. This is in line with what a primary judge of the Federal Court noted in a case from 2020. In that case, the primary judge found that it was an error to defer a non-refoulement assessment from a visa cancellation procedure to a future protection visa application. This is because such application would have to be rejected if the applicant did not pass the character test and it was difficult to understand how s 501 would not prevent the grant of a protection visa when the concerned migrant's criminality had already led to a visa cancellation (see FAK19 v Minister for Immigration, Citizenship, Migrant Services and Multicultural Affairs, [2020] FCA 1124). See also footnote 50 above. While there is no information on DMH16 about AJL20's visa cancellation procedure, the fact that his visa was cancelled indicates that despite his arrival in Australia at a young age and his years living in the country prior to his criminal conviction, the overall balance of all elements led to the conclusion that he should not keep his visa. It is not known, however, if non-refoulement obligations were assessed during the visa cancellation.

100 DMH16 v Minister for Immigration and Border Protection, [2017] FCA 448, para. 26.

grant a visa – to AJL20.[101] Even before the Minister pronounced themselves in this regard, procedures started to return AJL20 to Syria, his country of nationality. Indeed, already in January 2019, AJL20's case was referred to the 'removal space' within the Department of Immigration and Border Protection and officers of the Department started exploring how to obtain Syrian travel documents to AJL20. In February, however, an Assistant Director in the Complex and Controversial Cases section of the Department questioned AJL20's referral for involuntary removal as he was considered to engage Australia's protection obligations. After internal discussions within the Department, all efforts to remove AJL20 to Syria were stopped as he was owed non-refoulement obligations.[102]

This led to the AJL20 case mentioned in the previous subsection, in which AJL20 challenged the legality of his detention by arguing that his detention was unlawful since no efforts were being taken to remove him (despite the requirement to do so regardless of non-refoulement, according to pre-2021 Amendment s 197C). As also noted in the previous section, a primary judge of the Federal Court agreed with his arguments and ordered his release.

In practice, the primary judge thus deemed that by taking efforts to comply with Australia's international non-refoulement obligations and, consequently, not violate AJL20's right to life and to be free from torture, Australian authorities violated his right to liberty. After the primary judge's decision, AJL20 was released into a situation of limbo, as "(…) he is in the community without a visa, and he is not a citizen."[103] This is not prescribed in Australian law, as

101 Thus providing another evidence that these options are unlikely to be applied to those with a criminal history.

102 AJL20 v Commonwealth of Australia, [2020] FCA 1305, paras. 100–105. In November 2019, the Department started pursuing the possibility of removing AJL20 to Lebanon, as his parents were Lebanese citizens and thus AJL20 might be eligible for Lebanese citizenship as well. Lebanese authorities were contacted in this regard. With the COVID-19 crisis that arose in the beginning of 2020, however, Lebanese authorities became unresponsive, and it was considered unlikely that any removal to Lebanon would take place in the near future due to the pandemic. These facts had legal relevance in the legal procedure before the Federal Court but did not influence the Court's final finding that AJL20's detention was unlawful. They also do not have significant influence on the narrative of the main text, which is why they are only briefly mentioned here.

103 Gregoire, P. (9 January 2021). Australia: The indefinite detention Achilles Heel: An interview with Human Rights for All director principal Alison Battisson. Mondaq. Available at: https://www.mondaq.com/australia/human-rights/1023966/the-indefinite-detention-achilles-heel-an-interview-with-human-rights-for-all-director-principal-alison-battisson.

the Migration Act determines the mandatory detention of migrants without a visa in the country. The case was thus brought before the High Court of Australia.[104]

The High Court, with a small majority (4 against 3), dismissed the primary judge's decision. According to the High Court, the Migration Act is clear when it says that an unlawful non-citizen must remain in detention until they are either granted the right to enter Australia or removed from the country, neither of which has happened in AJL20's case. The High Court continues by saying that in the months the executive did not take steps to return AJL20, it did not fulfil its duty prescribed by the law and thus it was liable to be subjected to a *writ of mandamus* in that regard, but that nothing justified the release from detention of AJL20. After the High Court's decision, AJL20 was returned to detention.[105]

AJL20 shows how those with a criminal history have little chances of being allowed to stay in Australia. Despite having arrived in the country at a young age and thus having strong ties to Australia, which is likely to weigh in favour of continued stay in the country, he had his visa cancelled after being criminally convicted. He then asked for protection, but his visa was refused due to the same criminal conviction. Although the Minister recognised that AJL20 was owed protection obligations, they still refused to use discretionary powers to grant AJL20 a visa, leading to multiple years of immigration detention. Indeed, cases such as that of AJL20 have led Australia's character provisions to be described as a catch-22 by judges of the Federal Court of Australia[106] and undesirable but unreturnable migrants to be considered 'totally screwed'[107] by scholars.

As noted earlier in this chapter, however, in 2023, the High Court of Australia made a landmark decision[108] overruling Al-Kateb and thus potentially

---

104 Commonwealth of Australia v AJL20, [2021] HCA 21.

105 Human Rights for All, Our Stories. Available at: https://www.hr4a.com.au/services-4. In view of the High Court's 2023 decision (NZYQ v Minister for Immigration, Citizenship and Multicultural Affairs [2023] HCA 37), however, migrants in the same situation as AJL20 have started to be released, as explained in Subsection 5.5 below.

106 See, e.g. DOB18 v Minister for Home Affairs, [2019] FCAFC 63, para. 36; BAL19 v Minister for Home Affairs, [2019] FCA 2189, para. 43; AEM20 v Minister for Home Affairs, [2020] FCA 623, para. 110.

107 Pillai, S. (8 August 2021). AJL20 v Commonwealth: Non-refoulement, indefinite detention and the 'totally screwed.' Australian Public Law. Available at: https://auspublaw.org/2021/09/ajl20-v-commonwealth-non-refoulement-indefinite-detention-and-the-totally-screwed/.

108 NZYQ v Minister for Immigration, Citizenship and Multicultural Affairs [2023] HCA 37.

changing the fate of undesirable but unreturnable migrants in the country. This decision and some of its consequences are thus discussed in the next subsection.

5.5 *Recent Developments in Australia Affecting Undesirable but Unreturnable Migrants: The Case of* NZYQ *and Its (Expected) Consequences*

As explained above, the High Court of Australia first confirmed Australia's strict detention regime, which could lead to indefinite detention, in the 2004 Al-Kateb decision. Since then, the Court reasserted that position multiple times, including in 2021 in the abovementioned AJL20 case. In November 2023, the Court was once again asked to consider the lawfulness of indefinite detention in the country in the NZYQ case.[109] This time, however, the outcome was different, as the High Court overruled Al-Kateb and, consequently, its acceptance of indefinite detention when there is no real prospect of removal of the concerned migrant in the reasonably foreseeable future.

The NZYQ case concerned a stateless Rohingya Muslim born in Myanmar, who applied for a protection visa in Australia as he feared persecution in Myanmar. While it was recognised that he would be at risk in Myanmar and could not be returned there, his protection visa request was denied due to a conviction, in Australia, for a sexual offence against a child.[110] As his visa was denied, he was placed in detention after his release from prison. As was the case with AJL20, however, measures to remove him to Myanmar were not taken since it was known that he would be at risk there. NZYQ then turned to the High Court of Australia, as AJL20 did, to challenge his detention.

NZYQ's case was quite similar to that of AJL20, but with one important difference. While AJL20 only questioned the statutory construction of the Migration Act, that is, whether indefinite detention in his case was a consequence of the correct interpretation of the Act, NZYQ questioned both the statutory construction of the Migration Act and its compliance with the Australian constitution. Regarding the statutory construction of the Migration Act, in both the AJL20 and the NZYQ cases, the High Court concludes that there is no reason to deviate from Al-Kateb as indefinite detention can be a consequence of the mandatory detention regime prescribed in the Migration

---

109 Ibid.

110 Ibid., para. 3.

Act.[111] In NZYQ, however, the High Court also assesses whether NZYQ's detention is compatible with Australia's constitution. When examining this question, the High Court noted that previously established constitutional principles determined that detention is penal or punitive in character.[112] In view of this, detention for non-punitive (criminal) reasons must be exceptional and limit itself to what is necessary to achieve the legislative objective of the detention. In migration cases, the objective of detention would be either to remove a migrant from Australia or keep them outside the Australian society while waiting for a decision on a visa application. If the objective is unachievable (for example, because there is no pending visa application or because there is no prospect of removal taking place as the concerned migrant is stateless or would be at risk upon return), then the detention loses its purpose and is unlawful.[113] As that was the case regarding NZYQ, his detention was considered unlawful.

This reasoning of the High Court has thus been interpreted to mean that while the Migration Act does grant the executive power to detain a person to pursue their removal from Australia, this power does not extend to situations where there is no prospect of the removal taking place.[114] Consequently, following the decision, it was said that "[T]he ruling could trigger further immigration detention releases. There are reportedly 92 people in similar positions [sic] who have largely been refused visas on character grounds. Most could not be deported to their home countries because they had a well-founded fear of persecution."[115] Indeed, in the days following the decision, it was reported that about 50 migrants were estimated to have been released from immigration

111 See ibid., paras 22–23.

112 These principles were first discussed in the context of immigration detention in the Lim case: Chu Kheng Lim v Minister for Immigration, Local Government and Ethnic Affairs [1992] HCA 64 (High Court of Australia, 8 December 1992).

113 NZYQ v Minister for Immigration, Citizenship and Multicultural Affairs [2023] HCA 37, paras. 44–46.

114 See Gregoire, P. and Nedim, U. (5 December 2023). The Reasons the High Court Ruled Indefinite Detention Is Unlawful in Australia. NSW Courts. Available at: https://nswcourts.com.au/articles/the-reasons-the-high-court-ruled-indefinite-detention-is-unlawful-in-australia/.

115 Hennessy, A. (9 November 2023) Landmark Australian Ruling Rejects Indefinite Immigration Detention: Longstanding Practice to Deter Asylum Seekers Found Unlawful. Human Rights Watch. Available at: https://www.hrw.org/news/2023/11/09/landmark-australian-ruling-rejects-indefinite-immigration-detention. See also: Karp, P. (8 November 2023) Indefinite immigration detention ruled unlawful in landmark Australian high court decision. The Guardian. Available at: https://www.theguardian.com/australia-news/2023/nov/08/australia-high-court-indefinite-detention-ruling-government.

detention,[116] a number that was said to have risen to 93 on 22 November 2023[117] and later to 148 in February 2024.[118]

To avoid a situation in which these migrants are in the territory without a visa, an amendment to the Migration Act[119] providing a new visa regime was quickly enacted. This amendment allows the Minister to grant a pending removal visa to persons for whom there is no real prospect of removal from Australia becoming practicable in the reasonably foreseeable future. The visa granted in these cases includes mandatory conditions such as notifying authorities of the persons who reside with the visa holder and of any interstate travel as well as obtaining prior authorisation before performing any work or regular organised activity involving more than incidental contact with a minor or vulnerable person. Furthermore, two additional conditions may be imposed if the Minister believes they are necessary to protect the Australian community. These conditions are subjecting the concerned migrant to a curfew from 10pm to 6am and mandating them to wear a monitoring device.

Some of the migrants initially subjected to these two latter conditions challenged the legislation authorising them,[120] yet, once the legal challenges were filed, these conditions were lifted for them,[121] leading the concerned migrants to drop the legal cases.[122] Legal challenges against the new legislation, how-

116 See Knaus, C. and Karp, P. (12 November 2023) Malaysian hitman released from Australian immigration detention after high court ruling. The Guardian. Available at: https://www.theguardian.com/australia-news/2023/nov/12/malaysian-hitman-released-from-australian-immigration-detention-after-high-court-ruling?CMP=Share_AndroidApp_Other.

117 Doran, M. (22 November 2023) Emergency powers regarding people released from immigration facing High Court challenge, less than a week after passing parliament. ABC News. Available at: https://www.abc.net.au/news/2023-11-22/emergency-powers-immigration-detention-high-court-challenge/103139022.

118 Doran, M. (1 February 2024) Immigration detainees drop High Court challenges after ankle monitoring bracelets removed. ABC News. Available at: https://www.abc.net.au/news/2024-02-01/immigration-detainee-challenges-dropped-ankle-monitoring-lifted/103409080.

119 Migration Amendment (Bridging Visa Conditions) Act 2023: https://www.legislation.gov.au/C2023A00093/asmade/text. See also: Human Rights Law Centre (17 November 2023) Summary: Migration Amendment (Bridging Visa Conditions) Bill 2023. Available at: https://www.hrlc.org.au/reports-news-commentary/2023/11/17/summary-migration-amendment-bridging-visa-conditions-bill-2023.

120 See Doran, M. (22 November 2023).

121 Karp, P. (14 December 2023) Immigration minister lifts ankle bracelet and curfew conditions for two ex-detainees suing Australian government. The Guardian. Available at: https://www.theguardian.com/australia-news/2023/dec/15/immigration-minister-lifts-ankle-bracelet-and-curfew-conditions-for-two-ex-detainees-suing-australian-government.

122 Doran, M. (1 February 2024).

ever, may still be expected. This is because, considering that most of the conditions imposed are mandatory and thus apply regardless of the personal situation of the concerned visa holder, they may constitute a disproportionate interference with concerned migrants' human rights, such as the right to private and family life and the right to freedom.[123] Indeed, the principal lawyer of the organisation representing one of the migrants who started legal proceedings to challenge the legislation noted that the new law had "(…) devastating implications for the liberty, bodily integrity, privacy and dignity of refugees and migrants."[124] In this regard, she noted that while the curfew and monitoring device usage conditions were lifted in the case of the migrant her organisation represented, he "(…) remains on an insecure visa subject to a suite of oppressive other conditions."[125] Indeed, as the new visa regime provided to the migrants released after the High Court's 2023 decision is a pending removal one, it implies that Australia will continue its efforts to remove such visa holders. Undesirable but unreturnable migrants holding such visas, however, are unlikely to be returned as there are human rights concerns preventing their removal. They may thus find themselves with insecure visas and under strict conditions for lengthy periods. While it is unclear what will happen to these migrants in the long term in Australia, it is worth noting that undesirable but unreturnable migrants in Canada may find themselves in a similar situation – that is, living under temporary permits with conditions attached for lengthy periods, without the possibility of permanent residence. This situation is thus discussed in more detail in Chapter 4 of this book.

Lastly, it is worth noting that while the High Court of Australia considered indefinite detention to be unlawful when there is no real prospect of removal of the concerned migrant in the reasonably foreseeable future in NZYQ, a different decision taken by the Court in the ASF17 case in May 2024[126] seems to indicate that some migrants will still face indefinite detention in Australia. This is because, in ASF17, the Court found that where removal is not possible due to the concerned migrant's voluntary lack of cooperation in removal procedures, detention can continue. As ASF17's claims of fear of harm upon return

123 See, e.g. Human Rights Centre (16 November 2023) Albanese Government must respect High Court ruling and stop punishing migrants and refugees. Available at: https://www.hrlc.org.au/news/2023/11/16/rushed-legislation.

124 Doran, M. (1 February 2024).

125 Ibid.

126 ASF17 v Commonwealth of Australia [2024] HCA 19 (High Court of Australia, 10 May 2024). See also: Human Rights Law Centre (10 May 2024) Explainer: High Court's decision in ASF17 v Commonwealth. Available at: https://www.hrlc.org.au/reports-news-commentary/2024/05/10/asf17-high-court.

were rejected in his visa application, it was considered that he would not be at risk in his country of origin, although he later claimed different reasons to fear harm upon return, which were not taken into account in his visa application. The High Court, however, was not asked to assess his fear of persecution, only the legality of his detention. Thus, the Court concluded that "[I]n the absence of an extant protection finding"[127] his removal was permissible and only required his cooperation. As such, his detention could continue since he could voluntarily choose to contribute to his return.

6 Conclusions: "Jesus Knew That There Was a Place for Everything and It's Not Necessarily Everyone's Place to Come to Australia"[128]

The path(s) undesirable but unreturnable migrants may take in Australia can be summarised in a simplified manner in Figure 2.1.

This image exemplifies how Australia has a complex migration system in place, which, as explained in Section 2, is regulated by the Migration Act. The Act is the instrument through which Australia internalised its interpretation of the Refugee Convention and thus determines the requirements to be met by those who seek international protection to be granted a protection visa. The Migration Act sets stricter requirements than the Refugee Convention, limiting the application of that treaty in the national context. At the same time, it extends protection to those who may not fit the refugee definition but to whom non-refoulement obligations stemming from other international human rights treaties apply.

Besides setting specific criteria and exclusion clauses for protection visas, Australia also demands that everyone passes a strict character test to be granted a visa to enter or remain in Australia. For those who have been granted a visa and no longer meet the character test, their visa may be cancelled. In most cases, the reasons why a person would not pass the character test are linked to involvement in criminal activity.

To cancel an existing visa, however, a decision-maker cannot rely solely on the character test. Instead, an assessment of multiple factors, including,

127 ASF17 v Commonwealth of Australia [2024] HCA 19, para. 46.

128 This quote is the answer given by former Australian Prime Minister, Tony Abbott, when asked about what Jesus would do regarding asylum seekers. See Harvey, M. (6 April 2010). Jesus would not accept every asylum-seeker: Abbott. Perth Now. See also: abcqanda, Tony Abbott joins Q&A. Available at: https://www.youtube.com/watch?v=foN4SQ4R5K4.

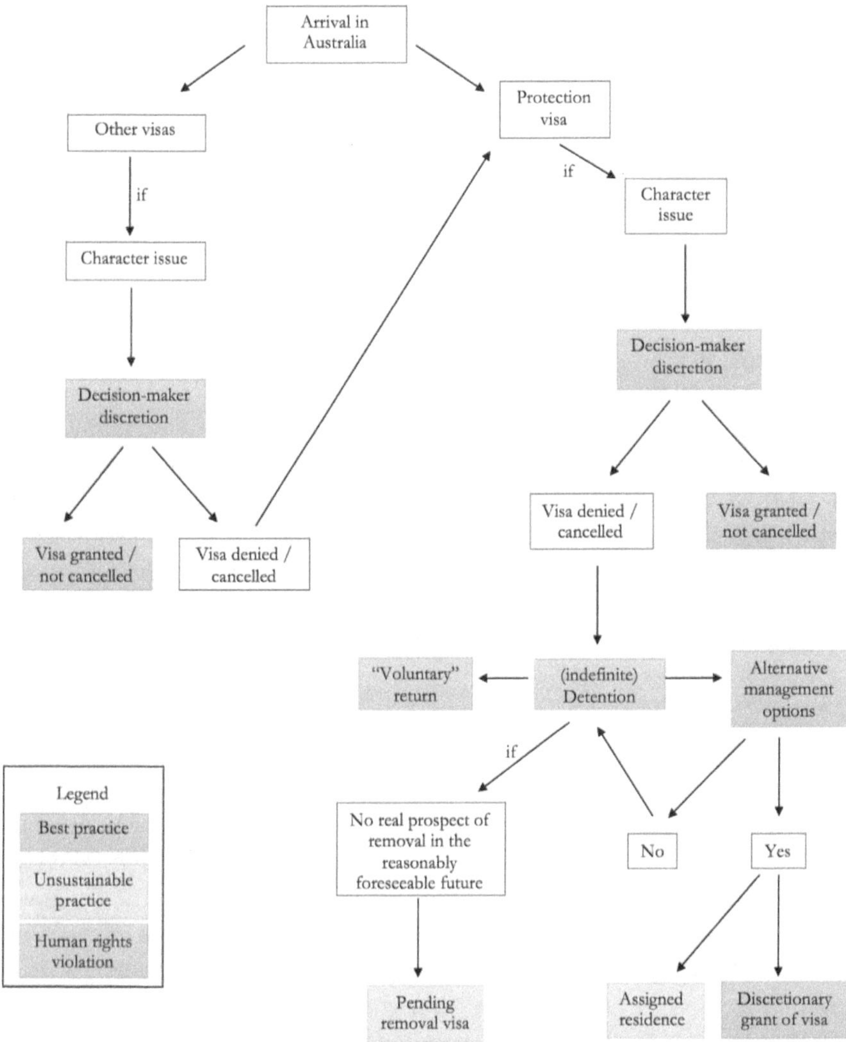

FIGURE 2.1 Paths for undesirable but unreturnable migrants in Australia

among others, the danger the person poses to the Australian community, the interests of minor children in Australia, the expectations of the community, the person's ties to the country and non-refoulement obligations that may be owed to that person need to be considered and weighed before a visa cancellation. This shows that Australia applies a balancing test when determining who is undesirable.

When such assessment does not weigh favourably for those concerned, undesirable but unreturnable migrants will be subjected to mandatory detention, as all migrants who do not have a visa to enter or remain in Australia. In

2014, an Amendment to the Migration Act indicated that those detained should be returned as soon as reasonably possible regardless of whether non-refoulement applied to them. The government's position, however, was not to return them in violation of non-refoulement as a matter of policy. This discrepancy between law and policy was greatly debated before the Federal Court of Australia, mandated to perform judicial review in cases of visa cancellation or refusal based on character grounds. After years of cases, that Court concluded that the correct interpretation of the law was that the concerned person should be returned regardless of Australia's international obligations. This has led to a new Amendment, in 2021, that specifies that those who are owed non-refoulement are not to be returned in violation of such obligations.

The explanatory memoranda of both the 2014 and 2021 Amendments mention that the Migration Act grants the Minister discretionary powers to comply with Australia's non-refoulement obligations, which include the power to grant a visa to a migrant in detention, even when the person did not apply for one, as well as to place them in assigned residence (or community detention). Both alternatives come with restrictions and, in practice, it seems to be the government's policy not to apply such measures to those who had a visa cancelled or refused in character grounds.

Thus, for many years, the most likely fate of undesirable but unreturnable migrants in Australia was indefinite detention, a practice that is deemed to be incompatible with international human rights obligations. The NZYQ case, decided by the High Court of Australia in November 2023, however, changed that situation, as in that case, the High Court deemed that detention would be unlawful when there is no real prospect of removal of the concerned migrant in the reasonably foreseeable future (which is likely to be the case for undesirable but unreturnable migrants). Following this decision, many migrants were released from detention and legislation changes were enacted to allow the Minister to grant these migrants a pending removal visa with conditions attached. This development, however, may also raise human rights concerns, as mandatory visa conditions limiting human rights may be disproportionate, since they do not take into account the individual situation of the concerned migrants and the appropriateness of the conditions to their case. Furthermore, as this visa remains a pending removal one, it does not seem to provide a long-term solution for undesirable but unreturnable migrants. Since temporary permits with conditions attached are also used in Canada as a way to regulate the situation of undesirable but unreturnable migrants, this solution is further explored in Chapter 4 of this book.

CHAPTER 3

Belgium: Is Protection against Refoulement Enough?

1 Introduction

As explained in the introduction to this book, the case studies aim to present a variety of regions and legal systems. In this context, Belgium was chosen to present how a State operating under the European system and a civil law regime regulates the situation of undesirable but unreturnable migrants. As a European country and a member State of the European Union (hereafter EU), Belgium is bound by the Charter of Fundamental Rights of the European Union (hereafter EU Charter), the European Convention on Human Rights (hereafter ECHR) and the decisions of the Court of Justice of the European Union (hereafter CJEU) and the European Court of Human Rights (hereafter ECtHR) interpreting these instruments. Thus, this important oversight should help ensure respect for the rights of undesirable but unreturnable migrants and contribute to the development of human rights-compliant measures. Whether the country complies with its international obligations when regulating the situation of undesirable but unreturnable migrants will be evaluated throughout this chapter.

Before looking at how Belgium regulates the situation of undesirable but unreturnable migrants, however, this chapter will start by presenting the relevant national instruments to situate the topic of migration in Belgian law, and by identifying the decision-makers that act in this field. This is done in the next section.

2 Who Is Making the Decisions? The Law and the Authorities in Charge of Migration

In Belgium, the main legal instrument that regulates migration issues is the law of 15 December 1980 on the entry, stay, settlement and removal of foreign nationals[1] (hereafter 1980 Migration Law). Many other national and regional

1 In the original language: Loi du 15 décembre 1980 sur l'accès au territoire, le séjour, l'établissement et l'éloignement des étrangers / Wet van 15 December 1980 betreffende de

 | DOI:10.1163/9789004719910_005

instruments, however, complement this law in regulating migration and the rights of migrants in Belgium. These include, for example, the Royal Decree of 8 October 1981 on the entry, stay, settlement and removal of foreign nationals[2] (hereafter the 1981 Royal Decree). Other instruments will be referred to in this chapter where relevant.

At the international level, Belgium is bound by the legal framework of the EU, including the EU Charter and the EU asylum framework (explained in Section 3.4 of Chapter 1), as well as by the ECHR, the application of which is overseen by the ECtHR. Belgium is also a party to the Refugee Convention and many other human rights treaties, including the International Covenant on Civil and Political Rights (hereafter ICCPR) and the Convention against Torture and Other Cruel, Inhuman or Degrading Treatment or Punishment (hereafter Convention against Torture). These instruments should thus guide Belgium's actions in relation to migrants in the country.

Institution-wise, migration issues fall under the competency of the State Secretary for Asylum and Migration (hereafter State Secretary), the policies of whom are implemented by the Immigration Office. Multiple bodies act in immigration decision-making in Belgium. Requests for international protection are decided by the Office of the Commissioner General for Refugees and Stateless Persons[3] (hereafter office of the Commissioner General or CGRA,[4] following its French acronym). Decisions of the CGRA may be appealed to the Aliens Litigation Council (hereafter CCE,[5] following its French acronym).6 The CCE has full jurisdiction only when deciding appeals from decisions regarding international protection (taken by the CGRA). For other migration decisions, it only assesses legal errors.[7] Decisions of the CCE may not be appealed; however, they may be revised for legal error by the Council of State.[8]

---

toegang tot het grondgebied, het verblijf, de vestiging en de verwijdering van vreemdelingen.

2 In the original language: Arrêté royal du 8 octobre 1981 sur l'accès au territoire, le séjour, l'établissement et l'éloignement des étrangers / Koninklijk besluit van 8 oktober 1981 betreffende de toegang tot het grondgebied, het verblijf, de vestiging en de verwijdering van vreemdelingen.

3 See articles 51/5 and 57/6, 1980 Migration Law.

4 Commissariat général aux réfugiés et aux apatrides.

5 Conseil du Contentieux des Étrangers.

6 Articles 39/1 and 39/2, 1980 Migration Law.

7 Article 39/2, 1980 Migration Law.

8 Article 39/67, 1980 Migration Law and article 14, §2, Coordinated Law of 12 January 1973 on the Council of State. In the original language: Lois coordonées du 12 janvier 1973 sur le Conseil d'État / Gecoördineerde wetten van 12 januari 1973 op de Raad van State.

Decisions of these two bodies (when exercising judicial review) are thus relied upon to identify the correct application of migration legislation.[9]

Against this background, the next sections will look at who is considered an undesirable migrant within this framework.

3 Who Are the Undesirables?

Overall, it can be said that Belgian law provides two different categories of undesirability. First, those based on the exclusion clauses of the Refugee Convention (largely mirrored in the EU asylum framework), which serve to exclude migrants from protective statuses. Second, broad clauses relating to national security and public order, which serve to exclude migrants from most statuses in the country (including protective ones). Thus, subsection 3.1 will address the first category, that is, the provisions that serve to exclude from international protection or from other exceptional statuses those who are excluded from refugee status according to the Refugee Convention and the European asylum framework.[10] Subsection 3.2, in turn, will explore the second category, that is, the provisions referring to the broader concepts of public order and national security, which serve to exclude migrants from most migration statuses in the country.

3.1 *Undesirables in Protection Procedures*

3.1.1 Those Who Committed International Crimes

Article 55/2 of the 1980 Migration Law explicitly refers to the Refugee Convention, providing that those who are excluded from refugee status in accordance with the international treaty will also be excluded in Belgium. Article 55/2 further clarifies that those who incite or in any way participate in the crimes listed in article 1F of the Refugee Convention will also be excluded from refugee status.[11]

As a reminder, article 1F(a) of the Refugee Convention excludes from refugee status those who have committed a crime against peace, a war crime, or a

9 See the introduction to this book for the case selection and reference period of the research on which the book is based.

10 Explained in Section 3.4 of Chapter 1.

11 This latter clarification is in accordance with article 12(3) of the Qualification Directive and of the upcoming Qualification Regulation, explained in Section 3.4 of Chapter 1.

crime against humanity. In Belgian law, not only are those who commit these crimes excluded from refugee protection, but also from subsidiary protection,[12] temporary protection[13] and from being granted an exceptional status for health reasons.[14]

Regarding the practical application of this undesirability clause, Rikhof noted that Belgium relies on the definitions of these crimes contained in international instruments such as the Statute of the International Criminal Court.[15] He further notes that defences, such as duress, are taken into account and, when accepted, prevent an undesirability finding.[16] Lastly, he noted that membership in an organisation that commits international crimes alone is not sufficient for an exclusion finding. In this regard, he said that "[M]embership as a heading for liability has been usually rejected,"[17] and that, instead, substantial (personal) contribution with knowledge of the crime is required.[18]

In 2018, the CCE considered a case[19] involving a man from Rwanda who, after being convicted in Belgium for war crimes and serving his sentence, applied for asylum. He was considered to be excluded and his request was denied. While the case before the CCE did not concern his asylum procedure,[20] the fact that he was excluded many years after the crimes were com-

12 Article 55/4, § 1er(a), 1980 Migration Law.

13 Article 57/32 § 1(1), 1980 Migration Law. Temporary protection refers to the EU's third protection status, which applies in the event of a mass influx of displaced persons to EU Member States. It is regulated by Council Directive 2001/55/EC of 20 July 2001 on minimum standards for giving temporary protection in the event of a mass influx of displaced persons and on measures promoting a balance of efforts between Member States in receiving such persons and bearing the consequences thereof. At the time of writing, this status was only enacted once, in 2022, to grant status to Ukrainians fleeing the armed conflict in Ukraine. See Council implementing decision (EU) 2022/382 of 4 March 2022 establishing the existence of a mass influx of displaced persons from Ukraine within the meaning of Article 5 of Directive 2001/55/EC, and having the effect of introducing temporary protection.

14 Article 9*ter* § 4, 1980 Migration Law.

15 Rikhof, J. (2023). Exclusion and Refoulement: Criminality in International and Domestic Refugee Law. Irwin Law Inc., pp. 235–238.

16 Ibid., p. 413–414.

17 Ibid., p. 314.

18 Ibid., p. 313.

19 Arrêt n° 213 120 (Conseil du Contentieux des Etrangers, 29 November 2018).

20 Instead, it concerned his removal from Belgium, which was a consequence of the asylum rejection.

mitted and after having served his sentence indicates that this type of undesirability persists over time and is not overcome by prosecution.[21]

3.1.2 Those Who Committed a Serious Crime

Article 1F(b) of the Refugee Convention excludes from refugee status those who have committed a serious non-political crime before arriving in the country of refuge. Following the Convention, Belgian law excludes those who have committed a serious crime from refugee protection,[22] subsidiary protection,[23] temporary protection[24] and the exceptional grant of status for health reasons.[25] Furthermore, beneficiaries of subsidiary protection may have their status revoked when it is deemed that they committed a crime in their country of origin, which would entail a prison sentence in Belgium, if they left their country of origin to escape the penalty.[26]

Rikhof notes that for a crime to be considered serious in Belgium, a number of factors should be taken into account, including: the nature of the act, the penalty, the actual damage inflicted upon a person or property and the rules of procedure surrounding the crime.[27] He also noted that some of the older cases involving this type of exclusion related to crimes committed by criminal organisations (such as the Turkish Dev-Sol Organisation, the LTTE, the MQM in Pakistan and the Radical Students Union in India).[28] In this regard, he notes that, as is the case for exclusion under article 1F(a) of the Refugee Convention in Belgium, a person must make a "substantial contribution with an immediate effect on the crime along with the intention of committing this crime"[29] to be excluded.

3.1.3 Those Who Committed Acts Contrary to the Purposes and Principles of the United Nations (UN)

The last exclusion clause under the Refugee Convention (article 1F(c)) concerns those who were found guilty of acts contrary to the purposes and prin-

21 This case thus exemplifies some of the limits of prosecution as a solution for regulating the situation of undesirable but unreturnable migrants, as shown in Section 4.2 of Chapter 1.
22 Article 55/2, 1980 Migration Law.
23 Article 55/4 § 1er(c), 1980 Migration law.
24 Article 57/32 § 1(2), 1980 Migration Law.
25 Article 9*ter* § 4, 1980 Migration Law.
26 Article 55/5/1, 1980 Migration Act.
27 Rikhof, J. (2023), p. 469.
28 Ibid., pp. 469–470.
29 Ibid., p. 470.

ciples of the United Nations (hereafter UN). Again, this provision is mirrored in Belgian law to exclude migrants from refugee protection,[30] subsidiary protection,[31] temporary protection[32] and the exceptional grant of status for health reasons.[33]

Regarding the practical application of this provision, Rikhof noted that it has increasingly been used in terrorism cases.[34] In this regard, the Council of State found, in 2017, that the mere fact of being convicted for participating in a terrorist group, without a conviction for participation in terrorist acts, could be enough to exclude someone from refugee status as participation in a terrorist group in itself can be considered an act contrary to the purposes and principles of the UN.[35]

3.2 *Undesirables for Reasons of National Security or Public Order*

Besides excluding from protective and exceptional statuses those who are deemed undesirable in the Refugee Convention, Belgian law contains multiple provisions that serve to exclude migrants from migration statuses. In this regard, the terms national security and public order are used throughout the 1980 Migration Law as reasons that would lead to a migrant being undesirable and thus being denied the right to enter or stay in the country.

In the international protection context, the provisions addressing national security mainly follow article 33(2) of the Refugee Convention,[36] which, as explained in Chapter 1, sets an exception to the principle of non-refoulement, despite it being the cornerstone of refugee protection. In Belgium, article 33(2) is included in Article 52/4 of the 1980 Migration Law, which allows the Office of the Commissioner General to refuse refugee status to those who are considered a danger due to a previous conviction. Thus,

30 Article 55/2, 1980 Migration Law.

31 Article 55/4 § 1er(b), 1980 Migration law.

32 Article 57/32 § 1(3), 1980 Migration Law.

33 Article 9*ter* § 4, 1980 Migration Law.

34 Rikhof, J. (2023), pp. 545–546.

35 Arrêt nº 238.210 (Conseil d'État, 16 May 2017). It is worth nothing that Rikhof references a 2011 CCE case to affirm that, in Belgium, "(…) membership in a terrorist organization is not in itself a sufficient ground for exclusion from refugee status" (Rikhof, J. (2023), p. 546). The 2017 case from the Council of State cited here, however, points to a change in this interpretation by Belgian courts.

36 Article 33(2) prescribes as follows: "[T]he benefit of the present provision [protection from refoulement] may not, however, be claimed by a refugee whom there are reasonable grounds for regarding as a danger to the security of the country in which he is, or who, having been convicted by a final judgment of a particularly serious crime, constitutes a danger to the community of that country."

the 1980 Migration Law merges 1F and 33(2) into requirements to recognise someone as a refugee, instead of framing 33(2) as an exception to non-refoulement.[37] Similarly, being considered a danger to security after a criminal conviction also serves to exclude migrants from temporary protection.[38] Article 55/3/1 of the 1980 Migration Law further prescribes that recognised refugees may have their status revoked if they are convicted of a serious crime and are thus considered a threat to society or national security.

In subsidiary protection, article 55/4 of the 1980 Migration Law more broadly excludes those who are a danger to society or national security, thus dropping the criminal conviction requirement. The same applies to the exceptional grant of status for health reasons.[39]

Outside the international protection (and exceptional grant of status for health reasons) context, article 3(7) of the 1980 Migration Law more generally states that the right to enter Belgium may be denied to those who may compromise the country's public tranquillity, public order or national security.[40] Similarly, Article 43 establishes that EU citizens and their family members may be denied the right to enter or stay in Belgium for reasons of public order, national security or public health.

Different provisions of the 1980 Migration Law also allow the withdrawal of the right to stay in Belgium for reasons of public order. These include, for example, articles 21 and 22 (regarding non-EU citizens)[41] and article 44*bis* (regarding EU citizens and their family members). Thus, public order and national security seem to be the key terms that will define when a migrant is undesirable in Belgium. These terms, however, are not defined in Belgian law.

---

37 This is in line with the EU asylum framework, since, as explained in Section 3.4 of Chapter 1, the Court of Justice of the European Union (CJEU), when assessing the compatibility of the EU framework with the Refugee Convention, noted that the former grants greater protection than the latter, as it does not allow a non-refoulement exception, even in cases of national security. See Joined Cases C-391/16, C-77/17 and C-78/17 (Court of Justice of the European Union, 14 May 2019), paras. 94–95.

38 Article 57/32 § 1(4), 1980 Migration Law.

39 Article 9*ter* § 4, 1980 Migration Law.

40 At the European level, Regulation (EU) 2016/399 of the European Parliament and of the Council of 9 March 2016 on a Union Code on the rules governing the movement of persons across borders (Schengen Borders Code) establishes in Article 6(e) that non-EU nationals shall not be allowed to enter the Schengen space if they are considered a threat to public order or internal security.

41 These two latter provisions do not apply to beneficiaries of international protection according to article 20 of the 1980 Migration Law, however, as mentioned earlier in this chapter, they may lose their protection status in accordance with other provisions, including, in some cases, for reasons of national security.

In the Refugee Convention context, Farmer notes that national security is also undefined in article 33(2), as the article "(...) does not identify the types of acts that could trigger the national security exception but rather leaves that to the discretion of the states, allowing for the possibility of broad application."[42] This lack of definition, however, has been criticised by human rights bodies and scholars.[43]

In this regard, when assessing Belgium's compliance with the ICCPR, the UN Human Rights Committee noted that Belgium had "(...) ambiguous definition of offences related to terrorism, national security and public order."[44] Similarly, when the UN Committee against Torture assessed Belgium's compliance with the Convention against Torture, it expressed concern over the lack of precision of the clauses allowing the refusal or withdrawal of refugee status or subsidiary protection when the refugee is considered a danger to national security.[45] These blurred notions may thus undermine legal certainty.

Some indications as to the practical application of these notions, however, can be found in legal provisions and Case Law. The efforts to clarify the implementation of these terms are presented in the next subsection.

3.2.1 National Security or Public Order in Practice: What Needs to Be Taken into Account? Some Discretion on Deciding Who Is Undesirable

As noted above, multiple provisions in Belgian law serve to deny or revoke the right to enter or stay in the country for reasons of national security or public order. These concepts, however, are not defined in law. Some articles of the 1980 Migration Act try to remedy this by giving decision-makers some guidance on the practical application of these notions.[46] For example, articles 23

---

42 Farmer, A. (2008). Non-refoulement and Jus Cogens: Limiting anti-terror measures that threaten refugee protection. Georgetown Immigration Law Journal, 23(1), 1–38, p. 9.

43 See, e.g. Macq, C. (2018). Le point sur le retrait du droit au séjour et l'éloignement pour motifs d'ordre public des étrangers en séjour legal. Revue du droit des étrangers, 198, 179–219, para. 53.

44 Human Rights Committee (2019). Concluding observations on the sixth periodic report of Belgium (CCPR/C/BEL/CO/6). United Nations, para. 11.

45 Original quote in French: "(...) les clauses permettant le refus ou le retrait du statut de réfugié ou de la protection subsidiaire quand le réfugié est considéré comme un danger pour la sécurité nationale sont rédigées de manière imprécise." Committee against Torture (2021). Observations finales concernant le quatriéme rapport périodique de la Belgique (CAT/C/BEL/CO/4). United Nations, para. 25.

46 In this regard, article 62 of the 1980 Migration Act provides that when revocation of the right to stay is envisaged, the concerned migrant will be notified and given the opportu-

and 45 establish that, for the purpose of withdrawing the right to stay of a migrant, the behaviour of the concerned person must represent a real, current and sufficiently serious threat to a fundamental interest of society. Article 23, addressing non-EU citizens, further states that when deciding to end someone's right to stay, the decision-maker must take into account the nature of the public order or national security infraction and the danger the concerned individual presents. According to that article, the length of the concerned migrant's stay in Belgium and their links to the country, as well as the links to the country of origin and the consequences of the decision to the concerned individual and their family members must also be taken into account.[47]

Regarding international protection holders, once the CGRA decides to revoke a protection status,[48] article 11 §3 of the 1980 Migration Act allows decision-makers to end the concerned person's temporary right to stay and issue an order to leave the territory. The decision must, however, take into account the nature and strength of the migrant's family links, the length of their stay in Belgium, as well as the existence of family, cultural or social links with the country of origin.

Concerning EU citizens, in turn, article 45 says that past criminal convictions alone do not suffice to justify the denial or withdrawal of a migration status.[49] In this regard, the Council of State clarified that the article's precision

---

nity to present the relevant arguments that may influence the decision. Thus, the elements mentioned in the guidance that is exposed below can be presented by migrants to decision-makers. The disrespect of article 62 will lead to an annulment of the decision. For example, through its Arrêt n° 243.808 (Conseil d'État, 26 February 2019) the Council of State annulled an initial return order since the concerned migrant had not been heard. The decision, however, also shows that the presence of a lawyer is not needed when the State representative meets with the migrant for this purpose. See also Arrêt n° 197 240 (Conseil du Contentieux des Etrangers, 22 December 2017); Arrêt n° 197 241 (Conseil du Contentieux des Etrangers, 22 December 2017); Arrêt n° 197 242 (Conseil du Contentieux des Etrangers, 22 December 2017).

47 Similarly, Article 74/13 establishes that when taking a decision to return someone, the minister or their delegate must consider the best interest of the child, the family life and the state of health of the concerned migrant.

48 Articles 55/3/1 and 55/5/1 also require that, upon reaching a revocation decision, the CGRA issues an opinion regarding the compatibility of a return decision with the inclusion criteria for refugee and subsidiary protection prescribed in articles 48/3 and 48/4.

49 In this regard, in a decision from 2015, the CCE annulled an order to leave the Belgian territory against an EU citizen as the decision was taken based only on previous criminal convictions, without explaining how the personal behaviour of the concerned migrant would represent a real and sufficiently serious threat affecting a fundamental interest of society. See Arrêt n° 157 475 (Conseil du Contentieux des Etrangers, 30 November 2015), para. 3.1. Similarly, the CCE found that a conviction alone could not justify the rejection

that the existence of previous criminal convictions cannot, in itself, motivate an expulsion measure means that there cannot be an automatism between the existence of criminal convictions and the expulsion decision. Instead, it is necessary to examine whether the personal behaviour of the foreigner constitutes a threat to public order.[50]

While article 23 does not explicitly say, as article 45 does, that criminal convictions alone cannot justify the revocation of a right to stay, multiple decisions of the Council of State and the CCE indicate that even though criminal acts, due to their nature,[51] seriousness and repetition in time,[52] may justify considering someone a threat to national security or public order, a criminal conviction alone is not sufficient to withdraw the right to stay of a non-EU national.[53] Furthermore, in specific cases, the Council of State noted that deci-

of a family reunification application for reasons of public order. See Arrêt n° 194 086 (Conseil du Contentieux des Etrangers, 24 October 2017), para. 3.5.

50 The Council's words were: "La précision selon laquelle l'existence de condamnations pénales antérieures ne peut, à elle seule, motiver une mesure d'expulsion signifie qu'il ne peut pas y avoir d'automatisme entre l'existence d'une ou de certaines condamnations pénales et la décision d'expulsion: il faut examiner si le comportement personnel de l'étranger constitue une menace pour l'ordre public." Arrêt n° 243.152 (Conseil d'État, 6 December 2018), p. 9. For example, in Ordonnance n° 13.078 (Conseil d'État, 29 November 2018), the Council of State accepted that some of the elements that may be considered include the behaviour displayed by the person concerned, their background, the recurrent and serious nature of the incriminating facts and the lack of proof that the person has made amends. In the same line, in Arrêt n° 173 880 (Conseil du Contentieux des Etrangers, 1 September 2016), the CCE annulled a decision in which the decision-maker did not explain how the personal behaviour of the concerned person justified the withdrawal of their right to stay in Belgium, instead relying solely on their conviction.

51 For example, the terrorist nature of a criminal act led the Council of State to confirm a decision deeming a migrant a permanent threat to national security and thus justifying a decision to expel him. The concerned migrant had participated in a terrorist group and been convicted for his involvement in the group's activities. See Arrêt n° 240.734 (Conseil d'État, 16 February 2018).

52 Recidivism with lack of proof of rehabilitation was also accepted as a factor that could lead to the rejection of status to EU citizens and their family members by the CCE in Arrêt n° 174 351 (Conseil du Contentieux des Etrangers, 8 September 2016).

53 See, e.g. Ordonnance n° 11.515 (Conseil d'État, 3 September 2015); Ordonnance n° 12.204 (Conseil d'État, 17 November 2016); Ordonnance n° 12.333 (Conseil d'État, 3 March 2017); Ordonnance n° 12.882, p. 3 (Conseil d'État, 5 June 2018); Arrêt n° 243.788 (Conseil d'État, 22 February 2019); Arrêt n° 159 074 (Conseil du Contentieux des Etrangers, 21 December 2015); Arrêt n° 210 425 (Conseil du Contentieux des Etrangers, 2 October 2018). Similarly, the CCE found that convictions alone could not justify a lengthy entry ban based on the fact that the concerned person was considered a grave threat to public order. See, e.g. Arrêt n° 176 961 (Conseil du Contentieux des Etrangers, 27 October 2016), p. 13; Arrêt n° 177 215 (Conseil du Contentieux des Etrangers, 31 October 2016), para. 3.2;

sion-makers should take into account the reasons for offending and possible releases granted;[54] whether concerned migrants have not reoffended for a certain period of time,[55] if they were acquitted in the relevant criminal proceedings,[56] and, in the case of ongoing criminal procedures, whether loss of status and expulsion would impact the right to a fair trial in Belgium.[57]

At the same time, both the CCE and the Council of State have deemed that a conviction or even a criminal procedure is not necessary when the person's behaviour and attitude alone constitute a threat to national security.[58] In this regard, they found that a Dutch citizen[59] who preached extremist ideas represented a threat to national security and thus upheld his expulsion from Belgium, despite the fact that he had not been pursued criminally for his actions.[60] In another case, in which a migrant was caught during a robbery,

---

Arrêt n° 177 216 (Conseil du Contentieux des Etrangers, 31 October 2016), para. 4.2.2; Arrêt n° 178 845 (Conseil du Contentieux des Etrangers, 1 December 2016), para. 2.3; Arrêt n° 178 846 (Conseil du Contentieux des Etrangers, 1 December 2016), para. 3.3; Arrêt n° 179 112 (Conseil du Contentieux des Etrangers 9 December 2016), para. 3.3; Arrêt n° 190 701 (Conseil du Contentieux des Etrangers, 18 August 2017), para. 2.2.4; Arrêt n° 193 687 (Conseil du Contentieux des Etrangers, 13 October 2017), para. 3.6; Arrêt n° 213 507 (Conseil du Contentieux des Etrangers, 6 December 2018), para. 3.2.1; Arrêt n° 213 511 (Conseil du Contentieux des Etrangers, 6 December 2018), para. 3.6; Arrêt n° 229 831 (Conseil du Contentieux des Etrangers, 5 December 2019), para. 2.1.5.

54 See Arrêt n° 245 068 (Conseil du Contentieux des Etrangers, 30 November 2020).

55 See, e.g. Arrêt nº 242.627 (Conseil d'État, 11 October 2018); Arrêt n° 213 188 (Conseil du Contentieux des Etrangers, 29 November 2018).

56 Arrêt nº 240.760 (Conseil d'État, 20 February 2018).

57 Arrêt nº 241.632 (Conseil d'État, 29 May 2018).

58 See, e.g. Arrêt n° 176 498 (Conseil du Contentieux des Etrangers, 18 October 2016), p. 5; Arrêt n° 195 544 (Conseil du Contentieux des Etrangers, 24 November 2017), p. 8.

59 Thus entitled to a higher degree of protection as an EU national, as will be shown in the following section.

60 Arrêt n° 177.002 (Conseil du Contentieux des Etrangers, 28 October 2016); Ordonnance nº 12.254 (Conseil d'État, 22 December 2016). It should be noted, however, that the CCE also found, in another case, that the mere fact of attending a mosque known for its links with a fundamentalist and radical organisation did not suffice to deny the right to stay in Belgium without showing that the concerned individual had engaged in reprehensible activities or shared extremist views. See Arrêt n° 177 338 (Conseil du Contentieux des Etrangers, 4 November 2016). Similarly, the CCE also annulled a decision rejecting the right to settlement to a recognised refugee due to the fact that the concerned refugee was considered a threat to public order due to their contacts with extremist members of the Caucasus community in Belgium. The CCE found that the lack of explanation concerning the type of contact, the activities involved, or the persons concerned served to invalidate the decision. See Arrêt n° 229 938 (Conseil du Contentieux des Etrangers, 9 December 2019). This is in line with jurisprudence of the CJEU, which, in a case regarding Germany, noted that "(…) the mere fact that the refugee supported that [terrorist]

the CCE found it reasonable to consider that the concerned migrant may compromise public order based on the ongoing criminal procedures, in which the facts were not questioned by the concerned person.[61]

Lastly, it is important to note that the CCE mentioned, in a case involving the withdrawal of the right to stay for reasons of national security, that every decision must present clear and unequivocal reasoning to enable the recipient of the decision to understand the justifications for it and, where appropriate, to be able to challenge the decision in the context of an appeal as well as to enable the competent court to exercise its control on the subject.[62]

The abovementioned guidance seems to indicate that decision-makers should consider the overall situation of the concerned migrant, without focusing exclusively on their undesirability. Thus, it indicates that all elements surrounding a concerned person's situation in Belgium are to be taken into account when deciding whether they should be allowed to enter and remain in the country. This is further shown by the fact that Belgian law also indicates that those who have resided longer in the country or have strong links to it should be granted greater protection against losing their status, showing that settlement in Belgium is an important element to consider when deciding who is undesirable. The next subsection will thus explain how Belgian law affords greater protection for those who have strong ties to the country.

3.2.2 Can Long Settlers Still Be Considered Undesirable?

As noted above, Belgian law and judicial bodies suggest that decision-makers must take different factors into account when considering who is an undesir-

---

organisation cannot automatically mean that that person's residence permit is revoked," further noting that "(…) in the context of the judicial review of the assessment carried out by the competent authority, the referring court must examine the role that Mr. T. [the concerned migrant] actually played in supporting that organisation, by ascertaining in particular whether he himself has committed terrorist acts, whether and to what extent he was involved in planning, decision-making or directing other persons with a view to committing acts of that nature, and whether and to what extent he financed such acts or procured for other persons the means to commit them." See Case C-373/13 (Court of Justice of the European Union, 24 June 2015), paras. 87 and 90.

61 Arrêt n° 159 138 (Conseil du Contentieux des Etrangers, 22 December 2015).

62 The CCE's words were: "Il suffit, par conséquent, que la décision fasse apparaître de façon claire et non équivoque le raisonnement de son auteur afin de permettre au destinataire de la décision de comprendre les justifications de celle-ci et, le cas échéant, de pouvoir les contester dans le cadre d'un recours et, à la juridiction compétente, d'exercer son contrôle à ce sujet." Arrêt n° 204 918 (Conseil du Contentieux des Etrangers, 6 June 2018), par 3.3.2.2.1. See also Arrêt n° 204 919 (Conseil du Contentieux des Etrangers, 6 June 2018).

able migrant. As will be shown in this section, settlement in Belgium is an important factor to consider in this regard. This is because Belgian law affords greater protection to those who have resided in the country for longer periods or have strong links to Belgium (for example, through family members).

It is important to note, however, that this greater protection has been reduced as important legislative changes took place in 2017[63] regarding the denial and withdrawal of migration status.[64] Most of these changes were brought to the 1980 Migration Law by the Law of 24 February 2017 amending the law of 15 December 1980 on access to the territory, stay, establishment and removal of foreigners in order to strengthen the protection of public order and national security[65] (the 2017 amendment). Before the 2017 amendment, article 20 of the 1980 Migration Law[66] set as a general rule that migrants without the right to settle in Belgium could be returned in cases where they disrupted public order or national security. The same article established that migrants who had the right to settle in Belgium or those who had a long-term residence status in the country had a stronger protection and could only be returned in case of serious disruption of public order or national security. Lastly, article 21 of the pre-amended 1980 Migration Law defined certain categories of migrants that could not be expelled from Belgium under any circumstances. These included migrants born in Belgium or those who arrived in the country before the age of 12 as well as refugees whose refugee status was recognised in Belgium. Furthermore, article 21 also established a few categories of

63 These changes arose less than a year after terrorist attacks took place in Brussels, killing many. The attacks were conducted by Belgian nationals (and a French national) of foreign origin. This stricter migration law that followed the attacks thus seem to indicate that the foreign origin of the attackers, despite their Belgian nationality, was enough to further strengthen the association between immigration and threats to security, presented in Chapter 1. Thus, the amendment diminishes the security given to settled migrants against loss of status. Regarding the terror attacks in Brussels, see, e.g.: BBC News (22 March 2016) Brussels attacks: Zaventem and Maelbeek bombs kill many. Available at: https://www.bbc.com/news/world-europe-35869254.

64 The objective of this section is to analyse the current state of affairs and not conduct an in-depth analysis of the specific changes brought by the 2017 amendments. For a comprehensive overview of these changes, see: Macq, C. (2018).

65 In original language: Loi du 24 février 2017 modifiant la loi du 15 décembre 1980 sur l'accès au territoire, le séjour, l'établissement et l'éloignement des étrangers afin de renforcer la protection de l'ordre public et de la sécurité nationale / Wet van 24 februari 2017 tot wijziging van de wet van 15 december 1980 betreffende de toegang tot het grondgebied, het verblijf, de vestiging en de verwijdering van vreemdelingen, met het doel de bescherming van de openbare orde en de nationale veiligheid te versterken.

66 See archived version nº 92 of the 1980 Migration Law.

migrants that could only be expelled in case of grave breaches of public order or national security. These were migrants who had been regularly living in Belgium for at least twenty years; migrants who had not been sentenced to a prison sentence equal to or greater than five years and who exercised parental authority over a child legally residing in Belgium; migrants residing regularly in the country for at least ten years; migrants fulfilling the conditions to acquire Belgian nationality by declaration of nationality; spouses of Belgian citizens; and migrant workers suffering from a permanent incapacity for work. These rules changed significantly with the 2017 Amendment.[67]

Since the 2017 Amendment, there are no longer categories of migrants that cannot be expelled from Belgium under any circumstances in view of their settlement.[68] Furthermore, as noted above, post-amendment articles 3(7), 21 and 43 of the 1980 Migration Law provide that almost all migrants may be returned for reasons of public order or national security.[69]

A greater protection, however, is still afforded to those who have been in the country for longer. For example, article 22 specifies that non-EU citizens who obtained the right to settle in Belgium, who have the long-term resident status or who have regularly lived in Belgium for at least 10 years can only have their right to stay revoked for serious reasons of public order or national security. This is also the case for EU citizens and their family members, as article 44*bis* establishes that they may have their right to stay revoked for reasons of public order, national security or public health, but specifies in paragraph 2 that for those who obtained permanent residence, their right to stay may only be withdrawn by the State Secretary personally[70] for serious reasons of public order or national security while paragraph 3 determines that EU citizens who

---

67 While some of the judicial decisions mentioned in this section relate to the 1980 Migration Law as it was before the 2017 amendments, they remain valid in which they relate to the definition of public order or national security, which are still the main concepts associated to the refusal and withdrawal of status and expulsion from the Belgian territory, despite the different standards that may apply in relation to each concept.

68 As will be shown below, however, Belgian law does protect those who are owed non-refoulement obligations from return in any circumstance.

69 It should be noted, however, that beneficiaries of international protection are excluded from the application of articles 21 (explained above) and 22 (which will be explained below) according to article 20.

70 Indeed, the CCE annulled a decision that was taken by a delegate under this article, as a delegate does not have the competency to do so. See Arrêt n° 213 807 (Conseil du Contentieux des Etrangers, 13 December 2018).

have been living in the country for at least 10 years can only have their right to stay revoked for compelling reasons of national security.[71]

The practical application of these provisions, however, is not straightforward, since, as noted above, the concepts of public order and national security are not well-defined. The CCE tried to shed some light on the application of these different degrees of threat. For example, regarding the difference between serious reasons and compelling reasons, it noted that the concept of "serious reasons" must be interpreted less strictly than that of "compelling reasons," as it does not require the existence of "exceptional circumstances" or an infringement of a particularly high degree of seriousness, which is required when the standard is "compelling reasons."[72]

In academic literature, however, Macq said that it is impossible to determine precisely the degree of seriousness required to move from one concept to the other. According to her, an assessment of these different degrees depends on the intrinsic characteristics of the offence. In this regard, the assessment is to be carried out on a case-by-case basis, taking into account all the relevant elements, in fact and in law, specific to the case at hand. She claims that this leaves too much discretion to decision-makers to decide the seriousness requirements. Ultimately, this means the greater protection afforded to migrants with strong links to Belgium appears to be artificial since it is based on the use of vague, undefined concepts.[73]

Even though the practical implementation of the stronger protection given to long settlers can be questioned, this subsection and the previous one show that Belgian law and jurisprudence call on decision-makers not to limit themselves to the criminal actions (or threats thereof) migrants were involved in. Instead, the overall situation of the said migrant, including their links to Belgium, should be considered when deciding who is undesirable. This assessment, however, will not always favour continued stay and thus, in some cases, migrants may see their right to enter or stay in Belgium denied or terminated. Those who fear harm upon return, however, should be able to express this fear to prevent refoulement in violation of human rights. The next sections will thus present the options available for migrants to have their non-refoulement claims assessed in Belgium.

71 See Arrêt n° 177.002, para. 4.2.2.2.3.
72 Ibid. idem.
73 Macq, C. (2018), pp. 198–199.

4 Who Are the Unreturnable Migrants?

4.1 *Making a Non-refoulement Claim by Requesting International Protection*

In Belgium, a request for international protection is the main procedure through which a migrant's fear of harm upon return is assessed. Applications for refugee status and subsidiary protection are both made as requests for international protection in the country.[74] This means that everyone who requests international protection in Belgium will first be assessed in view of the refugee criteria and, if those are not met, they will be assessed on the subsidiary protection requirements.[75]

As a party to the Refugee Convention and as a member State of the EU, Belgium needs to take both frameworks (the international one and the EU one, explained in Chapter 1) into account in its national legislation regulating the grant of international protection.

In national law, Belgium regulates refugee and subsidiary protection in chapter II of title II of the 1980 Migration Law.[76] The first provision in this chapter, article 48, establishes that those who meet the requirements set in international treaties that Belgium is a part of may be recognised as refugees. In this regard, article 48/3, §1er specifically mentions that refugee status is granted to those who satisfy the conditions set in article 1 of the Refugee Con-

74 Article 49/3 of the 1980 Migration Law.

75 When Belgium included the subsidiary protection status in its national legal framework (through measures taken to internalise the now superseded Council Directive 2004/83/EC of 29 April 2004 on minimum standards for the qualification and status of third country nationals or stateless persons as refugees or as persons who otherwise need international protection and the content of the protection granted), it provided the possibility of those who received an opinion of the CGRA deeming that their return would put their life, physical integrity or liberty at risk before the insertion of the subsidiary protection in the national context being granted subsidiary protection nonetheless, as long as the risk upon return was still real and that the person did not present a risk to national security of public order (Article 77, §3 of the Law of 15 September 2006 modifying the law of 15 December 1980 on the entry, stay, settlement and removal of foreign nationals; loi du 15 septembre 2006 modifiant la loi du 15 décembre 1980 sur l'accès au territoire, le séjour, l'établissement et l'éloignement des étrangers / Wet van 15 september 2006 tot wijziging van de wet van 15 december 1980 betreffende de toegang tot het grondgebied, het verblijf, de vestiging en de verwijdering van vreemdelingen). This seems to have given an alternative status to those who were excluded from refugee status before October 2006, but it provided no solution to those who were also excluded from subsidiary protection afterwards or who were deemed a threat to national security or public order.

76 Temporary protection, in turn, is defined in Article 57/29 of the 1980 Migration Law.

vention, while other articles transpose different parts of the Qualification Directive (explained in Section 3.4 of Chapter 1). For example, subsidiary protection is provided in Belgian law and article 15 of the Qualification Directive (largely unchanged in the upcoming Qualification Regulation), defining serious harm for the purpose of assessing subsidiary protection, is transposed into the national context in article 48/4 of the 1980 Migration Law. In article 48/5, Belgium extends the principle of internal flight alternative to subsidiary protection, as allowed by the Directive (and as mandated by the upcoming Regulation in article 8). Following the Procedures Directive,[77] Belgium has also introduced the concepts of first country of asylum, safe country of origin and safe third country in its national legislation.[78] Thus, those who are considered to have protection elsewhere may be denied protection in Belgium.

In practice, the Council of State provided some guidance on when the feared acts in the country of origin are considered sufficient for the purposes of granting international protection, noting that the mere possibility of ill-treatment due to the situation of groups at risk in a country is not in itself enough. Instead, the person who wishes to justify the fear of ill-treatment must demonstrate that both the general situation in the country of origin and the specific circumstances of their personal case justify the risk of inhuman or degrading treatment upon return.[79] Regarding the evidence that proves that someone meets the set criteria, the Council of State notes that when decision-makers base their decisions on online or telephone communication with sources other than the applicant, these sources need to be disclosed to the applicant for international protection so that they have the opportunity to verify the information.[80]

As noted in Section 3.1 above, however, undesirable migrants may have their request for international protection denied when they fall under an exclusion clause. In this regard, articles 52/4,[81] 55/2 and 55/4 of the 1980 Migra-

---

77 Directive 2013/32/EU of the European Parliament and of the Council of 26 June 2013 on common procedures for granting and withdrawing international protection. This Directive will be replaced by a Regulation in 2026 (Regulation (EU) 2024/1348 of the European Parliament and of the Council of 14 May 2024 establishing a common procedure for international protection in the Union and repealing Directive 2013/32/EU). The Regulation continues to include the abovementioned concepts.

78 Articles 57/6, 57/6/1 and 57/6/6, 1980 Migration Law.

79 Ordonnance nº 11.681 (Conseil d'État, 21 December 2015).

80 See Arrêt nº 232.858 (Conseil d'État, 10 November 2015); Arrêt nº 232.859 (Conseil d'État, 10 November 2015); and Arrêt nº 232.949 (Conseil d'État, 19 November 2015).

81 This provision internalises article 33(2) of the Refugee Convention, which, in the international instrument, creates an exception to the (refugee law) non-refoulement princi-

tion Law require that, upon making an exclusion decision in a protection procedure, the CGRA issues an opinion on the compatibility of the concerned person's return with the inclusion clauses (that is, on the risk of harm upon return). Thus, even undesirable migrants will have their non-refoulement claims assessed, regardless of whether they are excluded or not.

It should be noted that a request for international protection, albeit the main means to assess harm upon return, is not the only way for migrants to have their non-refoulement claims analysed. The next subsections will thus present the other possibilities available for unreturnable migrants.

4.2 *Making a Non-refoulement Claim Based on Health Issues through a* 9ter *Application*

In Belgium, there is a specific procedure for those who fear harm upon return due to health reasons, that is, when return entails a real risk for the migrant's life or physical integrity or a real risk of inhuman or degrading treatment because there is no adequate treatment for their health condition in the country of origin.[82] This procedure is prescribed in article 9*ter* of the 1980 Migration Law. However, article 55/4, which regulates exclusion from subsidiary protection, also serves to exclude those who make an application under article 9*ter* of the 1980 Migration Law. In this regard, the CCE deemed that it was not a legal error to exclude someone who fell under article 55/4 without first assessing their health-related claim. According to the CCE, the assertion that a decision cannot result in exclusion from the benefit of article 9*ter* without first examining whether the illness in question reaches the seriousness threshold required by this provision cannot be accepted any more than the claim that it follows from a general principle of international law that, in matters of inter-

ple. The 1980 Migration Law provision, however, by requiring that the CGRA assesses compatibility of the concerned person's return with the inclusion clauses, differs from the Refugee Convention in that it calls on decision-makers to take non-refoulement into account, even if article 33(2) explicitly creates an exception to the principle.

82 This is in line with the Case Law of the ECtHR, which considers that returning someone to a place where they would not have access to adequate medical treatment would amount to a violation of non-refoulement. The Paposhvili case mentioned below exemplifies this Case Law. For a thorough analysis of the ECtHR's position regarding health-related non-refoulement claims, see section III. B. of the following contribution: Baker, C. (2022). No refuge for the sick: How the EU's health-based non-refoulement standard compounds the exclusionary nature of international refugee law. Washington International Law Journal, 31(2), 251–291.

national protection, the exclusion clauses must be examined after the inclusion clauses.[83]

This seems to indicate that protection-related claims in protection procedures also do not need to be considered before exclusion clauses.[84] However, as was noted in the previous section, even if someone is excluded from protection, the CGRA still needs to assess whether their return would be compatible with non-refoulement. This is not the case for 9*ter* applications and thus migrants may not have their claim of harm heard in such procedure if they are deemed to be undesirable.

In view of the absolute character of non-refoulement, however, Belgian law provides that every return decision must take non-refoulement into account. The possibility of having a non-refoulement claim assessed in return procedures is thus presented in the next subsection.

4.3 *Non-refoulement Assessment in Return Procedures*

Belgian law gives great emphasis to the principle of non-refoulement. In this regard, article 74/17 §1er of the 1980 Migration Law establishes that the return of a migrant will be deferred in cases where return would expose the concerned person to a violation of non-refoulement.[85] More specifically, the article states that return will not be possible when the CGRA recognises that Belgium owes protection obligations to a person, unless the State Secretary or a delegate shows that the CGRA's assessment is no longer applicable. Similarly, article 24 §3 of the same legal text provides that those who lose their right to

83 The words of the CCE were: "l'affirmation du requérant, selon laquelle « la décision querellée ne pouvait pas conclure à [son] exclusion du bénéfice de l'article 9*ter*, sans examiner au préalable si la maladie dont il souffre atteint le seuil de gravité exigé par cette disposition », ne peut être retenue, pas plus que celle selon laquelle « Il ressort d'un principe général de droit international qu'en matière de protection internationale, les clauses d'exclusion doivent s'examiner après les clauses d'inclusion », affirmation non étayée et qui ne peut nullement se déduire des extraits de jurisprudence reproduits en termes de requête." Arrêt n° 190 991 (Conseil du Contentieux des Etrangers, 29 August 2017), para. 3.1. See also Arrêt n° 194 142 (Conseil du Contentieux des Etrangers, 24 October 2017); Arrêt n° 196 796 (Conseil du Contentieux des Etrangers, 18 December 2017).

84 In this regard, the upcoming Qualification Regulation explicitly says, in article 12(4), that once a decision-maker finds that a person is excluded from refugee status, they "shall exclude the applicant from refugee status without performing a proportionality assessment linked to the fear of being persecuted." The same is provided in article 17(4) for subsidiary protection.

85 This is in line with article 9(1)(a) of Directive 2008/115/EC of the European Parliament and of the Council of 16 December 2008 on common standards and procedures in Member States for returning illegally staying third-country nationals (Return Directive).

stay for reasons of public order or national security shall not be returned to a place where they may be exposed to a non-refoulement violation.[86] Thus, to ensure compliance with these provisions, the Council of State considers that non-refoulement needs to be taken into account by decision-makers before a decision to order a migrant to leave the territory is taken.

In this regard, before the Council of State, the Belgian State has argued that non-refoulement only needs to be considered when the return of the migrant will be executed and not before a decision to order the concerned migrant to leave the territory is taken. As a general rule, the CCE and the Council of State used to uphold this position, noting that before a coercive measure is adopted, a non-refoulement assessment is premature.[87] The situation is different when a detention order is associated with the order to leave the territory, thus attaching a coercive measure to the decision. In these cases, the Council of State considers that, in view of the possibility that return violates a migrant's rights, especially those included in article 3 of the ECHR (that sets the right to be free from torture), non-refoulement should be taken into account before an order to leave the territory (with an associated detention measure) is issued.[88]

In some more recent decisions, however, the CCE and the Council of State seem to dissociate the need to consider non-refoulement from the coercive measure,[89] hinting at the fact that this should be considered at the moment of issuing an order to leave the territory in all cases. For example, in 2017, the Council of State said that it cannot be assumed that a migrant will not respect an order to leave the territory. Consequently, the State cannot refrain from ensuring that the execution of this order complies with non-refoulement on

86 At the European level, EU Member States' commitment to non-refoulement is prescribed in article 5 of the Return Directive and in article 19(2) of the EU Charter.

87 See Ordonnance n° 11.805 (Conseil d'État, 17 February 2016); Ordonnance n° 11.084 (Conseil d'État, 9 February 2015); Arrêt n° 152 020 (Conseil du Contentieux des Etrangers, 9 September 2015); Arrêt n° 159 147 (Conseil du Contentieux des Etrangers, 22 December 2015); Arrêt n° 159 164 (Conseil du Contentieux des Etrangers, 22 December 2015).

88 See, e.g.; Arrêt n° 230.956 (Conseil d'État, 23 April 2015).

89 See, e.g. Ordonnance n° 12.683 (Conseil d'État, 23 January 2018); Arrêt n° 240.691 (Conseil d'État, 8 February 2018); Arrêt n° 239.259 (Conseil d'État, 28 September 2017); Arrêt n° 196 796; Arrêt n° 207 878 (Conseil du Contentieux des Etranger, 20 August 2018); Arrêt n° 212 351 (Conseil du Contentieux des Etrangers, 15 November 2018); Arrêt n° 214 615 (Conseil du Contentieux des Etrangers, 24 December 2018); Arrêt n° 222 085 (Conseil du Contentieux des Etrangers, 28 May 2019); Arrêt n° 222 108 (Conseil du Contentieux des Etrangers, 28 May 2019); Arrêt n° 222 425 (Conseil du Contentieux des Etrangers, 7 June 2019); Arrêt n° 223 931 (Conseil du Contentieux des Etrangers, 12 July 2019); Arrêt n° 228 708 (Conseil du Contentieux des Etrangers, 13 November 2019).

the pretext that it could carry out such verification when taking coercive measures to ensure the removal of the concerned migrant.[90]

Thus, decisions not taking into account non-refoulement can be subjected to annulment.[91] While an annulment procedure is ongoing, article 39/82 § 2 of the 1980 Migration Law allows migrants to request the suspension of the execution of their return when there is a risk that fundamental rights (such as the right to life and the right to be free from torture) would be violated by the measure.[92] In practice, the CCE suspended multiple removal decisions that did not properly assess the concerned migrant's claim that their health conditions upon return could be so detrimental (for instance, due to lack of available treatment) as to amount to ill-treatment.[93] Similarly, the CCE also suspended decisions that did not properly consider a claim of fear of harm upon return when the concerned migrants made substantiated claims in that regard[94]

90 The words of the Council were: "[L]a circonstance qu'en cas d'irrespect de l'ordre de quitter le territoire, la partie adverse puisse adopter des mesures de contrainte pour procéder à l'éloignement de l'étranger au sens de l'article 1er, 7°, de la loi du 15 décembre 1980, soit à son transfert physique hors du territoire, et puisse s'assurer, à ce moment, que cet éloignement respecte l'article 3 de la Convention de sauvegarde des droits de l'homme et des libertés fondamentales, n'implique pas qu'elle ne doive pas veiller, dès la prise de l'ordre de quitter le territoire, à ce que son exécution ne méconnaisse pas l'article 3 précité. En effet, il ne peut pas être préjugé que l'étranger ne respectera pas l'ordre de quitter le territoire. En conséquence, la partie adverse ne peut pas s'abstenir de veiller à ce que l'exécution de cet ordre respecte l'article 3 de la Convention de sauvegarde des droits de l'homme, sous prétexte qu'elle pourrait opérer une telle vérification lors de la prise de mesures de contrainte destinées à l'éloignement de l'étranger en cas d'inexécution de l'ordre de quitter le territoire." Arrêt nº 239.259, p. 5.

91 See, e.g. Arrêt n° 156 593 (Conseil du Contentieux des Etrangers, 18 November 2015); Arrêt n° 214 067 (Conseil du Contentieux des Etrangers, 14 December 2018).

92 This is particularly important when the reasons for the order to leave the territory are compelling reasons of national security since article 39/79 §3 of the 1980 Migration Law establishes that remedies against decisions based on these reasons do not have a suspensive effect.

93 See, e.g. Arrêt n° 153 269 (Conseil du Contentieux des Etrangers, 24 September 2015); Arrêt n° 174 380 (Conseil du Contentieux des Etrangers, 8 September 2016); Arrêt n° 196 682 (Conseil du Contentieux des Etrangers, 15 December 2017); Arrêt n° 205 737 (Conseil du Contentieux des Etrangers, 21 June 2018); Arrêt n° 222 419 (Conseil du Contentieux des Etrangers, 7 June 2019); Arrêt n° 224 331 (Conseil du Contentieux des Etrangers, 26 July 2019); Arrêt n° 233 525 (Conseil du Contentieux des Etrangers, 3 March 2020).

94 See, e.g. Arrêt n° 204 589 (Conseil du Contentieux des Etrangers, 4 April 2018); Arrêt n° 203 271 (Conseil du Contentieux des Etrangers, 27 April 2018); Arrêt n° 204 346 (Conseil du Contentieux des Etrangers, 24 May 2018); Arrêt n° 204 588 (Conseil du Contentieux des Etrangers, 29 May 2018); Arrêt n° 204 605 (Conseil du Contentieux des Etrangers, 30 May 2018); Arrêt n° 204 797 (Conseil du Contentieux des Etrangers, 1 June 2018); Arrêt n° 205 297 (Conseil du Contentieux des Etrangers, 13 June 2018); Arrêt

or (claimed to) have started/succeeded in asylum applications (in other countries).[95]

For the CCE to conclude that there is a risk upon return, similarly to the assessment made in international protection procedures, it must examine the foreseeable consequences of the removal of the concerned migrant, taking into account the general situation in the country of return and the specific circumstances of the case of the concerned migrant.[96] Exceptionally, in cases where the concerned person claims to be part of a group systematically exposed to a practice of ill-treatment, article 3 ECHR (establishing the prohibition of torture) will be engaged when the concerned migrant demonstrates that there are serious and proven grounds to believe in the existence of the practice in question and that they belong to the targeted group.[97]

n° 204 798 (Conseil du Contentieux des Etrangers, 18 June 2018); Arrêt n° 207 579 (Conseil du Contentieux des Etrangers, 8 August 2018); Arrêt n° 211 193 (Conseil du Contentieux des Etrangers, 18 October 2018); Arrêt n° 213 616 (Conseil du Contentieux des Etrangers, 6 December 2018); Arrêt n° 223 833 (Conseil du Contentieux des Etrangers, 9 July 2019); Arrêt n° 226 101 (Conseil du Contentieux des Etrangers, 13 September 2019); Arrêt n° 228 708.

95 See, e.g. Arrêt n° 159 337 (Conseil du Contentieux des Etrangers, 23 December 2015); Arrêt n° 196 685 (Conseil du Contentieux des Etrangers, 15 December 2017); Arrêt n° 205 094 (Conseil du Contentieux des Etrangers, 8 June 2018); Arrêt n° 205 434 (Conseil du Contentieux des Etrangers, 18 June 2018); Arrêt n° 208 222 (Conseil du Contentieux des Etrangers, 27 August 2018); Arrêt n° 211 232 (Conseil du Contentieux des Etrangers, 18 October 2018); Arrêt n° 212 351; Arrêt n° 222 425; Arrêt n° 222 630 (Conseil du Contentieux des Etrangers, 14 June 2019); Arrêt n° 223 863 (Conseil du Contentieux des Etrangers, 10 July 2019); Arrêt n° 224 927 (Conseil du Contentieux des Etrangers, 13 August 2019).

96 In this regard, the CCE follows the guidance from the ECtHR. More specifically, the CCE refers to the following cases: "Cour EDH 4 décembre 2008, Y./Russie, § 78; Cour EDH 28 février 2008, Saadi/Italie, §§ 128–129; Cour EDH 30 octobre 1991, Vilvarajah et autres/ Royaume-Uni, § 108 in fine." See, e.g. Arrêt n° 153 269, p. 10; Arrêt n° 174 380, p. 11; Arrêt n° 196 044 (Conseil du Contentieux des Etrangers, 1 December 2017), p. 7; Arrêt n° 203 271, p. 28; Arrêt n° 223 833, p. 9; Arrêt n° 246 394 (Conseil du Contentieux des Etrangers, 17 December 2020), p. 23.

97 In this regard, the CCE follows the guidance from the ECtHR. More specifically, the CCE refers to the following cases: "Cour européenne des droits de l'Homme, 28 février 2008, Saadi/Italie, § 132"; "Cour européenne des droits de l'Homme, 4 décembre 2008, Y./ Russie, § 80; Cour européenne des droits de l'Homme, 23 mai 2007, Salah Sheekh/Pays-Bas, § 148." See, e.g. Arrêt n° 154 705 (Conseil du Contentieux des Etrangers, 16 October 2015), p. 9; Arrêt n° 178 953 (Conseil du Contentieux des Etrangers, 5 December 2016), p. 6; Arrêt n° 193 479 (Conseil du Contentieux des Etrangers, 12 October 2017), pp. 19–20; Arrêt n° 213 120, p. 12.

Regarding Dublin decisions, that is, when the decision-maker deems that another EU State (other than Belgium) is responsible for assessing the asylum request according to the European rules on shared responsibility for asylum applications, and consequently that the asylum seeker should be transferred to the responsible State, it is also required that decision-makers take into account claims of ill-treatment in the European State to which the asylum seeker is to be sent for assessment of their claim.[98] Furthermore, a decision to transfer a migrant to another EU member State also needs to consider whether the latter may remove the concerned migrant to their country of origin or another State where they face harm (indirect refoulement).[99]

When it comes to rejections or withdrawals of permits, however, the Council of State deems that there is no legal error committed in not considering non-refoulement if the denial or withdrawal of a permit is not accompanied by any expulsion measure as in this case a non-refoulement assessment would be premature.[100] Similarly, the CCE also found that a non-refoulement assessment would be premature when the withdrawal of a permit was not accompanied by a removal order.[101]

In sum, Belgian law and jurisprudence ensure that a non-refoulement assessment is made before a migrant is removed from the country to ensure Belgium's compliance with non-refoulement. Thus, non-refoulement should always be taken into account in return procedures. In the case of a permit denial or withdrawal with no associated removal order, however, such an assessment is not required.

4.4 *Non-refoulement Assessment in Belgium: Some Conclusions*

Overall, there seems to be a great emphasis on the broader principle of non-refoulement in the 1980 Migration Law. For example, regarding international protection, even in cases where the Refugee Convention would provide an exception to that principle (according to article 33(2)) or exclude someone from protection altogether (following article 1F), the Belgian legislator

98 See, e.g. Ordonnance n° 12.926 (Conseil d'État, 12 July 2018); and Ordonnance n° 12.927 (Conseil d'État, 12 July 2018); Arrêt n° 213 378 (Conseil du Contentieux des Etrangers, 3 December 2018).

99 See Arrêt n° 194 542 (Conseil du Contentieux des Etrangers, 30 October 2017).

100 See Ordonnance° 10.993 (Conseil d'État, 5 January 2015); and Ordonnance n° 11.929 (Conseil d'État, 26 April 2016). Similarly, in Arrêt n° 230.503 (Conseil d'État, 12 March 2015), even though the concerned migrant could not be returned to her country of origin, her permit request was denied without any legal error.

101 See, e.g. Arrêt n° 230 558 (Conseil du Contentieux des Etrangers, 19 December 2019); Arrêt n° 230 778 (Conseil du Contentieux des Etrangers, 23 December 2019).

requests that an assessment of the risk of harm upon return for the person being excluded from refugee or subsidiary protection or having an existing status revoked takes place. This is further complemented by multiple provisions, that also apply outside the international protection framework. These provisions provide that no return should be conducted in disrespect of non-refoulement. This strong level of protection against non-refoulement in Belgian law derives not only from Belgium's international human rights commitments but also from the EU human rights and asylum frameworks, which, as noted above, also provide strong protections against refoulement.[102]

To ensure compliance with these legal provisions preventing refoulement, Belgian law and jurisprudence require that all removal decisions take non-refoulement into account. Consequently, these mechanisms seem, *a priori*, to ensure that undesirable migrants will have their non-refoulement claims assessed in the country and will not be removed in disrespect of that principle. Against this background, the next section will thus explore what happens in practice after a migrant has been deemed to be undesirable but unreturnable in Belgium.

5 Solutions for Undesirable but Unreturnable Migrants

5.1 *Residence Permit. An Impossible Dream?*

As noted in Section 3.2 above, decisions to refuse or withdraw the residence status of migrants need to take into account a range of elements going beyond public order or national security. Thus, it is possible that undesirable but unreturnable migrants may still be able to obtain or keep a residence status in the country and thus (continue to) reside regularly in Belgium, especially if they have strong ties to the country. When the overall assessment does not weigh in favour of granting or continuing the right to reside in Belgium, the concerned migrant will not be granted or will lose their residence status.

In this regard, certain categories of migrants, including those who cannot return to their country of origin due to reasons outside their control, may request a regularisation of their status in Belgium.[103] However, those who

---

102 Indeed, as previously noted, the CJEU concluded that the EU asylum framework provides broader protection than the Refugee Convention, as it does not prescribe an exception to non-refoulement. See Section 3.4 of Chapter 1.

103 Article 2 of the Law of 22 December 1999 relating to the regularisation of stay of certain categories of migrants staying in the territory of the Kingdom (Loi du 22 décembre 1999 relative à la régularisation de séjour de certaines catégories d'étrangers séjournant sur le

are deemed a threat to public order or national security are excluded from this benefit,[104] which limits this possibility for undesirable migrants.

In exceptional circumstances, migrants may also request the right to stay in Belgium according to article 9*bis* of the 1980 Migration Law. While exceptional circumstances are not specified in the article, it is explicitly stated that the elements which have already been invoked in support of an asylum application and which have been rejected by the asylum authorities, as well as the elements which should have been invoked during the asylum procedure will not be taken into account. This restriction also extends to elements linked to subsidiary protection, as an asylum application in Belgium will look at both.[105] Thus, this does not seem to be the appropriate procedure for unreturnable migrants who fear harm upon return, as their claims may coincide with claims that would fall under the international protection procedure. Furthermore, a 9*bis* request is unlikely to benefit undesirable migrants, as this is an exceptional procedure, which grants the decision-maker a broad margin of appreciation when assigning weight to past acts.[106] For example, the Council of State accepted that decision-makers could reject such a request due to the seriousness of the crime committed, even if the crime was committed long ago and thus the alleged threat posed by the migrant would no longer be current.[107]

When a migrant in Belgium does not have a residence permit, the State Secretary or one of their delegates is often allowed to order them to leave the Belgian territory. In this regard, article 7 of the 1980 Migration Law pre-

territoire du Royaume / Wet van 22 december 1999 betreffende de regularisatie van het verblijf van bepaalde categorieën van vreemdelingen verblijvend op het grondgebied van het Rijk).

104 Ibid., article 5.

105 Indeed, the CCE found no error in decisions refusing to consider a 9*bis* application in which the applicant made similar claims to those already presented during an application for international protection. See, e.g. Arrêt n° 152 020; Arrêt n° 152 940 (Conseil du Contentieux des Etrangers, 21 September 2015).

106 In this regard, NANSEN noted that some undesirable but unreturnable migrants apply for a residence permit based on article 9*bis*, but that, if they have previously received an order to leave the territory, they may also be subjected to an entry ban, which can lead these applications to be declared without object. When that is not the case, applications are often rejected for reasons related to public order. NANSEN. (2021). CONTRIBUTION A LA RÉFLEXION 2021/2 – Pour un statut d'inéloignable. Available at: https://nansen-refugee.be/wp-content/uploads/2021/09/2.-Pour-un-statut-dinéloignable.pdf, p. 4.

107 Arrêt n° 232.397 (Conseil d'État, 1 October 2015).

scribes that, if needed, migrants who receive an order to leave the Belgian territory may be detained to ensure their return. Detention is thus addressed in the next section.

5.2 *A Brief Section for a Brief Detention*

As noted above, when a migrant is ordered to leave the territory, they may be detained to ensure their removal. In Belgium, detention is limited to a period of 2 months (renewable) and, according to article 7 of the 1980 Migration Law, in cases of migrants who pose a threat to public order or national security, may not exceed 8 months (as opposed to 5 months for others).[108] Similarly, according to article 74/5 of the same Law, those arrested trying to enter the country irregularly can be detained for the same period in view of their return. For those who request international protection, article 74/6 of the Law limits detention in case of national security or public order to a maximum of 6 months. Article 110 quaterdecies, §1 of 1981 Royal Decree, in turn, provides for alternative measures (other than detention), including the duty to report and financial guarantees, to be applied to ensure a foreigner's voluntary return.

As noted above, however, multiple provisions in the 1980 Migration Law act to ensure respect for the principle of non-refoulement and thus, according to national law, undesirable migrants who are also unreturnable would not be returned to a place where they face harm, as the removal order against them is likely to be suspended and annulled. Their detention would consequently be deprived of a legal basis, as return is not envisaged in their case,[109] unless a suitable third country to which they can be removed is identified. In this regard, article 71 of the 1980 Migration Law allows detainees to challenge their detention judicially and thus seek release.

Detention of undesirable but unreturnable migrants, however, will only end when the mechanisms in place ensure that a return, in violation of non-refoulement, does not proceed. To assess whether that is always the case, the

108 At the EU level, article 15(5) and (6) of the Return Directive establishes an absolute maximum of 18 months for pre-return detention.

109 In this regard, the CCE noted that a coercive measure such as detention presupposes that the return is being envisaged and, when return is not possible, it cannot stand. It said: "Le Conseil rappelle que l'objectif d'une mesure d'éloignement est précisément l'éloignement du territoire belge et que si celui-ci n'est pas possible au moment de la prise de l'acte, la mesure perd sa finalité première" (Arrêt n° 211 193, p. 5). See also: Arrêt n° 213 616, p. 6; Arrêt n° 213 699 (Conseil du Contentieux des Etrangers, 10 December 2018), p. 12; Arrêt n° 214 622 (Conseil du Contentieux des Etrangers, 26 December 2018), p. 9; Arrêt n° 228 708, p. 12.

next subsection will thus look at whether the return of undesirable but unreturnable migrants is a possibility in Belgium, despite the country's strong commitment to non-refoulement in law.

5.3 *Return. Possible Human Rights Violation?*

As mentioned above, multiple provisions of the 1980 Migration Law act to ensure respect for the principle of non-refoulement and thus, according to national law, undesirable migrants who are also unreturnable would not be returned to a place where they face harm, as the removal order against them is likely to be suspended or annulled.

In this regard, it is worth noting that suspensions are granted regardless of the acts engaged in by the undesirable migrant, as the CCE recognises the absolute character of the article 3 ECHR (setting the right to be free from torture) and thus no balancing with public order is possible.[110] Similarly, the CCE deems that an order to leave the territory can be annulled if, after the order was issued, a change in the situation leads to the migrant risking harm upon return.[111]

Despite this strong commitment to upholding non-refoulement, Belgium's practices in this regard have been questioned. For example, the UN Human Rights Committee expressed concern about "(…) the absence of an effective procedure for the individual assessment of asylum seekers on the one hand and of persons who are subjected to deportation or expulsion on the

110 For example, in a case from 2015, the CCE said: "[L]es arguments de la partie défenderesse [the Belgian State], lors de l'audience, relatifs aux motifs présents dans la décision, et en particulier le motif relatif au trouble à l'ordre public y figurant et qui permettraient à eux seuls de motiver cette décision, ne sont pas de nature à entraîner un autre constat que celui qui précède, dès lors que l'article 3 de la Convention européenne des droits de l'Homme fondant la suspension de l'acte ci-avant ne peut souffrir d'aucune dérogation." Arrêt n° 153 269, para. 6.2.

111 That was the case in Arrêt n° 236.849 (Conseil d'État, 20 December 2016), where it was accepted that the migrant risked harm if returned due to his health condition, even though these health issues arose after the order to leave the territory was issued. Since it was accepted by the State that the migrant could face harm, the Council of State saw no legal error in the CCE annulling the order to leave the territory for this reason. In another case, the CCE similarly noted that "lorsqu'un laps de temps significatif s'est écoulé entre la prise de la décision d'éloignement sous la forme d'un ordre de quitter le territoire et la mise en oeuvre effective de cet ordre, la partie défenderesse doit effectuer un nouvel examen du risque de violation des articles 3 et 8 de la [CEDH], au moment de l'exécution de l'ordre de quitter le territoire" (Arrêt n° 246 394, para. 3.3.2.2). See also: Arrêt n° 196 044; Arrêt n° 197 401 (Conseil du Contentieux des Etrangers, 30 December 2017); Arrêt n° 197 404 (Conseil du Contentieux des Etrangers, 30 December 2017). These last three cases, however, concerned the suspension of the decision, and not its annulment.

other,"[112] calling on the Belgian State to "(...) take all necessary measures to ensure that an individual assessment is carried out for each case of asylum, deportation or expulsion, with full respect for the principles of non-refoulement and safe third countries"[113] and to "(...) ensure the effective and independent monitoring of deportation operations."[114] These observations seem to indicate that despite the requirement that an individual assessment on human rights impacts, including non-refoulement, be made before starting procedures to remove someone, in practice, migration decisions in Belgium sometimes fail to abide by this obligation.[115] Indeed, the UN Committee against Torture expressed concern over Belgium's practices of extraditing foreigners with diplomatic assurances and of returning migrants to countries at war,[116] showing that the mechanisms in place to ensure respect for non-refoulement may carry some flaws.

The ECtHR[117] reached similar conclusions in cases concerning undesirable but unreturnable migrants in Belgium. For example, on 2 September 2015, the

112 Human Rights Committee (2019). Concluding observations on the sixth periodic report of Belgium, para. 31.

113 Ibid., para. 32.

114 Ibid. idem.

115 Regarding human rights assessments beyond non-refoulement, the ECtHR found in 2016 that Belgium had not properly taken into account the family life of Mr. Paposhvili when ordering him to leave the Belgian territory, where he had resided irregularly for years with his family and where he also engaged in criminal activities. In that case, further explored below, the former fifth section of the ECtHR deemed that Mr. Paposhvili's criminal conduct combined with the fact that he spent many years in Belgium as an irregular migrant had signification weight, adding to that the fact that his family, as Georgian nationals, could temporarily relocate to Georgia to stay with him, the former fifth section found no violation of his family life in returning him to Gerogia. The Grand Chamber, in turn, found that Belgium had not taken all facts into account, for example, not considering whether Mr. Paposhvili had become dependent on his family due to his deteriorating health, and thus, returning him without such consideration would have constituted a violation of his right to family life prescribed in Article 8 ECHR. See Paposhvili v. Belgium, 41738/10 (European Court of Human Rights, 13 December 2016).

116 Committee against Torture. (2021). Observations finales concernant le quatrième rapport périodique de la Belgique, paras. 25–26.

117 As explained in the introduction to this book, this research takes as its framework the UN core human rights treaties, which Belgium has ratified. Apart from the UN system, Belgium is also bound by the European human rights framework, the main instrument of which is the ECHR. Most of the rights prescribed in the European Convention are equivalent to those prescribed by the ICCPR and thus violations of the ECHR are likely to also be violations of the ICCPR. The ECtHR is the main body that assesses whether the ECHR has been violated. In this regard, considering the enforceability of the decisions of the ECtHR (see article 46 ECHR) combined with the fact that UN treaty bodies will not take

Court decided the Ouabour case,[118] which concerned a Moroccan national convicted in Belgium for participation in a terrorist group. While he was facing criminal proceedings in Belgium, Morocco requested his extradition to be prosecuted in the country for terrorism offences. Mr. Ouabour, however, claimed that he was likely to be tortured during the procedures in Morocco, as the country was known for ill-treating those accused of terrorism and using confessions obtained under torture to secure convictions. Mr. Ouabour presented multiple reports from UN human rights bodies and international NGOs supporting his claims. The judicial authorities in Belgium, however, deemed that these reports were general and did not refer to the individual situation of Mr. Ouabour, who then turned to the ECtHR to claim a violation of his rights. According to the Court, the information provided by Mr. Ouabour, taken from objective, diverse and consistent sources, established that the use of practices contrary to article 3 of the ECHR (which prescribes the prohibition of torture and ill-treatment in wording that is almost identical to article 7 ICCPR) against persons prosecuted in the context of the fight against terrorism is a lasting problem in Morocco. The ECtHR thus concluded that if Mr. Ouabour were extradited to Morocco, Belgium would violate its non-refoulement obligations under the convention.[119]

In the following year, on 13 December 2016, the Grand Chamber of the ECtHR decided Paposhvili.[120] The case concerned a Georgian national who arrived in Belgium in 1998 and spent many years irregularly residing in the country, during which he engaged in criminal activities. He tried to regularise his status in the country but his request for a permit was rejected due to his past crimes. While he was in prison in Belgium, he developed chronic lymphocytic leukaemia. The seriousness of his conditions required a stem cell transplant, which he could not have in the absence of a residence permit. Mr. Paposhvili was ordered to leave Belgium multiple times and proceedings started to return him to Georgia. His return, however, was postponed and halted until Mr. Paposhvili died in Belgium in 2016. At that time, he had

---

on cases that are being examined by another international human rights body (see article 5(1)(a) ICCPR and article 22(5)(a) Convention against Torture), such as the ECtHR, it seems logical that the jurisprudence of the UN treaty bodies regarding Belgium is scarce. However, considering the compatibility of rights between the UN and European systems, decisions of the ECtHR on the application of the ECHR provide an important indicator of whether internationally recognised rights of undesirable but unreturnable migrants are respected in Belgium and thus are also relied on for this analysis.

118 Ouabour v. Belgium, 26417/10 (European Court of Human Rights, 2 September 2015).

119 Ibid., paras. 75–79.

120 Paposhvili v. Belgium.

already started proceedings before the ECtHR claiming that his return to Georgia would be a violation of non-refoulement.[121] When evaluating the issue, the Grand Chamber observed that Mr. Paposhvili had claimed that the treatment he was undergoing in Belgium was not available in Georgia and he may not have access to the other treatments used to care for leukaemia patients in the country due to the shortcomings in the Georgian social insurance system. The Grand Chamber deemed that Belgium did not assess these claims and thus wrongly concluded that his return would not incur in risk of ill-treatment, finding that if Mr. Paposhvili had been returned to Georgia without such an assessment, Belgium would have violated article 3 ECHR.

The finding of possible violations in both cases indicates that Belgium does not always make a proper assessment before return, which is in line with the abovementioned UN Committees' recommendations that Belgium takes an individual assessment and carefully considers all elements, including non-refoulement, before taking asylum or return decisions. Thus, despite the mechanisms put in place by Belgian law to avoid non-refoulement violations, in practice, the assessment of non-refoulement is not always carried out as carefully as is required. This may lead to Belgium violating its international obligations.

When the assessment correctly identifies someone as unreturnable, however, their return will be halted, according to the 1980 Migration Act. At the same time, as noted in Section 5.1 above, they are unlikely to be granted a permit. Thus, undesirable but unreturnable migrants may have to live in limbo in the Belgian society. This alternative is presented below.

5.4 *Limbo. Guilty of Neglect?*

As noted in the previous section, undesirable but unreturnable migrants may end up in liberty in the Belgian territory but without a permit, thus in a state of legal limbo.[122] Those who remain in limbo may see certain measures imposed

---

121 His family chose to continue the case before the Court after his death. Regarding the risk of ill-treatment in Georgia, the former fifth section of the ECtHR deemed that return will be halted due to illness only on very exceptional cases and Mr. Paposhvili's case was not one of those at the moment the decision was taken (17 April 2014) as his health state was considered stable, and treatment was available in Georgia. The case was then taken to the Grand Chamber.

122 Indeed, with regards to undesirable but unreturnable migrants, it has been said that "[A] limited number of states (e.g. The Netherlands, Belgium) do not provide any temporary residence permit or leave to remain. This means that the UBUS [undesirable but unreturnable migrants] are considered undocumented migrants and are not allowed to work, rent a house or enjoy health insurance." Refugee Law Initiative, Arts & Humanities

against them. For example, article 26 of the 1980 Migration Law prescribes security measures that may be applied to migrants who infringed public order or national security. More specifically, the article mentions the possibility of forbidding the concerned person to go to specific places and/or to live away from them or the determination of assigned residence. Similarly, article 44 *sexies* of the same law establishes that when return is postponed, the concerned migrant may be subjected to preventive measures. Article 73, in turn, determines that a migrant may be placed in assigned residence when a judicial decision ends their detention. Article 68 of the 1980 Migration law then prescribes that migrants subjected to security measures, including assigned residence, may request that they be lifted every 6 months. Article 114 of the 1981 Royal Decree establishes that such request contains the arguments invoked by the concerned migrant.

Besides the abovementioned limitations, it is worth noting that article 75 of the 1980 Migration Law criminalises the action of staying illegally in the country. Furthermore, article 77 of the 1980 Migration Law criminalises acts assisting irregular migrants to reside in the country, except when such assistance is provided for humanitarian reasons. This provision may discourage migrants from seeking help or others from assisting them. In this regard, the European Commission against Racism and Intolerance noted that:

> (…) the obligation not to discriminate on the basis of residence status imposed by the European Union Victims Directive (2012/29/EU) has not yet been transposed into Belgian law. Migrant victims of discrimination who are irregularly present on Belgian territory may still refrain from exercising their right to complain to the police out of fear of being detained or deported.[123]

Research Council and Center for International Criminal Justice (2016). Undesirable and Unreturnable? Policy challenges around excluded asylum seekers and other migrants suspected of serious criminality who cannot be removed (Policy brief), p. 4.

123 European Commission against Racism and Intolerance (ECRI), ECRI Conclusions on the Implementation of the Recommendations in Respect of Belgium – Subject to Interim Follow-Up (2022), p. 4. Available at: https://rm.coe.int/ecri-conclusions-on-the-implementation-of-the-recommendations-in-respe/1680a807d0. Similarly, the UN Committee on Economic, Social and Cultural Rights, when evaluating Belgium's implementation of the International Covenant on Economic, Social and Cultural Rights, expressed concern "(…) at the lack of effective protection for migrant women, particularly those in an irregular situation, who often refrain from reporting such violence for fear of being deported" and at the "(…) at the practical difficulties encountered by irregular migrants in accessing emergency health-care services." (Committee on Economic, Social and Cultural Rights (2020). Concluding observations on the fifth periodic report of Belgium

Article 175/1 of social penal code,[124] in turn, punishes those who employ migrants irregularly residing in the country. Chapter 3 of the law providing for sanctions and measures against employers of illegally staying third-country nationals,[125] however, requires those who employ irregularly staying migrants to pay for the work provided. Migrants irregularly residing in Belgium also have a right to urgent medical assistance.[126]

Despite these important restrictions imposed on migrants in limbo and the challenges they face to enjoy their rights, as noted in Section 4.4 of Chapter 1, the ECtHR accepted this approach in 2005 in the Bonger v. the Netherlands case.[127] In that case, the court stated that the ECHR did not guarantee to non-nationals the right to enter, reside or remain in a member State and, more specifically, that a right to a residence permit could not be derived from the prohibition of torture and its consequent prohibition of refoulement.[128]

As also noted in Section 4.4 of Chapter 1, however, certain fundamental rights should be guaranteed to all migrants, regardless of their status. In this regard, Belgium's Federal Institute for the protection and promotion of Human Rights argued that the absence of a residence permit should not

---

(E/C.12/BEL/CO/5). United Nations Economic and Social Council, paras. 34 and 52). See also: Federal Institute for the protection and promotion of Human Rights. (15 July 2021). Garantir les droits humains des personnes sans papiers. This shows that, in Belgium, there does not seem to be sufficient firewalls (see Chapter 1, Section 4.4) in place to ensure undesirable but unreturnable migrants in limbo can enjoy the rights they are entitled to.

124 In the original language: Code pénal social / Sociaal Strafwetboek.

125 In the original language: Loi prévoyant des sanctions et des mesures à l'encontre des employeurs de ressortissants de pays tiers en séjour illegal / Wet tot vaststelling van sancties en maatregelen voor werkgevers van illegaal verblijvende onderdanen van derde landen.

126 Article 57 of the Organic Law of 8 July 1976 on public centres for social action (Loi organique du 8 juillet 1976 des centres publics d'action sociale).

127 Teshome Goraga Bonger v. the Netherlands, 10154/04 (European Court of Human Rights, 15 September 2005).

128 Similarly, the CJEU considered that, according to the Return Directive, "a Member State cannot be obliged to issue an autonomous residence permit, or other authorisation conferring a right to stay, to a third-country national who has no identity documents and has not obtained such documentation from his country of origin, after a national court has released the person concerned on the ground that there is no longer a reasonable prospect of removal." See Case C-146/14 (Court of Justice of the European Union, 5 June 2014). While this statement does not refer to unreturnability due to non-refoulement, due to the similarity of the situation, it is likely that an analogous conclusion would be reached in cases of unreturnability due to non-refoulement.

deprive migrants of their human rights and that migrants in an irregular situation still enjoy the right to lead a life consistent with human dignity.[129] In the refugee context, the CJEU has noted, when clarifying the application of the Qualification Directive, that the refugee whose residence permit is revoked:

> (…) retains his refugee status, at least until that status is actually ended. Therefore, even without his residence permit, the person concerned remains a refugee and as such remains entitled to the benefits guaranteed by Chapter VII of that directive to every refugee, including protection from refoulement, maintenance of family unity, the right to travel documents, access to employment, education, social welfare, healthcare and accommodation, freedom of movement within the Member State and access to integration facilities.[130]

In Belgium, this would apply to those who had a permit revoked but whose refugee status has not been withdrawn by the CGRA. Although, as noted above, the Qualification Directive and Belgian law do authorise the CGRA to revoke the status of recognised refugees who are convicted of a serious crime and are thus considered a threat to society or national security.[131] These rights spelled out by the Court are thus not ensured to all undesirable but unreturnable migrants.

Article 14 of the Qualification Directive, however, determines that when member States revoke, end or refuse to renew the status granted to a refugee, the concerned refugee still retains their rights to non-discrimination, freedom of religion, access to courts, education, and non-refoulement.[132] Similarly, the Return Directive provides that all unreturnable migrants must be ensured family unity with family members present in the territory, emergency health-

129 Federal Institute for the protection and promotion of Human Rights. (15 July 2021).

130 Case C-373/13, para. 95.

131 As noted in Chapter 1, Section 3.4, the upcoming Qualification Regulation mandates that refugee status and subsidiary protection be withdrawn in certain cases. See articles 14 and 19 Qualification Regulation. Those who have their refugee status based on the EU framework revoked but who are considered refugees under the Refugee Convention, however, are still entitled to (some of) the rights laid down in that instrument, as also noted in Chapter 1, Section 3.4.

132 Article 14(6) Qualification Directive (article 14(3) of the upcoming Qualification Regulation). See also Joined Cases C-391/16, C-77/17 and C-78/17.

care, education for minor children, special needs of vulnerable populations,[133] as well as other basic needs.[134]

As noted above, Belgian law does provide that migrants in an irregular situation are entitled to emergency healthcare and provides a humanitarian exemption to those who assist these migrants stay in the country but, as also mentioned above, assisting or employing irregular migrants are criminalised acts in the country. This means that undesirable but unreturnable migrants may be faced with very precarious situations while living in limbo. For example, "(…) several reports revealed that some states do not provide accommodation or any access to housing at all to non-removable migrants (Italy, Cyprus, Belgium)."[135]

The main difficulties associated with limbo status are listed in Section 4.4 of Chapter 1 of this book and thus will not be repeated here. As concluded in that section, however, even though human rights bodies do not find this status to be a violation of international conventions, limbo states lead to a position of indefinite suspension and neglect, with very limited access to important socio-economic rights and benefits. Indeed, a lack of status may make the realisation of the rights that are owed to these migrants theoretical,[136] which has led organisations working on migration in Belgium to call for the grant of legal status for unreturnable migrants.[137]

133 Article 14 Return Directive. The UN Human Rights Committee also referred to the need to grant migrants in an irregular situation access to emergency healthcare in Communication No. 2348/2014, CCPR/C/123/D/2348/2014 (Human Rights Committee, 24 July 2018).

134 See Case C-562/13 (Court of Justice of the European Union, 18 December 2014).

135 Eckert, G. (2021). Caught in limbo: The precarious (legal) situation of non-removable migrants stranded in Europe. Journal of Immigration, Asylum and Nationality Law, 35(3), 252–277, p. 263.

136 Farcy, J.-B. (June 2019). Sécurité nationale et exclusion du statut de protection internationale: Vers une autonomie croissante du droit européen ? Cahiers de l'EDEM. Available at: https://cdn.uclouvain.be/groups/cms-editors-cedie/newsletter/Cahiers%20juin%20 2019.pdf.

137 See NANSEN. (2021); Myria. (2020). Avis de Myria, le Centre fédéral Migration, sur la proposition de loi modifiant la loi du 15 décembre 1980 sur l'accès au territoire, le séjour, l'établissement et l'éloignement des étrangers, en vue d'y insérer des critères clairs, justes et précis de régularisation pour les personnes en situation de séjour irrégulier sur le territoire du Royaume et instituant une Commission indépendante de régularisation (DOC 55 1415/001). Available at: https://www.myria.be/files/Avis_Myria_FR_proposition _de_loi_55_1415_001.pdf.

5.5 *Solutions for Undesirable but Unreturnable Migrants: Some Conclusions*

The previous subsections showed that undesirable but unreturnable migrants may face different fates in Belgium. Some may be granted or keep their residence status, as their undesirability may, on balance, not be considered enough to prevent them from residing in the country. Others will be denied or lose their status, which may lead to a period of detention. It is unlikely that such detention will last long, however, as Belgian law has multiple mechanisms that prevent unreturnable migrants from being sent back to their countries and when return is not envisaged detention cannot continue. It should be noted, however, that Belgium's non-refoulement assessment has been questioned and thus may fail in certain cases. Those who are considered unreturnable and then released may find themselves in a situation of limbo, as they do not have the right to reside in Belgium and options to obtain a permit are limited for undesirable but unreturnable migrants. In this situation, some may be subjected to different measures such as assigned residence to mitigate a possible risk they are considered to pose to public order or national security. Apart from these measures, their rights are also very limited in the country, since those who assist or employ them may be punished for doing so.

6 Conclusions: Protection from Non-refoulement Alone Is Not Sufficient

The path(s) undesirable but unreturnable migrants may follow in Belgium can be summarised in a simplified manner in Figure 3.1.

To unpack this scheme, it can be said that Belgium contains multiple provisions in its national legislation that serve to deny or withdraw the right to enter or stay in the country's territory to migrants considered undesirable. In international protection cases, these provisions mirror the exclusion clauses of the Refugee Convention. More generally, however, Belgium excludes all those who disrespect public order or national security.

When assessing who should be considered undesirable under these provisions, Belgian law calls for a thorough individual assessment of the concerned migrant's situation, making it harder for those with closer ties to Belgium to lose their right to stay in the country. In practice, however, blurred definitions of public order and national security may undermine the protection afforded to those who are well-settled in the country.

Even when a migrant is considered undesirable, however, their return is not inevitable, as Belgian law contains multiple safeguards against returns

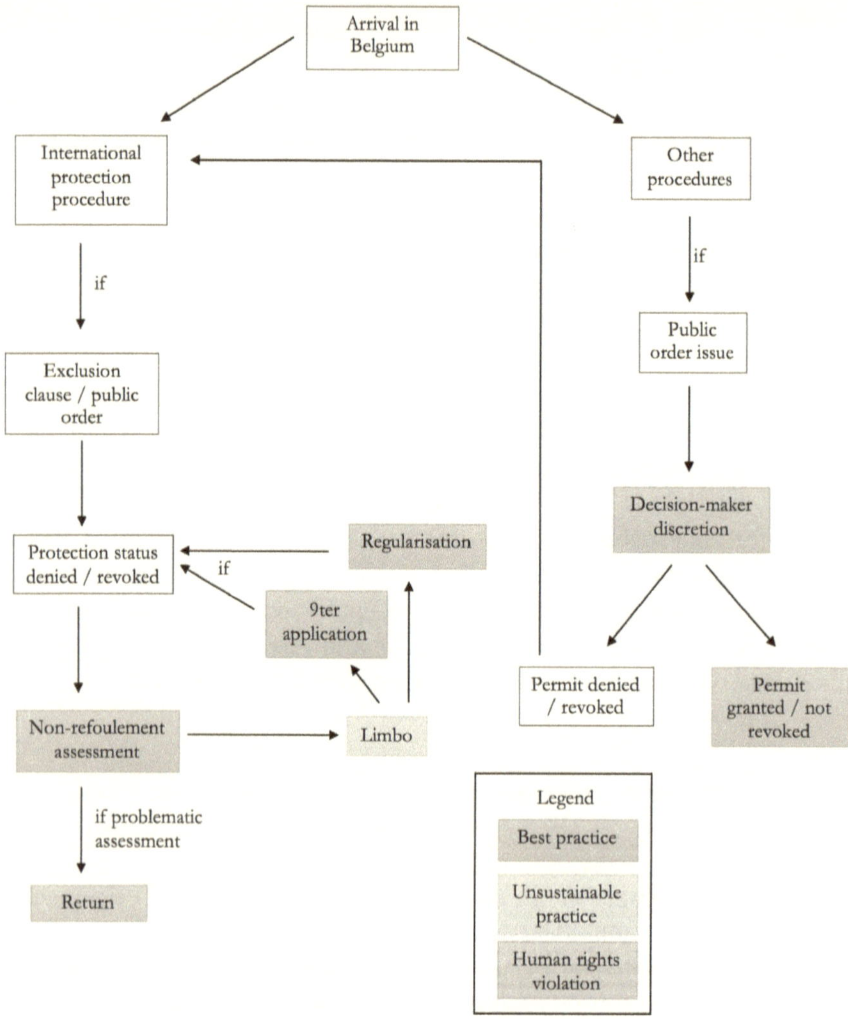

FIGURE 3.1 Paths for undesirable but unreturnable migrants in Belgium

that violate non-refoulement. For example, Belgium allows migrants fearing harm upon return to ask for international protection in the country. In Belgium, international protection is a concept that broadens the scope of the Refugee Convention, as it not only aims to protect those who meet the refugee definition of the Convention, but also covers those who fear harm upon return for reasons not listed in that instrument. This is in accordance with the EU asylum framework, explained in Section 3.4 of Chapter 1, which more broadly refers to international protection, including both refugees and those who qualify for subsidiary protection. Furthermore, even outside the scope of international protection, non-refoulement needs to be taken into account by decision-makers before ordering someone to leave Belgium. Once it is recognised that a person may face harm upon return, removal is no longer envisaged. This strong protection system provided in Belgian law reflects both the country's international and regional obligations. Belgium's assessment of the risk of harm upon return, however, has sometimes been criticised by international human rights bodies, showing that the practice may not be as protective as the law.

Migrants considered undesirable but unreturnable in Belgium are likely to be deprived of a permit to reside in the country yet be protected from removal, leaving them in a situation of legal limbo. While some rights are still to be assured to migrants regardless of their legal status in the country, the irregular situation in which undesirable but unreturnable migrants may find themselves in Belgium limits their access to rights and is thus questioned by scholars and organisations working with migrants.

In sum, Belgian law, at first glance, seems very protective of the rights of undesirable but unreturnable migrants, calling for a thorough individual assessment to be made before considering someone as undesirable and creating multiple safeguards against return in disrespect of the principle of non-refoulement. At a closer look, however, the lack of a definition of public order and national security may undermine the principle of legality and the individual assessment is not always carried out as thoroughly as provided in law. In practice, migrants who are considered undesirable but unreturnable may be subjected to short-term measures such as detention and assigned residence, but often find themselves free yet in limbo, with limited access to rights. Thus, while Belgian law initially indicates itself to be compliant with the applicable international human rights framework, its application may lead to violations.

CHAPTER 4

Canada: The Limits of a Limited Status

1 Introduction

This chapter continues the analysis of the measures applied at the national level to regulate the situation of undesirable but unreturnable migrants. In this context, the third and last country to be explored is Canada. Similar to the previous two chapters, this one will also start by briefly presenting the relevant instruments and decision-makers that act in the field of migration in the country. It will continue by identifying who is considered undesirable within the applicable migration framework. Afterwards, it will present the procedures available for migrants to have their unreturnability, that is, their non-refoulement claims, assessed. Lastly, it will analyse the available solutions for undesirable but unreturnable migrants in the country and provide some conclusions.

2 Who Is Making the Decisions? The Law and the Authorities in Charge of Migration

In Canada, the main piece of national legislation regulating migration is the Immigration and Refugee Protection Act of 2001 (hereafter IRPA),[1] the provisions of which are complemented by the Immigration and Refugee Protection Regulations (hereafter IRPA Regulations).[2] Canada is a party to the Refugee Convention and many other human rights treaties, including the International Covenant on Civil and Political Rights (hereafter ICCPR) and the Convention against Torture and Other Cruel, Inhuman or Degrading Treatment or Punishment (hereafter Convention against Torture). While Canada is a dualist country, thus requiring that international treaties be incorporated into domestic legislation to be applicable nationally, the Supreme Court of Canada has affirmed that "(…) the values and principles of customary and conventional international law form part of the context in which Canadian laws are

1 Immigration and Refugee Protection Act (S.C. 2001, c. 27) (hereafter IRPA): https://laws.justice.gc.ca/eng/acts/i-2.5/.

2 Immigration and Refugee Protection Regulations (SOR/2002–227) (hereafter IRPA Regulations): https://lawslois.justice.gc.ca/eng/regulations/sor-2002-227/.

 | DOI:10.1163/9789004719910_006

enacted."[3] According to the Supreme Court, this creates the presumption that national law conforms with Canada's international obligations. Regarding the migration context specifically, ss 3(2)(b) and 3(3)(f) of the IRPA explicitly mention that the Act aims to be applied in compliance with Canada's international obligations with respect to refugees and human rights instruments to which the country is a signatory.[4] Thus, the international framework should be taken into account to interpret national provisions.

S 4(1) IRPA determines that the Minister of Citizenship and Immigration (hereafter Minister) is responsible for the administration of the Act, which grants them specific powers, as will be mentioned below. Other ministers, however, are also assigned certain functions, such as the Minister of Public Safety and Emergency Preparedness, who, among others, is charged with the enforcement of the IRPA, including arrest, detention and removal.[5] The Minister heads the Department of Immigration, Refugees and Citizenship (hereafter Department),[6] whose officers are responsible for, among others, deciding on visa applications. Asylum applications considered eligible by the Department are sent to be decided by the Refugee Protection Division (hereafter RPD)[7] of the Immigration and Refugee Board of Canada (hereafter IRB), an independent administrative tribunal.[8] Decisions of the RPD may be appealed to the Refugee Appeal Division (hereafter RAD)[9] of the IRB. The IRB also has an Immigration Division (hereafter ID),[10] which is tasked with determining the admissibility[11] of foreigners to Canada and reviewing the detention of foreign nationals. Certain immigration decisions made by the ID or the Department can be appealed[12] to the Immigration Appeal Division (hereafter IAD)[13] of the IRB.

---

3 B010 v. Canada, 2015 SCC 58 (Supreme Court of Canada, 27 November 2015), para. 47. See also van Ert, G. (2019). The Domestic Application of International Law in Canada. In C. A. Bradley (ed.), The Oxford Handbook of Comparative Foreign Relations Law (pp. 501–518). Oxford University Press.

4 See also B010 v. Canada, 2015 SCC 58, para. 49.

5 S 4(2)(b) IRPA.

6 See Department of Citizenship and Immigration Act (S.C. 1994, c. 31): https://laws-lois.justice.gc.ca/eng/acts/C-29.4/page-1.html.

7 Ss 169.1–170.2 IRPA.

8 Ss 151–156 IRPA.

9 Ss 171–171.1 IRPA.

10 Ss 172–173 IRPA.

11 Inadmissibility in Canada is directly linked to the determination of who is undesirable and is thus explained in detail in Section 3 below.

12 Ss 62–71 IRPA.

13 Ss 174–175 IRPA.

Finally, immigration decisions are subject to judicial review by the Federal Court.[14] If, when making a judgement, the Federal Court identifies a serious question of general importance,[15] that question can be referred to the Federal Court of Appeal.[16] Decisions of the Federal Court and Federal Court of Appeal are relied on in this chapter to clarify the application of the provisions of the IRPA.[17] Decisions of the Federal Court of Appeal may only exceptionally be appealed to the Supreme Court of Canada.[18] As this is an exceptional case, decisions of the Supreme Court were not included in this chapter, although they may be referred to when they are referenced in decisions of the Federal Court and Federal Court of Appeal.

Against this background, the next section will explore who is considered an undesirable migrant within this framework.

3 Who Are the Undesirables?

In a 2018 decision, the Federal Court of Appeal recalled that the objectives of the IRPA, set out in subsection 3(1), include, among others, "(...) the security of Canadian society and the promotion of international justice and security by fostering respect for human rights and denying access to Canadian territory to persons who are criminals or security risks."[19] To achieve these objectives, the IRPA considers undesirable those who engage in international crimes, in (serious) criminality, in acts contrary to the principles and purposes of the United Nations (hereafter UN), as well as those who are considered a threat to security and those who engage in organised criminality. Migrants who fall under one of these categories "(...) may be denied entry to, or required to leave

14 S 72(1) IRPA.

15 According to the Federal Court of Appeal, for a question to be considered of general importance to justify a referral, "[T]he question must be a serious question that is dispositive of the appeal, transcends the interests of the parties and raises an issue of broad significance or general importance. This means that the question must have been dealt with by the Federal Court and must arise from the case itself rather than merely from the way in which the Federal Court disposed of the application." Lunyamila v. Canada, 2018 FCA 22 (Federal Court of Appeal, 19 January 2018), para. 46.

16 S 74(d) IRPA.

17 See the introduction to this book for the case selection and reference period of the research on which the book is based.

18 S 37.1 Supreme Court Act (R.S.C., 1985, c. S–26): https://laws-lois.justice.gc.ca/eng/acts/s-26/FullText.html.

19 Lunyamila v. Canada, 2018 FCA 22, para. 5.

Canada."[20] These different categories of undesirability are thus explored in the next subsections.

3.1 *Those Who Committed International Crimes*

In the international protection context, Canada makes a direct reference to the Refugee Convention, mentioning in s 98 of the IRPA that those referred to in articles 1E and 1F of the said Convention are excluded from both refugee and subsidiary or complementary protection. In this regard, article 1F(a) of the Convention excludes from refugee status those who have committed a crime against peace, a war crime, or a crime against humanity.

Outside the scope of international protection, ss 35 and 35.1 of the IRPA more generally deem inadmissible any foreign national who committed genocide, crimes against humanity or war crimes; was a senior official in the service of a government that engaged in these crimes, in terrorism or in systematic or gross human rights violations; or is the subject of sanctions under specific regimes.

Regarding the practical application of these provisions, a shift in the understanding of the standard required to consider someone guilty of international crimes came with the 2013 Ezokola decision by the Supreme Court. This decision changes the standard to be applied when assessing culpability through complicity for crimes against peace, war crimes, or crimes against humanity.

According to the Federal Court[21] "(...) the Supreme Court determined in *Ezokola* that the Canadian approach to criminal participation in crimes against humanity or war crimes had been overextended and it refined the test to fix that problem."[22] Before the Ezokola decision, the standard applied by the Federal Court was "personal and knowing participation," which was defined in the 1992 Ramirez decision of the Federal Court. In that decision, the Federal Court found that mere membership in an organisation that sometimes engages in international offences was not sufficient to exclude someone from refugee status. However, where an organisation is principally directed to

---

20 Mason v. Canada, 2019 FC 1251 (Federal Court, 2 October 2019), para. 39. Other reasons that may serve to deny or withdraw the right to enter or stay in Canada include health grounds, financial grounds and misrepresentation (see ss 38–40 IRPA). As these reasons are outside the scope of this book they are not analysed in this chapter.

21 Nota bene: some of the Federal Court cases mentioned in this section do not refer to exclusion cases. This is because the test for complicity applied in exclusion cases is the same test applied for complicity in inadmissibility cases (explained below). Thus, reference to inadmissibility cases is needed to provide a complete overview of the standard applied to complicity in exclusion.

22 Aazamyar v. Canada, 2015 FC 99 (Federal Court, 26 January 2015), para. 33.

a limited, brutal purpose, mere membership may involve personal and knowing participation in the organisation criminal acts.[23] After Ezokola, however,

> (…) mere association becomes culpable complicity only "when an individual makes a significant contribution to the crime or criminal purpose of a group" (Ezokola at para 87). Furthermore, a claimant must be aware of the organization's crime or criminal purpose and be aware that "his or her conduct will assist in the furtherance of the crime or criminal purpose (Ezokola at para. 89)."[24]

Thus, the Federal Court considered that Ezokola rejected a "guilty by association" approach,[25] as "[W]hile the test encompasses a broad range of actions, the requirement of a significant contribution ensures that not all individuals who are part of an organisation can be excluded under article 1(F)."[26] Over the following years, multiple cases based on the Ezokola test were brought before the Federal Court,[27] allowing that Court to further clarify the applicable standard for complicity. In this regard, in 2017, the Federal Court noted that the Ezokola test on voluntariness requires a full contextual factual analysis in view of the concerned migrant's circumstances and should not be limited to an evaluation of whether the person was acting under duress.[28]

When it comes to the commission of international crimes under s 35 (thus outside the international protection context), the Federal Court also confirmed that "[T]he test for inadmissibility under paragraph 35(1)(a) of the IRPA, as set out in Ezokola, is whether the PA [principal applicant] made a knowing, voluntary and significant contribution to the crimes against humanity."[29]

---

23 Simeon, J. C. (2015). The Application and Interpretation of International Humanitarian Law and International Criminal Law in the Exclusion of those Refugee Claimants who have Committed War Crimes and/or Crimes Against Humanity in Canada. International Journal of Refugee Law, 27(1), 75–106, p. 96.

24 Aazamyar v. Canada, 2015 FC 99, para. 34.

25 Habibi v. Canada, 2016 FC 253 (Federal Court, 26 February 2016), para. 19.

26 Khudeish v. Canada, 2020 FC 1124 (Federal Court, 8 December 2020), para. 73.

27 See, e.g. Bajraktari v. Canada, 2016 FC 1136 (Federal Court, 12 October 2016); Oladele v. Canada, 2017 FC 851 (Federal Court, 25 September 2017); Sarwary v. Canada, 2018 FC 437 (Federal Court, 24 April 2018); Yousif v. Canada, 2019 FC 128 (Federal Court, 30 January 2019); Niyungeko v. Canada, 2019 FC 820 (Federal Court, 17 June 2019).

28 Al Khayyat v. Canada, 2017 FC 175 (Federal Court, 13 February 2017), para. 56. The need to assess voluntariness was also mentioned in Ghirme v. Canada, 2019 FC 805 (Federal Court, 12 June 2019), para. 25.

29 Yousif v. Canada, 2019 FC 128, para. 24.

3.2 *Those Who Engage in (Serious) Criminality*

In the international protection context, article 1F(b) of the Refugee Convention (referenced in s 98 IRPA) excludes from refugee status those with respect to whom there are serious reasons for considering that they committed a serious non-political crime before arriving in the country of refuge.

Outside the international protection context, section 36 of the IRPA considers inadmissible those who engage in criminality or serious criminality. In this context, criminality refers to involvement in an offence that is indictable in Canada or in two offences not arising from the same occurrence. Serious criminality, in turn, refers to offences punished by a maximum term of imprisonment of at least 10 years in Canada or to which a person was convicted, in Canada, to a term of imprisonment of at least six months. As will be shown below, whether someone is considered inadmissible due to criminality or serious criminality has consequences for the remedies available to them. Furthermore, an application for asylum made by those who are found inadmissible to the country for reasons of serious criminality is considered ineligible (s 101(1)(f) IRPA). Lastly, permanent residents may only be considered inadmissible for serious criminality (not for criminality).

Despite both provisions (s 98 and s 36 of the IRPA) sharing the same aim of keeping criminals away from Canada, their practical application slightly differs. The following subsections will thus present the application of the serious crime exclusion in the international protection context, make some remarks on the interpretation of serious criminality in the inadmissibility context and explain the interaction between the two provisions.

3.2.1 Serious Crime in the International Protection Context

Regarding the practical application of article 1F(b) of the Refugee Convention in Canada, the Federal Court was seized multiple times in cases questioning the definition of a serious crime in the international protection context.[30] As the test to be applied in 1F(b) cases was refined by the Supreme Court in its 2014 Febles decision, in 2015, the Federal Court referred to the Febles test in multiple decisions, noting that the Supreme Court followed previous guidance from the Federal Court of Appeal. This previous guidance considered that a crime is presumed to be serious if the Canadian equivalent carries a maximum sentence of at least 10 years. At the same time, this presumption may be rebutted as the consideration of seriousness should take into account other factors,

30 Unlike in the context of inadmissibility, where the concept of serious criminality is defined in the IRPA and mainly relates to the maximum sentence attached to the crime in Canada, no such clear definition exists in the international protection concept.

such as "(…) the elements of the crime, the mode of prosecution, the penalty prescribed, the facts and the mitigating and aggravating circumstances underlying the conviction."[31]

While the Supreme Court endorses this analysis in Febles, it also stresses the importance of a contextual assessment, cautioning against a mechanistic, rigid application of the seriousness presumption. The Supreme Court also adds a new factor into the mix of considerations to be taken into account, that is, the Canadian sentencing range.[32] More specifically, the Supreme Court specified that when an offence is linked to a large sentencing range, where the maximum sentence is 10 years or more yet the minimum sentence is quite low, a person whose crime would fall at the less serious end of the range in Canada should not be presumptively excluded.[33] In the following years, the Federal Court thus continued to affirm that the seriousness presumption should not be understood as a rigid presumption and that the sentencing range needs to be taken into account.[34] The Federal Court also noted in its decisions that the Supreme Court in Febles confirmed that facts extraneous to the crime, such as completion of sentence, rehabilitation and the person no longer posing a threat to society, should not be taken into consideration to determine whether a crime was serious.[35]

Regarding the standard of proof for a 1F(b) exclusion (serious grounds to believe), the Federal Court clarified that it does not require a conviction. Indeed, the Federal Court found reasonable an exclusion decision based on police reports and credibility findings, even though the charges brought against the asylum applicant for the alleged crime basing the 1F(b) exclusion were not proceeded with.[36]

---

31 Jung v. Canada, 2015 FC 464 (Federal Court, 15 April 2015), para. 44.

32 Ibid., para. 38. See also Tabagua v. Canada, 2015 FC 709 (Federal Court, 4 June 2015), para. 21.

33 Jung v. Canada, 2015 FC 464, para. 34. See also Mohamed v. Canada, 2015 FC 1006 (Federal Court, 25 August 2015), para. 20.

34 See, e.g. A. B. v. Canada, 2016 FC 1385 (Federal Court, 16 December 2016); Ma v. Canada, 2018 FC 252 (Federal Court, 6 March 2018); Nwobi v. Canada, 2018 FC 317 (Federal Court, 20 March 2018).

35 See, e.g. Jung v. Canada, 2015 FC 464, paras. 41–42; Nwobi v. Canada, 2018 FC 317, para. 29.

36 Abbas v. Canada, 2019 FC 12 (Federal Court, 7 January 2019). Similarly, in Hashi v. Canada, 2020 FC 309 (Federal Court, 26 February 2020), the Federal Court also found that an exclusion decision based on dropped charges was reasonable, considering that "[T]he RPD is not constrained by the exact characterization of the conviction, or whether there was a conviction at all. There must simply be 'serious reasons for considering' that this type of crime was committed" (para. 29).

3.2.2 Serious Criminality as a Ground for Inadmissibility

In the inadmissibility context, the Federal Court of Appeal found, in 2015, that it was reasonable to consider the punishment associated with the offence at the moment of deciding on the inadmissibility, and not at the moment of the commission of the crime.[37] The case at hand concerned a man who was convicted for his involvement in a marijuana operation. At the time of the acts and his indictment, the crime was punishable with a maximum term of 7 years. Shortly after, however, the maximum term was increased to 14 years. At the time of conviction, the maximum term was 14 years, but it could not apply to him due to the non-retroactivity of penal law. He was, however, considered inadmissible due to serious criminality, as it was considered that the maximum term of imprisonment for the crime exceeded 10 years at the time of the inadmissibility assessment. The Federal Court of Appeal found no error in the inadmissibility finding.[38]

For crimes committed abroad, the Federal Court recalled that the standard of proof is reasonable grounds to believe (as prescribed in s 33 IRPA), not beyond a reasonable doubt.[39] In those cases, the decision-maker must conduct "(...) an equivalency analysis between the foreign offences pondered and the equivalent suggested in Canadian legislation,"[40] in which "(...) the officer must look at the essential ingredients of the two offences and be satisfied that they are comparable."[41] Such an assessment must take into account possible defences and/or immunities applicable to the offence.[42]

3.2.3 Serious Criminality: Differences between the International Protection and Inadmissibility Contexts

As serious crimes committed abroad may give rise to both an inadmissibility finding (under ss 36(1)(b) and (c) IRPA) and exclusion from refugee status (under Article 1F(b) of the Refugee Convention and s 98 IRPA), the Federal Court has in some cases compared the two provisions and assessed how they

37 Canada v. Tran, 2015 FCA 237 (Federal Court of Appeal, 30 October 2015), para. 60.

38 In the same case, the Court also found that a conditional sentence of imprisonment may reasonably be construed as a term of imprisonment for the purposes of assessing serious criminality. See Ibid., para. 88.

39 Halilaj v. Canada, 2017 FC 1062 (Federal Court, 23 November 2017), para. 20.

40 Randhawa v. Canada, 2020 FC 905 (Federal Court, 17 September 2020), para. 31.

41 Ibid. idem.

42 Ibid. idem; Bellevue v. Canada, 2018 FC 926 (Federal Court, 19 September 2018), para. 44; Bellevue v. Canada, 2020 FC 560 (Federal Court, 28 April 2020), para. 34. See also: Canada v. Aly, 2018 FC 1140 (Federal Court, 13 November 2018).

interact with each other. In this regard, it is important to note that crimes committed abroad may give rise to an inadmissibility finding when a person is convicted of a crime abroad (s 36(1)(b) IRPA) or when the person committed acts that would constitute an offence in Canada (s 36(1)(c) IRPA). The former provision is the one that was compared with article 1F(b) by the Federal Court. In this regard, the Court found that a determination that a person is inadmissible for serious criminality for having been convicted of a crime abroad does not necessarily mean that they are also excluded from refugee protection under article 1F Refugee Convention. The inadmissibility determination only creates a presumption that the crime was serious for the purposes of article 1F(b) of the Refugee Convention.[43] The inadmissibility decision, however, does not assess all the issues that are assessed under a 1F(b) exclusion. For example, it does not address in depth whether the conviction basing the inadmissibility was politically motivated. The Federal Court thus said that:

> The language of Article 1F(b) requires consideration whether the applicant for refugee status has committed a crime, while the language of s 36 (1)(b) requires consideration whether a person has been convicted of crime. As such, Article 1F(b) affords scope for consideration of arguments surrounding politically motivated prosecution or other flaws in a foreign legal system, as the fact of a conviction does not necessarily translate into a conclusion that a crime has been committed. However, s 36(1)(b) is triggered by the conviction itself.[44]

Even though an asylum claim will not proceed when someone is considered inadmissible due to serious criminality (as mentioned above), these differences are important as less remedies are available to those excluded from international protection, as will be shown below. It should be noted, however, that crimes committed abroad will not give rise to an inadmissibility finding if the concerned migrant satisfies the Minister that they have been rehabilitated (s 36(3)(c) IRPA). In this regard, "(…) the risk of reoffending is the key factor to weigh"[45] in a rehabilitation assessment.[46]

---

43 Go v. Canada, 2015 FC 635 (Federal Court, 14 May 2015), para. 15.
44 Gurbuz v. Canada, 2018 FC 684 (Federal Court, 6 July 2018), para. 29.
45 Tahhan v. Canada, 2018 FC 1279 (Federal Court, 18 December 2018), para. 21.
46 See also Zhang v. Canada, 2020 FC 927 (Federal Court, 24 September 2020), para. 64.

3.3 *Those Who Engage in Acts Contrary to the Principles and Purposes of the United Nations*

Article 1F(c) of the Refugee Convention (referenced in s 98 IRPA) excludes from refugee status those who are guilty of acts contrary to the purposes and principles of the United Nations (hereafter UN). Regarding the practical application of article 1F(c) in Canada, Rikhof noted that "[B]efore 1998, this exclusion ground was primarily used to exclude persons who had been convicted of drug trafficking offences after being admitted to Canada."[47] This, however, changed in 1998 when the Supreme Court concluded that article 1F(c) aimed to exclude those responsible for serious, sustained or systematic human rights violations, which amount to persecution in non-war contexts.[48] Drug trafficking would thus not fall under this article.[49] Since then, Rikhof noted that the article had been used scarcely in relation to terrorism and systemic human rights violations.[50]

Terrorism can also lead to inadmissibility under s 34 of the IRPA, which is discussed in the next subsection.

3.4 *Those Who Are Considered a Threat to Security*

Section 34 of the IRPA considers inadmissible those who engage in espionage, the subversion of a government or terrorism, as well as members of organisations that engage in those actions; those who are a danger to the security of Canada or those who commit acts of violence endangering the lives of persons in Canada.

With regard to this section, the Federal Court was called upon a few times to clarify the definition of terrorism, as the IRPA does not provide one. The Federal Court was thus confronted with the question of whether, in this situation, applying the Criminal Code definition of terrorist activity[51] was reasonable. In 2017, the Court found that it was "(…) appropriate and harmonious to use the definition of terrorist activity"[52] set out in the Criminal Code to inform the meaning of terrorism in the IRPA. In a decision from 2018, however, the Federal Court called for caution when using the Criminal Code definition, as criminal and immigration law are different legal frameworks with different

47 Rikhof, J. (2023). Exclusion and Refoulement: Criminality in International and Domestic Refugee Law. Irwin Law Inc., p. 547.

48 Ibid., p. 549.

49 Ibid., p. 550.

50 Ibid., pp. 552–553.

51 Terrorist activity is defined in s 83.01 of the Criminal Code (R.S.C., 1985, c. C-46): https://laws-lois.justice.gc.ca/eng/acts/c-46/index.html.

52 Ali v. Canada, 2017 FC 182 (Federal Court, 14 February 2017), para. 44.

purposes (although some purposes such as protecting security may overlap). Thus, it was said that a decision-maker cannot blindly rely on the criminal code definition without explaining why they have done so.[53] Lastly, in 2019, in a decision summarising previous Case Law on the matter, a judge of the Federal Court found that the definition of terrorist activity in the Criminal Code was compatible with the definition of terrorism applied by the Supreme Court in a migration case and thus it was reasonable to rely on it.[54]

Regarding membership in a terrorist group, both the Federal Court[55] and the Federal Court of appeal[56] noted that, unlike in the abovementioned Ezokola test, membership alone suffices for the purpose of inadmissibility under s 34 IRPA. Furthermore, s 34(1)(f) says inadmissibility is based on membership to an "(…) organization that there are reasonable grounds to believe engages, has engaged or will engage" in terrorist acts. Thus, the Federal Court concluded that "(…) there is no temporal component,"[57] that is, there is no requirement that the dates of an individual's membership coincide with the dates on which the organisation engaged in terrorism.[58]

3.5 *Those Who Engage in Organised Criminality*

Finally, section 37 finds inadmissible to Canada those who engage in organised criminality. As for a finding of criminality, the standard of proof is reasonable grounds to believe (s 33 IRPA).[59] In this regard, the Federal Court found unreasonable to rely on charges in and of themselves to reach an inadmissibility finding,[60] but noted that charges can be relied on as part of the evidence.[61] The Court also noted that the acts giving rise to an organised criminality finding, if committed abroad, do not need to constitute a criminal offence in the country where they were committed, as long as they constitute a crime in Canada.[62] For a finding of inadmissibility on organised criminality

53 Rana v. Canada, 2018 FC 1080 (Federal Court, 29 October 2018).

54 Saleheen v. Canada, 2019 FC 145 (Federal Court, 5 February 2019).

55 Alam v. Canada, 2018 FC 922 (Federal Court, 17 September 2018), para. 25.

56 Kanagendren v. Canada, 2015 FCA 86 (Federal Court of Appeal, 7 April 2015), paras. 21–22.

57 S.A. v. Canada, 2017 FC 494 (Federal Court, 12 May 2017), para. 13.

58 Ibid. idem.

59 See also Odosashvili v. Canada, 2017 FC 958 (Federal Court, 26 October 2017), para. 36.

60 Abdi v. Canada, 2017 FC 950 (Federal Court, 26 October 2017), para. 36.

61 Pascal v. Canada, 2020 FC 751 (Federal Court, 9 July 2020), para. 24; see also Odosashvili v. Canada, 2017 FC 958.

62 Nguesso v. Canada, 2015 FC 879 (Federal Court, 17 July 2015), para. 208.

to be made, however, the criminal organisation in question must be identified, as that is an essential element of s 37.[63]

Not all those who fall under the provisions mentioned in the current and previous subsections will be considered inadmissible, however, as decision-makers are afforded some discretion in their decisions. The elements that may influence an undesirability finding are thus explained in the next subsection.

3.6 *Discretion in Inadmissibility Decisions: Not as Many Undesirables as Initially Foreseen?*

In practice, when an officer of the Department or of the Canada Border Services Agency[64] is of the opinion that a foreigner is inadmissible, they may prepare a report setting out the relevant facts to be sent to the Minister (or their delegate) (s 44(1) IRPA). If the Minister (or their delegate) is of the opinion that the report is well-founded, they may refer the report to the ID for an admissibility hearing or issue a removal order against the concerned migrant (s 44(2) IRPA).[65]

Both the officer and the Minister (or their delegate) are afforded some discretion in their decisions. However, these are limited discretions,[66] especially in the abovementioned cases involving security and criminality, as security is considered a top priority by the IRPA (ss 3(1)(h) and (i)).[67] Within the constraints of such limited discretion, decision-makers may take into account personal circumstances of the concerned migrant, including, among others, whether they are beneficiaries of international protection, the longevity of their stay in Canada, whether a removal order has already been issued against them, and whether, in cases of minor criminality, the person may be considered rehabilitated.[68] In this regard, the Federal Court clarified that "(...) the prevailing jurisprudence establishes that there is no obligation on the

---

63 Ibid., para. 191.

64 While it is not relevant for this chapter to explain which officer is responsible for the initial report in which situation, this information can be found in: Canada Border Services Agency, ENF 6 – Review of reports under subsection A44(2), section 4. Available at: https://www.canada.ca/content/dam/ircc/migration/ircc/english/resources/manuals/enf/enf06-eng.pdf.

65 The specific situations in which a removal order may be ordered without a hearing before the ID are set out in s 228(1) IRPA Regulations.

66 Canada Border Services Agency, ENF 5 Writing 44(1) Reports, sections 8.1–8.2. Available at: https://www.canada.ca/content/dam/ircc/migration/ircc/english/resources/manuals/enf/enf05-eng.pdf; Canada Border Services Agency, ENF 6, section 8.2; Sharma v. Canada, 2016 FCA 319 (Federal Court of Appeal, 21 December 2016), paras. 22–23.

67 Sharma v. Canada, 2016 FCA 319, para. 22–23.

68 Canada Border Services Agency, ENF 5, sections 9.1–9.2, 10.1.

Officer or Minister's Delegate to consider H&C [humanitarian and compassionate] factors, but where they do so, in the context of reaching a recommendation [for an inadmissibility hearing], their consideration must be reasonable."[69] The Federal Court noted, however, that when a migrant makes a claim regarding their rights under the Canadian Charter of Rights and Freedoms (for example, due to their fear of refoulement), the decision-maker must consider the implications of their decision on the concerned migrant's Charter rights.[70] Despite this requirement to take into account Charter arguments when they are invoked, the Federal Court[71] and the Federal Court of Appeal[72] both noted that a finding of inadmissibility alone will not violate non-refoulement, as it does not necessarily lead to deportation since there are remedies available to the concerned migrant (as will be discussed in the next sections).

After considering all the elements, should the Minister (or their delegate) decide to refer the case to an admissibility hearing before the ID, the ID is mandated to make a removal order, if it is satisfied that the concerned migrant is inadmissible (s 45(d) IRPA). As a general rule, removal orders made by the Minister's delegate or following an inadmissibility finding by the ID may be appealed to the IAD (s 63(3) IRPA). No appeal, however, is allowed for those who have been found to be inadmissible on grounds of security, violating human or international rights, serious criminality or organised criminality (s 64(1) IRPA). For serious criminality, those convicted in Canada will only be prevented from filing an appeal when they have been convicted to a term of imprisonment of at least six months (s 64(2) IRPA). Although no appeal is allowed, those considered inadmissible on security grounds, for having been a member of a government that violated human rights, for being sanctioned under a specific regime, or on grounds of organised criminality may exceptionally be declared not inadmissible by the Minister. This may happen when, taking into account national security and public safety considerations, the Minister finds that such a declaration is not contrary to the national interest (s 42.1 IRPA).

---

69 McLeish v. Canada, 2020 FC 705 (Federal Court, 18 June 2020), para. 80.

70 Abdi v. Canada, 2018 FC 733 (Federal Court, 13 July 2018), paras. 72–79. See also: Canada Border Services Agency, ENF 6, section 9.

71 See Torre v. Canada, 2015 FC 591 (Federal Court, 6 May 2015); Suresh v. Canada, 2017 FC 28 (Federal Court, 10 January 2017); Revell v. Canada, 2017 FC 905 (Federal Court, 12 October 2017); Ching v. Canada, 2018 FC 839 (Federal Court, 16 August 2018); Kooner v. Canada, 2019 FC 806 (Federal Court, 12 June 2019).

72 See Tapambwa v. Canada, 2019 FCA 34 (Federal Court of Appeal, 31 May 2019); Revell v. Canada, 2019 FCA 262 (Federal Court of Appeal, 18 October 2019).

When an appeal is possible, the IAD will allow it when it finds that the appealed decision is wrong in law, fact or mixed law and fact; a principle of natural justice has not been observed; or when there are sufficient humanitarian and compassionate considerations to warrant special relief in light of all the circumstances of the case (s 67(1) IRPA). Regarding the last reason that allows an appeal, the Federal Court noted that:

> The factors in question [to find that there are humanitarian and compassionate grounds that would warrant special relief] are the following: 1) the seriousness of the offence or offences leading to the removal order; 2) the possibility of rehabilitation; 3) the length of time the appellant has spent in Canada and the degree to which the appellant is established in Canada; 4) the impact that the appellant's removal from Canada would have on his family; 5) the support available to the appellant not only within the family but also within the community; and 6) the degree of hardship that the appellant would face in the country to which he would likely be removed.[73]

About the second factor (possibility of rehabilitation), as mentioned above, the Federal Court also noted that reoffending is key in assessing it, stating that "(…) the likelihood of reoffending range is capped at not exceeding 50%. Any greater risk thereafter defines a likelihood of reoffending that results in the automatic rejection"[74] of the sought relief. A successful appeal means the IAD will set aside the original decision (s 67(2) IRPA) and thus can reverse the inadmissibility finding and consequent removal order.

In some cases, however, the abovementioned discretionary powers and appeals do not favour the continued stay of the concerned undesirable migrant. Should the migrant also be unreturnable, they need to present their non-refoulement claims, as that may impact their removal from the country. In Canada, two procedures aim at assessing harm upon return. The first one is the international protection procedure and the second one is the pre-removal risk assessment. The next section will thus explain these procedures.

---

73 Solmaz v. Canada, 2019 FC 736 (Federal Court, 24 May 2019), para. 6. See also Zhang v. Canada, 2020 FC 927, para. 10.

74 Zhang v. Canada, 2020 FC 927, para. 70.

4 Who Are the Unreturnable Migrants?

4.1 *Non-refoulement Assessment in an International Protection Procedure*

Canada allows most migrants in the country to ask for international protection. In this regard, as a party to the Refugee Convention, Canada's IRPA closely follows the inclusion clauses of the Refugee Convention in s 96, where it defines a Convention refugee as "a person who, by reason of a well-founded fear of persecution for reasons of race, religion, nationality, mem bership in a particular social group or political opinion," is outside their country of nationality or habitual residence (for stateless persons) and is, due to their fear, unwilling or unable to return and/or receive protection from that country.

Canada's legislation also goes beyond the Refugee Convention and extends subsidiary or complementary protection to those who may not be returned due to human rights concerns. In this regard, s 97 IRPA defines a person in need of protection as someone who, upon return to their country of nationality or habitual residence, may be subjected to torture, inhumane treatment or death. The provision specifies that the risk must be faced by the person in every part of that country and not be faced generally by other individuals in or from that country; the risk cannot be inherent or incidental to lawful sanctions, unless imposed in disregard of accepted international standards; and, lastly, the risk is not caused by the inability of that country to provide adequate health or medical care.

Like many countries, however, Canada will not grant protection status to those who came from a safe country or were granted refugee status in a safe country (s 101(1)(c.1), (d) and (e) IRPA), despite the Refugee Convention being silent about this. Safe countries are determined by taking into account whether they are parties to the Convention against Torture and the Refugee Convention, their policies and practices with regard to these Conventions, their human rights records, and whether they have an agreement with Canada for responsibility sharing in refugee protection (s 102(2) IRPA).

Furthermore, Canada also considers ineligible the applications of those who are found inadmissible to the country for reasons of security, violating human or international rights, serious criminality or organised criminality (s 101(1)(f) IRPA). In such cases, their asylum claims will not be heard. Similarly, migrants will not be granted protection when they fall under one of the exclusion clauses mentioned above. The IRPA provides, however, another procedure through which migrants can have their non-refoulement claims heard. This is the pre-removal risk assessment, which is explained below.

4.2 *Non-refoulement in Pre-removal Risk Assessments*

Apart from the international protection procedure described in the previous subsection, Canadian law also allows most of those subjected to removal from Canada[75] to apply for a pre-removal risk assessment (hereafter PRRA),[76] in which the risks the concerned migrant faces upon return will be assessed. Generally, a PRRA will assess whether the concerned migrant would face persecution (in accordance with the Refugee Convention) upon return or if their rights to life and to be free from torture would be at risk in their country of origin (human rights non-refoulement) (s 113(c) IRPA). Where it is found that the concerned migrant would be at risk upon return, they are granted refugee status (s 114(1)(a) IRPA).

Failed asylum seekers, however, will, in most cases, only be allowed to apply for a PRRA 12 months after the conclusion of their asylum proceedings (s 112(2) IRPA).[77] Migrants who were found inadmissible on grounds of security, violating human or international rights, organised criminality or serious criminality,[78] as well as excluded asylum seekers (according to article 1F Refugee Convention), in turn, can only apply for a restricted PRRA. In a restricted PRRA, only the risk to their rights to life and to be free from torture will be assessed (not a possible risk of persecution in accordance with the Refugee Convention) (s 113(d) IRPA). In case it is found that they would be at risk, they are not granted protection status but instead their removal from Canada is stayed (s 114(1)(b) IRPA). This stay, however, can be cancelled if the circumstances justifying the stay of the removal change (s 114(2) IRPA).

Should a person be considered a danger to the public in Canada during the PRRA procedure, the decision-maker (a member of the Department) must

---

75 See Government of Canada, Pre-removal risk assessment: Who can apply. Available at: https://www.canada.ca/en/immigration-refugees-citizenship/services/refugees/protection/refusal-options/pre-removal-risk-assessment/eligibility.html.

76 See s 112 IRPA and s 160 IRPA Regulations.

77 See also: Government of Canada, Pre-removal risk assessment – Exemptions to the 12-month wait period. Available at: https://www.canada.ca/en/immigration-refugees-citizenship/services/refugees/protection/refusal-options/pre-removal-risk-assessment/exceptions.html.

78 This restriction will not apply to those found inadmissible for serious criminality when they were convicted in Canada to a term of imprisonment of less than two years or to those convicted outside Canada for an offence that, if committed in Canada, would be punishable by a maximum term of imprisonment of at least 10 years, unless they were considered excluded from refugee protection under article 1F Refugee Convention (s 113 (e) IRPA). See also Gurbuz v. Canada, 2018 FC 684, para. 34.

weigh the risk to the concerned migrant upon return with the danger they pose "(...) to public safety in Canada and determine whether his PRRA should be refused and removal enforced."[79]

Apart from the PRRA, the Minister is also allowed to impose a general stay of removals to certain countries, where there is a generalised risk to the entire civilian population due to armed conflict, environmental disasters or other temporary and generalised situations.[80] Such a stay, however, does not apply to those found inadmissible on grounds of security, violating human or international rights, organised criminality or serious criminality, as well as excluded asylum seekers (according to article 1F Refugee Convention).[81]

5 Solutions for Undesirable but Unreturnable Migrants

Now that Section 3 has showed who is an undesirable migrant in Canada and Section 4 has presented the procedures that serve to recognise unreturnable migrants in the country, the current section will present the solutions available for undesirable but unreturnable migrants in Canada, while critically assessing their human rights compliance and sustainability.

In this regard, in the Refugee Survey Quarterly special edition[82] that followed the Refugee Law Initiative's project on undesirable but unreturnable migrants,[83] Bond made a similar attempt to identify the fate of undesirable but unreturnable migrants in an article focussing on undesirable migrants for (alleged) criminality who cannot be returned due to multiple reasons (not only human rights concerns). Bond found that these migrants may find themselves in one of the following five situations:

- eligible for permanent residence (PR);
- granted temporary stay of removal until impediment removed (TS);
- granted temporary status but removable due to an active removal order (SBR);
- placed in legal limbo, with no particular status (limbo); and

79 Canada v. Smith, 2019 FC 1454 (Federal Court, 19 November 2019), para. 16. See also s 115(2) IRPA, further discussed below.

80 S 230 IRPA Regulations.

81 S 230(3) IRPA Regulations.

82 Refugee Survey Quarterly, 36(1) (2017).

83 Project website: https://rli.sas.ac.uk/projects-0/undesirable-unreturnable-migrants.

- Subjected to suspect deportation, despite apparent impediment to removal (SD).[84]

Bond's analysis has a slightly different scope than the current book; however, most of these options generally apply to the undesirable but unreturnable migrants studied in this chapter, as shown in the following subsections.

5.1 *Return in Violation of Human Rights*

As noted in Section 3.1 of Chapter 1, apart from exclusion clauses, the Refugee Convention also provides that refugees considered a danger to security or who, convicted for a serious crime, constitute a danger to the community, cannot benefit from the (refugee law) non-refoulement protection. Following closely the Refugee Convention, Canada's IRPA establishes a prohibition of refoulement (as defined in the Refugee Convention) in s 115(1) and sets exceptions to such prohibition in s 115(2), which reads as follows:

> (2) Subsection (1) [establishing protection from non-refoulement] does not apply in the case of a person
> (a) who is inadmissible on grounds of serious criminality and who constitutes, in the opinion of the Minister, a danger to the public in Canada; or
> (b) who is inadmissible on grounds of security, violating human or international rights or organized criminality if, in the opinion of the Minister, the person should not be allowed to remain in Canada on the basis of the nature and severity of acts committed or of danger to the security of Canada.

As also mentioned in Chapter 1, however, human rights non-refoulement is broader than refugee law non-refoulement. In this regard, the Federal Court noted that "[A]lthough the paragraph [115(2) IRPA] itself contains no requirement that the risks to which an individual may be subject upon removal be assessed, such an assessment must be undertaken to ensure that any removal does not violate the individual's rights pursuant to section 7 of the [Canadian] Charter"[85] of Rights and Freedoms, which protects the right to life, liberty and

84 Bond, J. (2017). Unwanted but unremovable: Canada's treatment of "criminal" migrants who cannot be removed. Refugee Survey Quarterly, 36(1), 168–186, p. 181.

85 Murugamoorthy v. Canada, 2018 FC 650 (Federal Court, 21 June 2018), para. 18. Similar statements were made in Ezici v. Canada, 2017 FC 512 (Federal Court 18 May 2017), para.

security of person.[86] Indeed, s 3(3)(d) IRPA states that the Act must be applied in a manner that is consistent with the Canadian Charter of Rights and Freedoms. In this regard, the Federal Court noted that:

> The deportation of Convention Refugees to nations where they may face persecution or torture, known as refoulement, is exceptional in nature, and must be triggered by acts of "substantial gravity." When such recourse is considered, the delegate must balance the danger faced by applicant against the danger the applicant would present to the Canadian public if he was not removed. Given Canada's firm commitment to human rights, the rule of law and principles of fundamental justice, this balance will generally tip against expulsion[87] [references omitted].

The Federal Court further noted that the assessment of the risk faced by the applicant:

> (…) must be made contemporaneously; the Convention refugee or protected person cannot rely on his or her status to trigger the application of section 7 of the Charter. Continuing his analysis, the delegate must balance the danger to the public in Canada against the degree of risk, as well as against any other humanitarian and compassionate considerations[88] [references omitted].

As for the consideration of public danger, the Federal Court, referencing previous decisions, noted that it "(…) must refer to the possibility that a person who has committed a serious crime in the past may seriously be thought to be a potential re-offender."[89] In this regard, the Court found that the test to allow the overruling of the non-refoulement principle sets a very high threshold and

---

14; Baladie v. Canada, 2018 FC 706, para. 27 (Federal Court, 9 July 2018); and Shababy v. Canada, 2018 FC 810 (Federal Court, 1 August 2018), para. 4.

86 In A.B. v. Canada, 2020 FC 203 (Federal Court, 5 February 2020), para. 36, the Federal Court goes further, noting that the Minister must balance the danger to the public in Canada against the degree of risk upon return, as well as against any other humanitarian and compassionate considerations.

87 Balazuntharam v. Canada, 2015 FC 607 (Federal Court, 8 May 2015), para. 2. Similarly, in Yousif v. Canada, 2019 FC 128, the Federal Court noted that s 115(2) prescribes a very high threshold to be overcome, which is different from the test for inadmissibility (para. 23).

88 Ramanathan v. Canada, 2017 FC 834 (Federal Court, 22 September 2017), para. 39.

89 Ibid., para. 40. See also Makomena v. Canada, 2019 FC 894 (Federal Court, 5 July 2019), para. 28.

is a different test from inadmissibility.[90] For example, the Federal Court said that not every offence punishable by 10 years of imprisonment will lead to a danger opinion by the Minister allowing the removal of the concerned migrant.[91] At the same time, the Court stated that "(...) available case law unequivocally confirms that a crime need not be violent in order for the offender to constitute a danger to the public."[92]

It is worth noting that the onus to bring relevant elements (such as non-refoulement) to the attention of the Minister is on the concerned migrant.[93] Lastly, judicial appeal of danger opinions to the Federal Court is possible. In multiple cases, the Federal Court found that the danger posed by the concerned migrant or the risk they would face upon return was not properly considered and ordered a redetermination of the matter.[94]

In view of the above, it can be said that, from a legal perspective, removal in violation of non-refoulement is unlikely (but not impossible) to be the fate of some undesirable but unreturnable migrants in Canada. In practice, it has been said that Canada may deliberately use suspect deportations in violation of non-refoulement to handle problematic cases.[95]

In this regard, the UN Committee against Torture, when reviewing Canada's implementation of the Convention against Torture, expressed concern "(...) about exceptions to the principle of non-refoulement in the Immigration and Refugee Protection Act (subsection 115 (2),"[96] calling on Canada to "[C] onsider amending subsection 115 (2) of the Immigration and Refugee Protec-

90 Yousif v. Canada, 2019 FC 128, para. 23.

91 Makomena v. Canada, 2019 FC 894, para. 41.

92 Ramanathan v. Canada, 2017 FC 834, para. 45.

93 Barre v. Canada, 2017 FC 1091 (Federal Court, 1 December 2017), para. 20. See also: Immigration, Refugees and Citizenship Canada, ENF 28 - Ministerial opinions on danger to the public, nature and severity of the acts committed and danger to the security of Canada. Available at: https://www.canada.ca/content/dam/ircc/migration/ircc/english/resources/manuals/enf/enf28-eng.pdf.

94 See, e.g. Balazuntharam v. Canada, 2015 FC 607; Ahmed v. Canada, 2015 FC 1024 (Federal Court, 28 August 2015); Wafa v. Canada, 2015 FC 1153 (Federal Court, 9 October 2015); Reynosa v. Canada, 2016 FC 1058 (Federal Court, 20 September 2016); Ahmed v. Canada, 2018 FC 471 (Federal Court, 2 May 2018); Makomena v. Canada, 2019 FC 894; A.B. v. Canada, 2020 FC 203; Ahmed v. Canada, 2020 FC 507 (Federal Court, 9 April 2020).

95 Bond, J. (2017), p. 183. See also Inter-American Commission on Human Rights, Follow-up of the recommendations of the IACHR Report on asylum seekers in Canada (2000) (hearing), 7 September 2017. Available at: https://www.oas.org/en/iachr/sessions/hearings.asp?Country=CAN&Topic=0&Year=2017.

96 Committee against Torture (2018). Concluding observations on the seventh periodic report of Canada (CAT/C/CAN/CO/7). United Nations, para. 24.

tion Act to fully comply with the principle of non-refoulement."[97] The Committee further stated that "[T]he State party should under no circumstances expel, return or extradite a person to another State where there are substantial grounds for believing that he or she would be in danger of being subjected to torture."[98] The same concerns were expressed by the UN Human Rights Committee.[99] Indeed, considering the non-derogable character of the right to life and the right to be free from torture, removal to a place where the concerned migrants face a risk to these rights constitutes a human rights violation.

Not all undesirable but unreturnable migrants, however, will be returned to harm. Some, once the risk they face upon return is identified, will have their removal from Canada stayed for a certain period of time.[100] In some cases, there are alternatives to such situations. In this regard, inadmissible migrants can apply for permanent residence based on humanitarian and compassionate (often referred to as H&C in jurisprudence) grounds (s 25(1) IRPA), which would result in the removal of their inadmissibility. This option is explored in the next section.

5.2 *Permanent Residence*

Some inadmissible migrants in Canada can apply for permanent residence based on humanitarian and compassionate (or H&C) grounds (s 25(1) IRPA). Such requests must be considered by the Minister (or their delegate). In 2018, a decision of the Federal Court defined the process of deciding an application based on humanitarian and compassionate considerations as follows:

> An H&C application is a weighing exercise in which an immigration officer, on behalf of the Minister, must consider different and sometimes competing factors. When, as in the present case, an H&C exemption from criminal inadmissibility is sought, the officer must weigh the public policy reflected in section 36(1) of the IRPA against the individual circumstances of the case and determine whether the latter outweigh the former so as to warrant making an exception to the usual rule that serious criminality by a permanent resident leads to loss of status and removal from Canada.[101]

---

97 Ibid., para. 25.

98 Ibid., para. 29.

99 Human Rights Committee (2015). Concluding observations on the sixth periodic report of Canada (CCPR/C/CAN/CO/6). United Nations, para. 13.

100 While the removal is stayed, the removal order remains valid (just unenforceable).

101 Magsanoc v. Canada, 2018 FC 821 (Federal Court, 9 August 2018), para. 38.

The Court continued to say that relief (in the form of permanent residence) on humanitarian and compassionate grounds will be granted when, after an individual assessment of the circumstances of the case, the decision-maker finds that this is a situation in which a reasonable person would like to relieve the misfortunes of the concerned migrant.[102]

When weighing the criminal conduct of an undesirable migrant for the purpose of a humanitarian and compassionate assessment, the Federal Court noted that it was unreasonable for a decision-maker to consider only the criminal conduct and not take into account the other dimensions of the concerned migrant's criminal history, including mitigating considerations relating to the offences, sentencing and rehabilitation.[103] The Court also noted that the decision-maker should not impose an unattainable standard on the concerned migrant in a case in which the decision-maker dismissed the humanitarian and compassionate application because there was "no guarantee" that the concerned migrant would not re-offend. The Federal Court found, in that case, that it is impossible to guarantee that any person will not commit a criminal offence and that such an approach would prevent anyone with a criminal record from obtaining relief on humanitarian and compassionate grounds.[104]

Humanitarian and compassionate applications can thus serve to remove the undesirability (in this case represented by the inadmissibility finding) of certain migrants, when taking into account all their personal circumstances in Canada. This leads to some undesirable but unreturnable migrants being granted permanent residence in Canada despite the acts that gave rise to their undesirability. Thus, it reduces the number of undesirable migrants in the country and provides a long-term solution for some of those who were initially deemed undesirable but unreturnable migrants.

Not all undesirable migrants, however, are allowed to apply for permanent residence on humanitarian and compassionate grounds, as the IRPA explicitly excludes those found inadmissible under ss 34 (security), 35 (war crimes and crimes against humanity), 35.1 (sanctions) and 37 (organised criminality) from such relief (s 25(1) IRPA).

These latter migrants may be granted permanent status (and thus no longer be deemed inadmissible) by the Minister if the foreign national complies with any conditions imposed by the Minister and the Minister is of the opinion that the grant of permanent residence is justified by public policy considerations

102 Ibid., paras. 39–41.

103 Sivalingam v. Canada, 2017 FC 1185 (Federal Court, 21 December 2017), para. 12.

104 Aghayere v. Canada, 2018 FC 869 (Federal Court, 29 August 2018), para. 24.

(s 25.2 (1) IRPA). Regarding this possibility, the Federal Court of Appeal noted that it provides a similar discretion to a humanitarian and compassionate consideration, but the Court also notes that:

> (…) similarities aside, there is, however, a stark distinction between subsection 25(1) and section 25.2. The former contains mandatory language. The Minister "must" consider requests for humanitarian and compassionate relief. Section 25.2 in contrast, is discretionary. The Minister "may" consider granting relief. This is not a situation where the permissive or discretionary word, "may," can be read as mandatory.[105]

Thus, the Minister has greater discretion in these situations and will only act in cases justified by public policy, which is, in turn, defined by the Minister. As such, this is a more limited remedy, which is unlikely to apply to most cases of inadmissible migrants.

Undesirable but unreturnable migrants, who do not receive relief in the form of permanent residence (by a humanitarian and compassionate application or through a discretionary decision of the Minister), may still apply for a temporary permit. Temporary statuses are explored in the next subsection.

5.3 *Temporary Status*

As noted in the previous section, undesirable but unreturnable migrants who do not receive permanent residence may still apply for a temporary permit, which may, however, be cancelled at any time (s 24(1) IRPA). In this regard, the Federal Court noted, in the case of an inadmissible migrant who had a positive PRRA, that even though he was unable to obtain permanent residence, "(…) he is nevertheless permitted to remain in Canada and apply for a work or study permit because of Canada's international obligations against refoulement."[106] Bond, however, noted that temporary permits may make it challenging for these migrants to obtain employment. This is because, according to her, "(…) it is increasingly common for these work permits to be issued for a period of only six months, a limitation that necessitates a costly renewal process and makes it difficult for many individuals to find employment because employers are seeking longer term commitments."[107]

Challenges such as these may continue for a long period of time, as the IRPA Regulations explicitly exclude inadmissible migrants from being granted per-

105 Tapambwa v. Canada, 2019 FCA 34, para. 103.
106 Yousif v. Canada, 2019 FC 128, para. 14.
107 Bond, J. (2017), pp. 184–185.

manent residence (s 72(1)(e)(i) IRPA Regulations).[108] In practice, this can even be a barrier for recognised refugees to obtain permanent residence, since, as mentioned in Section 3.2.3, inadmissibility for criminality is not assessed in the same manner as exclusion from refugee status under article 1F(b) of the Refugee Convention. Indeed, in a case from 2018, the Federal Court found it reasonable to deny permanent residence to a recognised refugee due to a conviction abroad (which made him inadmissible under s 36(1)(b) IRPA), even though the Minister and the RPD, during his asylum procedure, recognised that he was denied due process in the criminal procedure that led to his conviction.[109]

The Federal Court did find in 2016, however, that where an inadmissible migrant asks for an exemption on humanitarian and compassionate grounds and brings forward arguments relating to the lack of permanent residence (such as difficulties that may arise from constantly having to renew work permits, limits to travel and the emotional impact of having no certain status), these need to be considered by the decision-maker.[110] If no specific and well-developed arguments are made about the consequences of not having permanent residence, in turn, the decision-maker has no obligation to consider them.[111] In any case, as noted above, not all undesirable but unreturnable migrants will be able to apply for an exemption based on humanitarian and compassionate grounds. Indeed, this has led Bond to conclude that "(…) permanent residence is never available to individuals found inadmissible for security, human or international rights violations, or organised criminality, regardless of the severity or duration of the impediment to removal."[112] Thus, should the circumstances in their country of origin change; they may be removed from Canada regardless of their ties and length of stay in that country. In other words, regardless of the private and family life they developed in Canada.

In this regard, the impossibility of most of these migrants obtaining permanent residence may disproportionately interfere with their rights. When examining a similar scheme that was applied in the United Kingdom (hereaf-

108 See also s 112(3)(a) IRPA. Abovementioned ss 25(1) and 25.2(1) IRPA are exceptions to this general rule.

109 Mansouri v. Canada, 2018 FC 144 (Federal Court, 7 February 2018).

110 Mirza v. Canada, 2016 FC 510 (Federal Court, 6 May 2016), paras. 48–49.

111 Horvath v. Canada, 2016 FC 1261 (Federal Court, 14 November 2016), para. 42.

112 Bond, J. (2017), pp. 182–183. It should be noted, however, that Bond does not take the Ministerial discretion provided by s 25.2 IRPA into account, as she considers that when such discretion is used migrants would no longer be considered inadmissible and thus excludes them from her analysis.

ter UK), Singer noted that UK courts seemed reluctant to find that such restricted status represented a disproportionate interference with the rights of migrants. At the same time, however, the courts did hint at the fact that there may be a point in which an individual has been in the country for so long and the possibilities of removal are so remote that there is no alternative but to grant permanent residence.[113] This end point hinted at by UK courts was mainly based on the right to private and family life of the concerned migrants, a right that has no equivalent in the Canadian Charter of Rights and Freedoms. The rights to private and family life, however, are enshrined in articles 17 and 23 of the ICCPR, to which Canada is a party. Indeed, the UN Human Rights Committee has considered cases of (alleged) violations of undesirable migrants' private and family life by Canada in multiple occasions (although most of these decisions were related to removal and not the grant of permanent status).[114]

Despite such international commitment, the Federal Court of Appeal rejected the possibility of upholding respect for the Covenant internally, since Canada is a dualist country and so international law may serve to guide the application of domestic law, but will not on its own create rights for individuals.[115] Thus, the argument that undesirable migrants should, at some point, benefit from the right to permanent residence in view of their rights to family and private life is unlikely to succeed in domestic courts. In some cases, however, the unavailability of permanent residence may put Canada in violation of its international human rights obligations as it may constitute a disproportionate interference with the concerned migrants' rights to private and family life.[116] Furthermore:

113 Singer, S. (2017). "Undesirable and unreturnable" in the United Kingdom. Refugee Survey Quarterly, 36(1), 9–34, pp. 31–33. See also (Kardi, R (On the Application Of) v Secretary of State for the Home Department, [2014] EWCA Civ 934, para. 32 (United Kingdom: Court of Appeal (England and Wales) 10 July 2014)).

114 See, e.g. Communication No. 3041/2017, CCPR/C/125/D/3041/2017 (Human Rights Committee, 19 March 2019); Communication No. 2264/2013, CCPR/C/122/D/2264/2013 (Human Rights Committee, 6 April 2018); Communication No. 2387/2014, CCPR/C/117/D/2387/2014 (Human Rights Committee, 15 July 2016); Communication No. 2060/2011, CCPR/C/116/D/2060/2011 (Human Rights Committee, 11 March 2016).

115 Revell v. Canada, 2019 FCA 262, paras. 130–134.

116 This may indeed be the case of Harkat, described below. Harkat has been in Canada for more than 25 years, over 15 of them living under strict conditions, despite the fact that the danger he presents to the public is considered to be on the lower side of the spectrum.

> For those individuals who are unremovable and remain in Canada without being eligible for permanent residence, life can be extremely challenging. The IRPA authorises immigration detention in certain circumstances, including where there are security concerns, identity issues, a perceived flight-risk, or ongoing inquiries into potential criminality.[117]

Indeed, s 55(1) IRPA allows the detention of a migrant who is considered a danger to the public or is a flight risk, and thus, unlikely to attend inadmissibility procedures.[118] The next subsection thus analyses the possibility of detention for undesirable but unreturnable migrants.

5.4 *Immigration Detention*

As noted in the previous subsection, s 55(1) IRPA allows the detention of a migrant who is considered a danger to the public or is a flight risk and thus unlikely to attend inadmissibility procedures.[119] Once a migrant is detained, the reasons to continue detention must be reviewed within 48 hours, then again in seven days and after that once every 30 days (s 57 IRPA). Reasons for continued detention are similar to the reasons for initial detention and include, among others, being a danger to the public, being a flight risk, or undergoing an inadmissibility procedure (s 58 IRPA). The factors to be considered when determining whether someone is a danger to the public or a flight risks are mentioned in ss 245 and 246 IRPA Regulations. As examples, some of the factors that should be taken into account to consider whether someone is a danger to the public are association with a criminal organisation, involvement in people smuggling or trafficking in persons, conviction for a sexual offence, and conviction for drug trafficking.

When determining whether a migrant should be released or kept in detention, the ID (responsible for reviewing detention and making release decisions[120]) should take into account the reason for detention, the length of time spent in detention, the expected length of continued detention, unexplained delays on the side of the Canadian administration, the existence of alternatives to detention, and the best interest of directly affected children (s 248 IRPA Regulations). According to the Federal Court, "[I]n considering these factors, the same weight need not be given to each of them. They must

117 Bond, J. (2017), p. 184.
118 See also ss 44(4) and (5) IRPA; s 244 IRPA Regulations.
119 See also ss 44(4) and (5) IRPA; s 244 IRPA Regulations.
120 See ss 57 and 58 IRPA.

rather be considered as a whole, and the reasons for detention will affect how each factor should be weighed and assessed."[121]

Over the years, the Federal Court and Federal Court of Appeal have provided further guidance on detention decision-making. For example, in 2020, the Federal Court of Appeal affirmed that "[T]he factors in section 248 of the Regulation, as law, must be followed. But on top of that, in order for continued detention to be legal under IRPA, there must be a nexus between detention and an immigration purpose. If that is missing, detention under IRPA is no longer possible."[122] The Court continued to note that detention is not possible when there is no possibility of removal, however, as long as removal is possible, the exact date of removal does not need to be known. In fact, removal does not need to be reasonably foreseeable to justify an immigration nexus, as long as it is still a possibility.[123] In this regard, the Federal Court stated that when a valid removal order exists, any of the factors for continued detention (s 58 IRPA) can be relied on to justify detention, even if the removal order is not enforceable, for example, because it was stayed due to a positive PRRA decision.[124] Thus, as long as a valid removal order exists, removal does not need to be the reason of detention, instead, being a danger to the public or a flight risk can, on their own, justify detention.[125]

Besides the reasons justifying detention, the Federal Court has also addressed another factor that needs to be considered when deciding whether or not to release a detained migrant, that is, the length of detention. It should be noted that IRB guidelines state that "[D]etention, even for valid reasons, cannot be indefinite."[126] In its Case Law, however, the Federal Court noted in 2015 that "[T]he indefinite nature of an individual's detention is only one factor to be considered when conducting a detention review. Indeed, it is an error of law to treat the indefinite nature of detention as a determinative factor."[127] This was repeated the Court in 2016, when it said that "[I]t is now settled law that the

121 Canada v. Lunyamila, 2018 FC 211 (Federal Court, 23 February 2018), para. 48. This case summarises the detention scheme in Canada in paras. 43–48. A similar summary is provided by the Federal Court of Appeal in Lunyamila v. Canada, 2018 FCA 22, paras. 5–12.

122 Brown v. Canada, 2020 FCA 130 (Federal Court of Appeal, 7 August 2020), para. 90.

123 Ibid., paras. 91–93. In this case, however, the concerned migrant was undesirable but not unreturnable, as he did not fear harm upon return.

124 Canada v. Taino, 2020 FC 427 (Federal Court, 25 March 2020), paras. 43–55.

125 Canada v. Lunyamila, 2018 FC 211, para. 85.

126 Immigration and Refugee Board of Canada, Chairperson Guideline 2: Detention. Available at: https://irb.gc.ca/en/legal-policy/policies/Pages/GuideDir02.aspx#s3, para. 3.1.14.

127 Ahmed v. Canada, 2015 FC 876 (Federal Court, 17 July 2015), para. 26.

indefinite nature of an individual's detention under the IRPA is only one factor to be considered when conducting a detention review, and cannot be treated as determinative."[128] In both cases where the Court made such statements the concerned migrants had been considered a danger to the public by the Minister and the removal order against them was consequently enforceable despite the fact that they were initially owed protection, as they were considered to fall under the non-refoulement exception. Since the Federal Court found (as noted above) that even a non-enforceable removal order can justify detention, however, it is unlikely that the Court would have reached a different conclusion (that is, that indefinite detention is a determinative factor) if the removal order had been stayed. Overall, the Federal Court found that:

> So long as there is "a meaningful process of ongoing review that takes into account the context and circumstances of the individual case," and other relevant factors that include those set forth in s. 248 of the Regulations, the continued detention of an individual or the continued imposition of conditions of release will not contravene the liberty interests protected by s. 7 of the Canadian Charter of Rights and Freedoms [establishing the right to life, liberty and security of the person].[129]

Thus, lengthy and potentially indefinite detention is accepted in Canada.

In this regard, the UN Working Group on Arbitrary Detention said it could not accept the Canadian government's argument that the country did not allow indefinite detention. According to the Working Group:

> (…) the fact that the Act [IRPA] does not authorize indefinite detention explicitly does not exclude the possibility that such indefinite detention could nevertheless occur, which is why the Working Group has required that a maximum period for the detention in the course of migration proceedings must be set by legislation and that upon the expiry of the period for detention set by law, the detained person must be automatically released.[130]

The Working Group continued to note that to accept the government's views would be to "(…) accept that individuals could be caught up in an endless

128 Canada v. Lunyamila, 2016 FC 1199 (Federal Court 27 October 2016), para. 32.
129 Canada v. Ali, 2018 FC 552 (Federal Court, 29 May 2018), para. 46.
130 Opinion No. 7/2019 concerning Ebrahim Toure, A/HRC/WGAD/2019/7 (Working Group on Arbitrary Detention, 25 April 2019), para. 64.

cycle of periodic reviews of their detention without any prospect of actual release. This is a situation akin to indefinite detention, which cannot be remedied even by the most meaningful review of detention on an ongoing basis."[131]

Also concerned about the length of detention in Canada, the UN Committee against Torture called on Canada to "[R]efrain from detaining irregular migrants and asylum seekers for prolonged periods, use detention as a measure of last resort only and for as short a period as possible, and continue the application of non-custodial measures;"[132] as well as to "[E]stablish a reasonable time limit on the duration of administrative immigration detention."[133] Similar recommendations were made by the UN Human Rights Committee.[134] Consequently, Canada's detention scheme, by *de facto* allowing indefinite detention, can lead to a violation of migrant's right to liberty.

If, however, after considering all the relevant factors, the ID decides to release the concerned migrant, the Division may impose any conditions that it considers necessary (s 58(3) IRPA). The concerned person will then be in the community and will be able to benefit from a temporary status (as noted in the previous subsection) but may have important limitations attached to it. This possibility is discussed in the next subsection.

5.5 *Temporary Status on Conditions*

The previous subsection briefly mentioned that when the ID decides to release a migrant from detention, the Division may impose any conditions that it considers necessary (s 58(3) IRPA). For example, to ensure the migrant reports to immigration procedures and does not present a danger to the public.[135] According to the IRB guideline on detention:

> Release with minimum conditions without a deposit or a guarantee should be the first consideration, and [ID] members should apply conditions of release as necessary to manage heightened risk. Release conditions imposed should be tailored to the specific circumstances of the

131 Ibid. idem.

132 Committee against Torture (2018). Concluding observations on the seventh periodic report of Canada, para. 35.

133 Ibid. idem.

134 Human Rights Committee (2015). Concluding observations on the sixth periodic report of Canada, para. 12.

135 See, e.g. Canada v. Arook, 2019 FC 1130 (Federal Court, 3 September 2019), in which the Federal Court found a release decision reasonable as the ID member imposed the necessary measures to mitigate the migrant's flight risk and danger to the public.

> case. They should be linked to risk and be effective in adequately mitigating those risk factors. The principles of proportionality and attainability must apply to every interference with or deprivation of liberty. Each condition imposed is a restriction on a person's liberty. There should be a justification for each condition. Therefore, any condition that is imposed should have a rational connection to the circumstances of the case and the specific ground of detention. This connection should be clearly explained in the reasons for decision.[136]

At the same time, the Federal Court noted that:

> The conditions of release imposed on persons who are inadmissible on grounds of serious criminality and have been found to constitute a danger to the public in Canada must ensure that the public is not exposed to any meaningful risk of harm. That is to say, they must virtually eliminate any risk to public safety, or any flight risk, presented by the person in question.[137]

Bond noted that these conditions[138] may include:

> (…) house arrest, use of electronic monitoring devices, mail and phone intercepts, prohibitions on computer and phone use, security cameras installed and monitored by CBSA [Canada Border Services Agency], restrictions on the ability to leave a particular geographical region, prohibitions on visitors without prior CBSA approval, and more. Cumulatively, these conditions can be so restrictive that one individual notoriously requested a return to detention as a preferable alternative.[139]

Conditions are not reviewed automatically but a change in conditions may be requested by the Minister or the person concerned.[140]

136 Immigration and Refugee Board of Canada, Chairperson Guideline 2: Detention, para. 3.1.2. See also Canada v. Hamdan, 2019 FC 1129 (Federal Court, 3 September 2019), para. 67.

137 Canada v. Ali, 2018 FC 552, para. 7.

138 IRB guidelines contain a list of conditions of release that may be resorted to by the ID. See Immigration and Refugee Board of Canada, Chairperson Guideline 2, para. 3.2.2.

139 Bond, J. (2017), p. 184.

140 Immigration and Refugee Board of Canada, Chairperson Guideline 2: Detention, para. 3.4.

In this regard, the case of Mohamed Harkat serves to illustrate the long-term use of multiple release conditions. Harkat arrived in Canada in 1995 and was granted refugee status in 1997. In 2002, he was considered inadmissible on grounds of national security and was detained until 2006, when he was released under strict conditions.[141] Over the years, the conditions of his release were changed[142] and revised by the Federal Court multiple times. At the time of writing, the last review of Harkat's release conditions by the Federal Court was in 2020, almost 15 years after his release. In that occasion, the Federal Court noted that "(…) the passage of time favours the relaxation of the conditions" and that "(…) the danger posed by Mr. Harkat continues to be situated at the lower end of the spectrum."[143] Despite this and the fact that the Federal Court relaxed some of the release conditions on that occasion, the Court continued to accept conditions limiting Harkat's use of mobile phones, computers and the internet, obliging him to provide the username and passwords of his emails and social media accounts to the Canada Border Services Agency, submitting his computer for inspection by the Agency every three months, limiting his possibilities to travel without notifying the Agency to a maximum of 96 hours within Ontario and Quebec, and being subjected to periodic physical surveillance, among others.[144] Thus, despite guidance determining that conditions of release should be linked to the risk factors, that each condition must be justified in view of the circumstances of the case and that the principle of proportionality should be followed,[145] undesirable but unreturnable migrants may still be subjected to multiple restrictions for lengthy periods, which may be a disproportionate interference with their rights.

Indeed, the most recent Federal Court decisions concerning the conditions Harkat is subjected to seem to assign disproportionate weight to a possible risk he presents to Canadian society. In the abovementioned 2020 decision, the Federal Court refers to its previous 2018 decision when addressing whether Harkat poses a danger to society, noting not much has changed

141 Harkat (Re), 2018 FC 62 (Federal Court, 23 January 2018), paras. 5–6.

142 According to IRB guidelines, "[A]n application for a change of conditions of release may be made by the Minister, the person concerned or his or her counsel." Immigration and Refugee Board of Canada, Chairperson Guideline 2: Detention, para. 3.4.1.

143 Harkat (Re), 2020 FC 715 (Federal Court, 19 June 2020), para. 33.

144 See ibid.

145 Immigration and Refugee Board of Canada, Chairperson Guideline 2, para. 3.1.2. See also Canada v. Hamdan, 2019 FC 1129, para. 67.

since then.[146] In the 2018 decision, the Court explains that the initial reasons behind the finding that Harkat was a danger to the community in 2002 were based on his involvement with a terrorist group and his connections to known terrorists.[147] In the same decision, the Federal Court notes that the last report regarding the danger Harkat posed dates from 2009, that no new evidence of his involvement in dangerous activities since had been presented, and that he had complied with the conditions imposed on him since 2006.[148] Overall, in the 2018 decision, the Federal Court concluded as follows:

> I am cognizant of the fact that the Ministers have adduced no new evidence regarding the level of danger posed by Mr. Harkat. The absence of such evidence clearly weighs in favour of Mr. Harkat. That being said, I cannot totally discount the findings contained in the decision upholding the security certificate and previous conditions review decisions. While the passage of time as well as Mr. Harkat's overall compliance with the conditions of release have significantly attenuated the level of danger he poses, I find that a danger still remains even though it is unclear to me whether the effectiveness of the conditions of release is responsible for the reduced threat or whether Mr. Harkat has truly turned a new leaf and abandoned his past ideologies.[149]

In making such a conclusion in 2018 and then following it in 2020, the Federal Court seems to have imposed an unattainable standard on Harkat. This is because despite the fact that no new evidence regarding the danger he posed to the community had been presented for over 10 years (in 2020) and that he complied with virtually all conditions of his release for almost 15 years, it was still considered that the finding that he presented a danger to the community (made in 2002 and last updated in 2009) could not be dismissed. As mentioned in Section 5.2, in a different case concerning the consideration of humanitarian and compassionate factors to exempt someone with a criminal history from an inadmissibility finding, the Federal Court stated that decision-makers should not impose unattainable standards on migrants, noting that

146 Harkat (Re), 2020 FC 715, paras. 29–30.

147 Harkat (Re), 2018 FC 62, paras. 15, 21, 37, 49 and 53.

148 Ibid., para. 61. Although in 2020 the Federal Court did find that he had breached a condition by changing his email password – allegedly unintendingly – without informing the Canada Border Service Agency. See Harkat (Re), 2020 FC 715, para. 23.

149 Harkat (Re), 2018 FC 62, para. 51.

it is impossible to guarantee that any person will not commit a criminal offence.[150] It must be recognised that this case related to a different procedure and Canada's IRPA does consider inadmissibility on security grounds to be more serious than inadmissibility based on criminality. However, imposing an unattainable standard in cases such as that of Harkat would be incompatible with existing guidance emphasising proportionality and the need for measures to be directly linked to risk factors. It may also be incompatible with the international human rights framework applicable to Canada, which similarly imposes limits on restrictions to human rights. Indeed, as it is impossible to guarantee that a person will not engage in criminal or terrorist acts, requiring such a standard would lead to a virtual risk of danger to the community always outweighing human rights concerns. Thus, when in practice an unattainable standard is applied to justify the conditions of release of an undesirable but unreturnable migrant, these conditions are not in compliance with the applicable human rights framework.

6 Conclusions: So Close and Yet So Far

The path(s) undesirable but unreturnable migrants may follow in Canada can be summarised in a simplified way in Figure 4.1.

To unpack this scheme, it can be said that Canada's main piece of immigration legislation, the IRPA, has as its objectives both the protection of those who may face danger in their country of origin and the denial of access to the Canadian territory to persons who are criminals or security risks (s 3 IRPA). To achieve the former, the IRPA grants protection to refugees, in accordance with the Refugee Convention, and to those who cannot be returned to their country of origin due to human rights concerns. This protection materialises through the asylum procedure as well as other remedies such as the PRRA, which aims to prevent the removal of migrants in violation of non-refoulement. To achieve the latter, in turn, the IRPA denies access to or requires to leave Canada those who are considered inadmissible due to their involvement in criminal activities or for being deemed a threat to security.

When it comes to undesirable but unreturnable migrants, however, these two objectives of the IRPA are likely to clash, as these migrants are both in need of protection and, *a priori*, part of the group of individuals the IRPA wishes to keep away from Canada. In such cases, the IRPA tries to reconcile

150 Aghayere v. Canada, 2018 FC 869, para. 24.

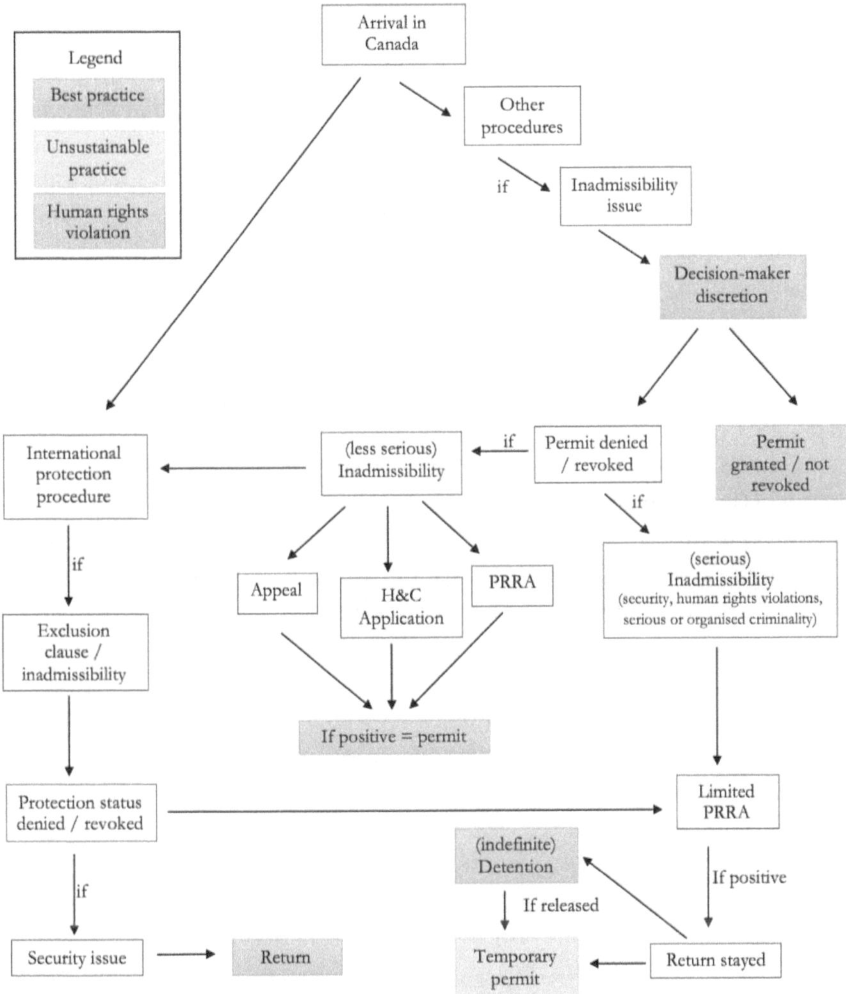

FIGURE 4.1 Paths for undesirable but unreturnable migrants in Canada

these opposing interests through mechanisms that allow undesirable migrants to be exempted from their inadmissibility to Canada when their personal circumstances, including humanitarian and compassionate factors, would favour such an outcome. In practice, this leads to the reduction of the number of undesirable migrants in Canada and provides a long-term solution to some of those initially deemed undesirable, as they can thus be granted permanent residence in the country.

Those who fall under the most serious cases of inadmissibility (that is, security concerns, international crimes or organised criminality), however, are unlikely to benefit from such relief as the IRPA limits their access to it. Furthermore, not all those who can request such a relief will be granted it, as the individual circumstances of their case may not lead to a positive outcome. These migrants may be subjected to different measures. Some of them may be returned to a place where they face irreparable harm, in violation of non-derogable human rights. This is because the IRPA provides an exception to both refugee law and human rights non-refoulement when undesirable migrants are considered a danger to the public in Canada, a possibility that has been criticised by human rights bodies.

Among the migrants who are not removed from Canada, some of them may be detained, if they are considered a flight risk or a danger to the community. Canadian law does not prescribe a maximum time limit for detention, which, in practice, can lead to lengthy and potentially indefinite detention. Indefinite detention is *per se* arbitrary and thus constitutes a violation of the right to liberty of those subjected to it.

Others, in turn, will be in liberty and allowed to remain in Canada due to the country's non-refoulement obligations towards them. In this case, they can apply for temporary study and work permits. As they are undesirable, however, the IRPA prevents them from obtaining permanent residence and thus, should the situation in their country of origin change; they may be removed, regardless of how long they have remained in Canada and of their ties to the country. In some cases, this may constitute a disproportionate interference with their rights to private and family life. Furthermore, some of these migrants may be subjected to certain conditions, which can be attached to the stay of their removal (due to non-refoulement) or their release from detention. In some cases, such conditions can last for several years and be very restrictive in limiting the movements and communications of those subjected to them, even when the risk they supposedly present is considered low. When that is the case, these conditions can also represent a disproportionate interference with their rights.

In sum, Canada's legal system limits the possibilities of removing unreturnable migrants through several remedies in place to assess the country's non-refoulement obligations. Despite this, a non-refoulement exception exists, for both refugee law and human rights law non-refoulement, allowing the return of certain migrants in violation of their non-derogable rights. Canada's IRPA also grants undesirable migrants different possibilities to obtain an exception to their inadmissibility and thus obtain permanent status in the country. For certain types of inadmissibility, however, these options are limited and these migrants may be subjected to detention or life in the community under strict conditions and with no possibility of permanent residence. In certain situations, these options will lead to a violation of their rights to liberty and private and family life. Thus, Canada's measures applied to undesirable but unreturnable migrants present both best practices and non-human-rights-compliant solutions.

CHAPTER 5

Towards a Solution for Undesirable but Unreturnable Migrants

1 Introduction[1]

After having studied at length the practices in place in three different countries, this concluding chapter will make some comparative remarks regarding the way the three States under analysis regulate the situation of undesirable but unreturnable migrants. These findings will then serve as the building blocks for proposing a solution to regulate the situation of these migrants.

In this regard, this chapter will propose to integrate the possibility to grant limited statuses to currently excluded migrants in international protection procedures, detailing how such statuses would be embedded in such procedures, which rights would be associated with them, and how to determine the measures that may be applied to limit such statuses. This proposal is based on best practices observed in the case studies.

2 Who Are the Undesirables?

All three countries analysed in this book have provisions in their national legislations (mainly the Australian Migration Act, the Belgian 1980 Migration Law and the Canadian IRPA) that aim to deny or withdraw the right to enter or stay in their territory to undesirable migrants. In this regard, the countries under assessment share three important similarities in their legal frameworks concerning who is an undesirable migrant.

First, all analysed States have provisions regarding undesirability that apply specifically to international protection procedures. In the three countries, these provisions closely follow article 1F of the Refugee Convention. This article serves to exclude from refugee protection those who commit international crimes, serious non-political crimes and acts that are contrary to the purposes and principles of the United Nations (hereafter UN). In all three States, courts

1 The main findings of this chapter were published in Zomignani Barboza, J. (2024). International Protection for Criminals: To Grant or Not to Grant? Lessons from Australia, Belgium, and Canada. International Journal of Refugee Law, 36(3), 223–247.

 | DOI:10.1163/9789004719910_007

provided clarifications as to the practical application of these provisions. For example, courts have deemed that membership in an organisation that commits international crimes alone is not sufficient for an exclusion finding and that defences such as duress should be taken into account.[2] At the same time, membership to terrorist organisations alone has been considered enough to justify exclusion.[3] Courts in Australia and Belgium have also considered that the crimes identified in article 1F can lead to exclusion regardless of whether the concerned person no longer represents a threat to society or has already completed their criminal sentence for the crime.[4] Lastly, regarding undesirables in international protection procedures, it is worth noting that, apart from article 1F, Australia[5] and Belgium[6] also frame the non-refoulement exception prescribed in article 33(2) of the Refugee Convention[7] as an additional exclusion clause in protection procedures. Canada, in turn, more closely follows the Refugee Convention and frames the situations related to article 33(2) as an exception to the principle of non-refoulement nationally, in spite of its human rights obligations.[8] Despite the different goals of the provision in the different countries, all three States see the national security component of article 33(2) as a forward-looking assessment and thus place (re)offending at the centre of the analysis.[9]

Second, the three analysed countries also include more general provisions in their legislation that may serve to consider any migrant undesirable. Belgium bases most of these provisions on the concerned migrant posing a threat to national security or public order, concepts that are not defined in national law.[10] Australia[11] and Canada,[12] in turn, provide more descriptive provisions regarding those who should not be allowed to enter or remain in their territo-

2 See Chapter 2, Section 3.1; Chapter 3, Section 3.1.1; and Chapter 4, Section 3.1.

3 This has been expressed by courts in Belgium and Canada. In Australia, it has not been said explicitly. See Chapter 2, Section 3.2; Chapter 3, Section 3.1.3; and Chapter 4, Section 3.3.

4 See Chapter 2, Section 3.2; and Chapter 3, Section 3.1.1.

5 See Chapter 2, Section 3.3.

6 See Chapter 3, Section 3.2.

7 As a reminder, this article states that the benefit of non-refoulement cannot "be claimed by a refugee whom there are reasonable grounds for regarding as a danger to the security of the country in which he is, or who, having been convicted by a final judgment of a particularly serious crime, constitutes a danger to the community of that country."

8 See Chapter 4, Section 5.1.

9 See Chapter 2, Section 3.3; Chapter 3, Section 3.2.1; and Chapter 4, Section 5.1.

10 See Chapter 3, Section 3.2.

11 See Chapter 2, Section 3.

12 See Chapter 4, Section 3.

ries. For example, both countries determine that those convicted to a certain amount of time in prison will be considered undesirable.[13] While in all three States most situations that lead to undesirability involve the commission of criminal activities, all analysed States provide that certain migrants may be considered undesirable even in the absence of a criminal conviction. This latter possibility is usually related to cases that involve undefined concepts such as national security, terrorism and public order, which can be challenging for decision-makers to interpret and/or lead to arbitrary decisions.[14]

Third, in cases where the right to enter or stay in the country is denied or withdrawn due a migrant's undesirability, all three countries require that multiple aspects, including, for example, the person's ties to the host country, be assessed.[15] Thus, decision-makers are called upon to balance the person's undesirability with other factors that may favour their stay in the country. This balancing exercise may in practice serve to evaluate whether the concerned migrant's rights to private and family life would not be disproportionately interfered with in case of withdrawal of status, as most factors that need to be considered in such assessment concern these rights. It also serves to reduce the pool of undesirable migrants, as some may, after the consideration of these elements, not be deemed undesirable. Furthermore, both Belgium and Canada offer greater protection to those who have been in the country for longer by setting higher thresholds for them to be considered undesirable in their laws,[16] further contributing to the reduction of the undesirable population in those countries. It should be cautioned, however, that decision-makers' discretion can play an important role in the aforementioned balancing exercise and thus a human rights-based approach may not always be taken.

3 Who Are the Unreturnable Migrants?

3.1 *International Protection as the Main Procedure to Assess Non-refoulement Claims*

In all three analysed States, a request for protection (or asylum) is the main procedure during which a migrant's non-refoulement claims will be ass-

---

13 See Chapter 2, Section 3.5; and Chapter 4, Section 3.2.

14 See e.g., Chapter 2, Section 3.3; Chapter 3, Section 3.2.1; and Chapter 4, Sections 3.2.1 and 3.4.

15 See Chapter 2, Section 3.6; Chapter 3, Section 3.2.1; and Chapter 4, Section 3.6.

16 See Chapter 3, Section 3.2.2; and Chapter 4, Section 3.2.

essed.[17] In this regard, all three analysed countries are parties to the Refugee Convention and thus added provisions in their national laws to internalise their international obligations deriving from the Convention. National law clarifies the domestic interpretation of the Refugee Convention. For example, both Australia[18] and Belgium[19] have enacted provisions referring explicitly to the internal flight alternative principle and its application in the national context. In this regard, some national clarifications seem to restrict the application of the Refugee Convention nationally. For example, Australia does not require that the area of internal relocation (in cases where there is an internal flight alternative) be practically, safely, and legally accessible to the individual, as suggested by the UN High Commissioner for Refugees (hereafter UNHCR) (and as this principle is applied in the EU context).[20] At the same time, however, all three countries go beyond the Refugee Convention and extend (subsidiary or complementary) protection[21] to those who cannot be returned to their country of origin due to human rights concerns. Thus, an international protection procedure in all three countries should assess non-refoulement from both a refugee law and a human rights law perspective.

In practice, however, migrants in Australia and Belgium have questioned whether such procedures would actually consider their non-refoulement claims. According to these migrants, since the international protection procedure contains exclusion clauses (as noted in the previous section), they argued that their claims could be dismissed without assessment if they were found to be excluded. The acceptance of this argument by Australian courts has led the Australian Minister for Immigration, Citizenship, Migrant Services and Multicultural Affairs to issue guidance to their Department calling on decision-makers to assess protection related claims (inclusion clauses) before exclusion clauses.[22] In Belgium, in turn, case law on exclusion seems to indicate that exclusion clauses can be assessed before inclusion in the country and, should a person be considered excluded, protection related claims do not need to be evaluated. At the same time, however, Belgian law determines that even if someone is excluded from protection, the commissioner general for refugees and stateless persons (in charge of asylum decisions) still needs to

17 See Chapter 2, Section 4.1; Chapter 3, Section 4.1; and Chapter 4, Section 4.1.

18 See Chapter 2, Section 4.1.

19 See Chapter 3, Section 4.1. Article 8 of the upcoming Qualification Regulation requires the consideration of internal flight alternative in all international protection cases.

20 Other ways in which Australia limits the application of the Refugee Convention nationally are presented in Section 4.1 of Chapter 2.

21 See Chapter 2, Section 4.1; Chapter 3, Section 4.1; and Chapter 4, Section 4.1.

22 See Chapter 2, Section 4.2.

assess whether their return would be compatible with non-refoulement.[23] These facts thus indicate that all those who make an application for international protection in these countries will have their protection-related claims taken into account, even if they are denied a protection status. In Canada, in turn, once an applicant has been considered excluded, their protection claims do not need to be considered.[24]

All three countries, however, bar certain third country nationals from applying for asylum. In Belgium, requests for protection will be deemed inadmissible when it is considered that, with regards to the applicant, there is a first country of asylum, a safe country of origin or a safe third country (articles 57/6, 57/6/1 and 57/6/6, 1980 Migration Law). Similar provisions can be found in Australia (ss 91A to 91D Migration Act) and Canada (s 101(1)(c.1), (d) and (e) IRPA). While these provisions presume that the concerned person has protection elsewhere and thus can benefit from the provisions of the Refugee Convention in another country, Australia and Canada also bar certain migrants who are not expected to have protection somewhere else from applying for protection nationally. This is because Australia bars unlawful maritime arrivals (that is, those who arrive in Australia irregularly by boat) from applying to any visa in the country,[25] unless the Minister exceptionally allows them to (s 46A Migration Act). Canada, in turn, considers ineligible international protection applications made by those who were found inadmissible to the country for reasons of security, violating human or international rights, serious criminality or organised criminality (s 101(1)(f) IRPA). Thus, not all migrants will have access to the international protection procedure in the analysed countries. Considering the absolute character of non-refoulement obligations, however, other mechanisms are prescribed to ensure migrants in these countries can have their non-refoulement claims assessed, as will be shown in the next section.

---

23 See Chapter 3, Section 4.2.

24 See Immigration and Refugee Board of Canada (31 December 2020), Interpretation of Convention Refugee and Person in Need of Protection in the Case Law, Chapter 11 – Article 1F, section 11.6. Available at: https://www.irb-cisr.gc.ca/en/legal-policy/legal-concepts/Pages/RefDef11.aspx#n116.

25 A similar bar being envisaged in the United Kingdom (UK) was considered to be "(…) clearly in breach of the UK's obligations under the 1951 Convention relating to the Status of Refugees." Singer, S. (14 March 2023). Undesirable but Unreturnable? Policy implications of the UK's Illegal Migration Bill. RLI Blog on Refugee Law and Forced Migration. Available at: https://rli.blogs.sas.ac.uk/2023/03/14/undesirable-but-unreturnable-policy-implications-of-the-uks-illegal-migration-bill/?utm_source=Refugee+Law+Initiative&utm_campaign=102cd30e2d-EMAIL_CAMPAIGN_2017_10_03_COPY_01&utm_medium=email&utm_term=0_304c0b75a9-102cd30e2d-581036941.

3.2 *Assessing Non-refoulement Outside International Protection Procedures*

As noted above, all States under study envisage means other than an international protection application through which non-refoulement claims will be assessed.

In Australia, there is no specific procedure, apart from a protection visa application that migrants can turn to, in order to have their non-refoulement claims assessed. However, when a decision-maker decides to deny or cancel a visa because the concerned migrant is deemed undesirable, decision-makers are asked to take non-refoulement claims into account.[26]

In Belgium, unlike in Australia and in Canada, there is a specific procedure in place for cases in which the feared harm upon return relates to a medical condition of the concerned migrant.[27] No other specific procedure exists to assess non-refoulement claims, however, before a removal decision is made, Belgian law requires decision-makers to give migrants the opportunity to present arguments (such as non-refoulement) that could prevent such a decision. Furthermore, the Belgian Council of State and the Aliens Litigation Council have both indicated that decision-makers should always consider non-refoulement before making a removal decision.[28]

Canada, in turn, unlike Australia and Belgium, has a specific procedure, apart from the international protection one, dedicated to assessing non-refoulement risks a migrant may face upon return. This procedure is the pre-removal risk assessment (hereafter PRRA),[29] which is available to most of those subjected to removal from Canada, but the consequences of which may be different for undesirable migrants.[30] In this regard, a positive PRRA may lead to the granting of refugee status, however, for migrants who were found inadmissible on grounds of security, violating human or international rights, organised criminality or serious criminality,[31] as well as excluded asylum seekers (according to article 1F Refugee Convention), a positive PRRA will

26 See Chapter 2, Section 4.3.

27 See Chapter 3, Section 4.2.

28 See Chapter 3, Section 4.3.

29 See s 112 IRPA; s 160 IRPA Regulations.

30 See Chapter 4, Section 4.2.

31 This restriction will not apply to those found inadmissible for serious criminality when they were convicted in Canada to a term of imprisonment of less than two years or to those convicted outside Canada for an offence that, if committed in Canada, would be punishable by a maximum term of imprisonment of at least 10 years, unless they were considered excluded from refugee protection under article 1F Refugee Convention (s 113 (e) IRPA). See also Gurbuz v. Canada, 2018 FC 684 (Federal Court, 6 July 2018), para. 34.

not grant them protection status but instead will halt their removal from Canada.

In sum, it can be concluded that, while only Canada has a specific procedure migrants can turn to in order to have their non-refoulement claims assessed, all three countries have mechanisms in place to ensure claims of harm upon return are taken into account before a migrant is removed.

Having identified who are undesirable migrants and who are unreturnable migrants in the countries under study, the next section will thus turn to the fate undesirable but unreturnable migrants face in the analysed States.

4 Solutions for Undesirable but Unreturnable Migrants: An Overview of Existing Measures

The previous chapters of this book showed that States have a web of measures and processes in place that undesirable but unreturnable migrants may find themselves caught in. This section will disentangle part of this web by presenting the main measures applied in the States under study to regulate the situation of undesirable but unreturnable migrants. These include two practices that violate internationally recognised human rights (namely, return to harm and indefinite detention); two best practices (namely the requirement to always balance undesirability with factors that may favour continued stay and the possibility to grant permanent residence in the country in exceptional circumstances); and two unsustainable practices (namely limbo and temporary stay with no possibility of obtaining permanent residence).

Before briefly outlining these practices, however, a short mention of absent practices is warranted. In this regard, diplomatic assurances (discussed in Section 4.1 of Chapter 1) did not appear in the analysed law, Case Law and literature regarding the countries under study, except in one case decided by the UN Committee against Torture regarding Canada.[32] In that case, however, the assurances did not influence the Committee's conclusion that there was no risk of torture upon return for the concerned migrant. This lack of information about the use of such assurances, however, does not mean they are not resorted to by States, just that they are not regulated by national law.

Similarly, prosecution of crimes committed before arrival in the host country (discussed in Section 4.2 of Chapter 1) also only appeared once, in a case decided in Belgium, in which a man was prosecuted in Belgium for having

32 Communication No. 488/2012, CAT/C/63/D/488/2012 (Committee against Torture, 11 May 2018).

been involved in the Rwandan genocide.[33] In this one case, it was clear that prosecution does not remove one's undesirability as, even after having completed his criminal sentence, the concerned migrant was still denied the right to stay in Belgium.

Now turning to the above-mentioned observed practices, the first human rights violation, that is, return in disrespect of non-refoulement, takes place in all three States under analysis, despite it being forbidden by law in Australia[34] and Belgium.[35] This is because the Australian Migration Act does allow for voluntary return to a place where migrants may suffer harm. As migrants may opt for that in situations where they find themselves in indefinite detention, the voluntariness of such a decision can be questioned and thus these returns may in practice amount to a violation of non-refoulement by Australia.

In Belgium, in turn, international human rights monitoring bodies questioned the practical implementation of the national legal provisions protecting migrants against non-refoulement. In this regard, they noted that the assessment made regarding the possible harm a migrant may face upon return does not always take into account all the relevant individual circumstances of the case at hand and may lead to removals in violation of non-refoulement.

Lastly, Canada is the only one of the three States that explicitly contains an exception to non-refoulement in its domestic law, mirroring the wording of article 33(2) of the Refugee Convention.[36] In this regard, the Federal Court found that the test to allow the overruling of the non-refoulement principle sets a very high threshold and is a different test from inadmissibility (which determines who is undesirable).[37] In practice, however, it has been said that Canada may deliberately use suspect deportations in violation of non-refoulement to handle problematic cases,[38] pointing to the fact that the fate of some undesirable but unreturnable migrants in Canada may be return to harm.

---

33 See Chapter 3, Section 3.1.1.

34 See Chapter 2, Section 5.3.

35 See Chapter 3, Section 5.3.

36 See Chapter 4, Section 5.1.

37 Yousif v. Canada, 2019 FC 128 (Federal Court, 30 January 2019), para. 23.

38 Bond, J. (2017). Unwanted but Unremovable: Canada's Treatment of "Criminal" Migrants Who Cannot be Removed. Refugee Survey Quarterly, 36(1), 168–186, p. 183. See also Inter-American Commission on Human Rights, Follow-up of the recommendations of the IACHR Report on asylum seekers in Canada (2000) (hearing), 7 September 2017. Available at: https://www.oas.org/en/iachr/sessions/hearings.asp?Country=CAN&Topic=0&Year=2017.

In this regard, all three States analysed were criticised by human rights monitoring bodies about their legislation and/or practices concerning return.[39]

The second practice that violates human rights, that is, indefinite detention[40] is still in place in Australia[41] and Canada.[42] This practice was also criticised by human rights monitoring bodies.[43]

The first best practice, that is, the requirement to always balance undesirability with factors that may favour continued stay before denying or revoking a visa or permit, in turn, is observed in all three analysed States.[44] This practice is very similar to what scholars involved in the Refugee Law Initiative research project[45] on undesirable but unreturnable migrants suggested as the most promising long-term solution for these migrants. In this regard, they suggested that decision-makers should

> (…) weigh the interests of the state to prolong the status of undesirability (level of acute security threat, seriousness of the alleged crimes, mode of complicity, level of responsibility) against the UBU's [undesirable but unreturnable] interests of having the status of undesirability

---

39 See Chapter 2, Section 5.3; Chapter 3, Section 5.3; and Chapter 4, Section 5.1.

40 In Belgium, migrants who are denied a permit or have their permit withdrawn may be placed in detention to ensure their removal from the territory. Belgian law, however, reinforces the absolute character of non-refoulement and thus, should a migrant in detention show that they would face a risk of harm upon return, their removal will be annulled. In this case, as the migration link (that is, return) no longer exists, detention would consequently be deprived of a legal basis. Indeed, in this regard, the CCE noted that a coercive measure such as detention presupposes that the return is being envisaged and, when return is not possible, it cannot stand. It said: "Le Conseil rappelle que l'objectif d'une mesure d'éloignement est précisément l'éloignement du territoire belge et que si celui-ci n'est pas possible au moment de la prise de l'acte, la mesure perd sa finalité première" (Arrêt n° 211 193, (Conseil du Contentieux des Etrangers, 18 October 2018), p. 5. See also: Arrêt n° 213 616, (Conseil du Contentieux des Etrangers 6 December 2018), p. 6; Arrêt n° 213 699, (Conseil du Contentieux des Etrangers, 10 December 2018), p. 12; Arrêt n° 214 622, (Conseil du Contentieux des Etrangers, 26 December 2018), p. 9; Arrêt n° 228 708, (Conseil du Contentieux des Etrangers, 13 November 2019), p. 12. Detention of undesirable but unreturnable migrants in Belgium is consequently expected to be short-lived, unlike in Australia and Canada where it can become indefinite. See Chapter 3, Section 5.2.

41 See Chapter 2, Section 5.1. It should be noted, however, that recent developments in Australia may reduce the use of this practice. See Chapter 2, Section 5.5.

42 See Chapter 4, Section 5.4.

43 See Chapter 2, Section 5.1; and Chapter 4, Section 5.4.

44 See Chapter 2, Section 3.6; Chapter 3, Section 3.2.1; and Chapter 4, Section 3.6.

45 Project website: https://rli.sas.ac.uk/projects-0/undesirable-unreturnable-migrants.

lifted (social, psychological, physical impact of protracted limbo situation).[46]

Indeed, granting or continuing the right to stay of undesirable but unreturnable migrants seems to be the only long-term solution that countries apply to regulate the situation of these migrants. Thus, such balancing, applied in all three States analysed in this book, can assist in reducing the number of migrants considered undesirable in any given country.

The second best practice, that is, the possibility to grant permanent right to stay in exceptional circumstances, is provided in all three analysed States,[47] but, for different reasons, this option is often limited for undesirable but unreturnable migrants.[48]

As for the two unsustainable practices, they are, first, leaving migrants in limbo (Belgium)[49] and, second, the grant of temporary permits (Canada).[50] As noted in the previous chapters, however, not only do these measures not provide for long-term solutions but they may also, in practice, lead to a violation of rights.

Limbo, as noted in Section 4.4 of Chapter 1, severely limits a person's access to rights, as without legal status they will have difficulties providing for themselves. Furthermore, this may go against States' interest of national security and public order since, as also mentioned in that section, having no means of survival, migrants in limbo may resort to begging or even stealing. Similarly, having no status can have detrimental effects on a person's mental health and further stimulate the commission of crimes, either for survival or out of frustration.

---

46 Refugee Law Initiative, Arts & Humanities Research Council and Center for International Criminal Justice (2016). Undesirable and Unreturnable? Policy challenges around excluded asylum seekers and other migrants suspected of serious criminality who cannot be removed (Policy brief), p. 5.

47 See Chapter 2, Section 5.2; Chapter 3, Section 5.1; and Chapter 4, Section 5.2.

48 Rikhof reached this same conclusion when analysing a broader sample of countries. He said: "[W]hile humanitarian solutions look useful on the surface, the countries under consideration are reluctant to extend this possibility to persons with a criminal background. When setting out general rules for humanitarian residence for persons who cannot be removed, an exception is frequently made for persons who have committed serious crimes or are a danger to the public order or national security." Rikhof, J. (2023) Exclusion and Refoulement: Criminality in International and Domestic Refugee Law. Irwin Law Inc., p. 735.

49 See Chapter 3, Section 5.4.

50 See Chapter 4, Section 5.3. This may also be the case in Australia following the legislative changes that took place in 2023, as noted in Section 5.5 of Chapter 2.

As for the temporary permits in Canada,[51] which are available for those who obtained a positive result in a limited PRRA, in the long-term, they can lead to situations such as the one Mohamed Harkat finds himself in. After over a decade in freedom in Canada, Harkat is still subjected to strict conditions, possibly in violation of his right to private life, and may still be subjected to return in violation of non-refoulement and/or his family and private life in Canada. Thus, while in the short-term this may provide a more robust solution than limbo, it is not a sustainable one.

Drawing lessons from the above analysis of the findings of the case studies, the next section will propose an outline for a national solution that could be adopted by States to regulate the situation of undesirable but unreturnable migrants.

5 Proposing a Solution for Undesirable but Unreturnable Migrants

As explained in the introduction to this book, the guiding question for this work was: what lessons can be learned from the experiences of Australia, Belgium and Canada when regulating the situation of undesirable but unreturnable migrants? Thus, building on the analysis of the practices in place in these countries, the remainder of this chapter will propose a solution to regulate the situation of undesirable but unreturnable migrants that could be applied by States faced with this challenge.

As shown throughout this book, regulating the situation of these migrants is a challenge for States, which often opt to apply solutions that either violate human rights law or are unsustainable. While all States somewhat follow what has been suggested by scholars in this field and balance undesirability with factors that may favour continued stay of undesirable but unreturnable migrants before denying or revoking a visa or permit, not all migrants will be allowed to enter or remain in the host country after such balancing exercise. Indeed, it was recognised by the scholars who proposed weighing the interests of the State to prolong the status of undesirability against the concerned migrants' interests of having the status of undesirability lifted that even if this is done, some individuals will not benefit from such exercise.[52]

---

51 As noted above, a similar scheme now also exists in Australia following the legislative changes that took place in 2023, as explained in Section 5.5 of Chapter 2.

52 Refugee Law Initiative, Arts & Humanities Research Council and Center for International Criminal Justice (2016), p. 5.

The solution proposed in this book thus fills a gap as it could be applied to all undesirable but unreturnable migrants, including those who do not benefit from the balancing exercise proposed by scholars and applied in the analysed States. Recognising such weighing as a best practice, however, the proposed solution incorporates it as a part of what is proposed, as will be shown below.

Before describing the proposed solution, some preliminary remarks are warranted. As the in-depth study of the practices in place in three different countries showed, it is clear that the issue of undesirable but unreturnable migrants is multi-layered[53] and that a solution needs to be more encompassing than simply proposing one measure. Consequently, the proposed solution needs to take into account different elements, including, for example, whether the concerned migrant poses a current threat to the State they are in, the entitlement of the concerned migrant to refugee status, and whether they are a new arrival or a long settler. These elements are important since even though national security and involvement in criminal acts can justify migration decisions and, in certain cases, limitations to rights, certain rights are owed to all migrants regardless of their status[54] and refugees are further entitled to certain rights regardless of whether they are considered dangerous.[55] Those who have been in the country for longer, in turn, are in a different situation than early arrivals. In this regard, long settlers are likely to have developed ties to the host country, which means the withdrawal of their right to stay and potential removal could interfere with their right to private and family life. They thus often receive greater protection against loss of status, as is the case in Belgium and Canada.[56] They may also be entitled to more rights due to the longevity of their stay as they may, for example, be permanent residents and thus entitled to socio-economic rights reserved to migrants with an unlimited right to stay.[57] Lastly, it is also important to recog-

---

53 This was also recognised by the scholars working on the Refugee Law Initiative research project on undesirable but unreturnable migrants, who noted that: "[T]he group of UBUs [undesirable but unreturnable migirants] is highly diverse." Ibid., p. 4.

54 See Chapter 1, Section 4.4.

55 See e.g. Chapter 1, Section 3.4.

56 See Section 2 above.

57 Besides this greater entitlement often offered to permanent residents, Pijnenburg noted that the duty of progressive realisation of Covenant rights imposed on States by the International Covenant on Economic, Social and Cultural Rights (ICESCR) means that "States' obligations towards people on the move [migrants] *de facto* increase over time" (Pijnenburg, A. (2021). At the Frontiers of State Responsibility: Socio-economic Rights and Cooperation on Migration (1st ed.). Intersentia, p. 120). When it comes to refugees, Chetail argues that the Refugee Convention envisages a progressive entitlement of rights and benefits to refugees, equating refugee status to an 'assimilative path' (Chetail,

nise that undesirable but unreturnable long settlers are frequently considered undesirable due to acts committed in the host country, which can be subjected to that country's criminal justice system. These different elements thus need to be properly reflected in the proposed solution.

Furthermore, in line with the idea that "(...) an effective response to security threats cannot be based on measures that restrict the movement of refugees and migrants and breach their rights,"[58] the proposed solution to the phenomenon of undesirable but unreturnable migrants should strike the correct balance between public order and national security and internationally recognised rights of the concerned migrants. Thus, a summary of the main rights these migrants are entitled to is also warranted before proposing a solution to regulate their situation. Regarding the civil and political rights of undesirable but unreturnable migrants, throughout this book, it has been repeated that their rights to life and to be free from torture, which are non-derogable rights, must be respected. This entails not only respect for such rights where these migrants are but also protection from return to a place where these rights would be violated (non-refoulement). In certain situations, especially regarding long settlers, return may likewise interfere with undesirable but unreturnable migrants' right to private and family life. This right is, to a certain extent, taken into account by States before revoking the status of undesirable migrants, as demonstrated in the case studies. As discussed during the analysis of detention practices in Australia and Canada as well as in Section 4.3 of Chapter 1, undesirable but unreturnable migrants also enjoy the right to liberty, which should protect them from indefinite detention, which is always considered arbitrary, as well as allow them to challenge the legality of their detention. They further enjoy the right to non-discrimination, which should protect them against discriminatory measures that can have the effect of depriving them of rights.[59] While the aforementioned rights appeared more prominently in the discussions of this book, this does not mean that undesirable but unreturnable migrants are not entitled to other civil and political rights. Indeed, as noted in Section 3.3 of Chapter 1, Chetail argues that in the context of the application of the International Covenant on Civil and Political

V. (2014). Are Refugee Rights Human Rights? An Unorthodox Questioning of the Relations between Refugee Law and Human Rights Law. In R. Rubio Marín, Human rights and immigration (pp. 19–72). Oxford University Press, p. 43).

58 Emmerson, B. (2016). Report of the Special Rapporteur on the promotion and protection of human rights and fundamental freedoms while countering terrorism (No. A/71/384; pp. 569–577). United Nations, p. 5.

59 See e.g. Chapter 1, Section 4.4.

Rights (hereafter ICCPR) "(…) the general applicability of human rights to noncitizens coupled with the prohibition of discrimination based on nationality substantially erode the traditional distinction between nationals and aliens."[60] Thus, as a general rule, undesirable but unreturnable migrants, regardless of their status in the host country,[61] should enjoy the rights prescribed by the ICCPR, including, for example, protection from slavery and forced labour, equality before courts and before the law, fair trial[62] and freedom of thought, conscience and religion.

As for social, economic and cultural rights, Pijnenburg noted that:

> (…) the principle of non-discrimination grants people on the move the same rights, in principle, as nationals. However, when realising socio-economic rights, States have a sovereign right to differentiate between people on the move and their own nationals, provided such limitation is proportionate and serves a legitimate aim. Crucially, the principle of non-discrimination on the ground of nationality allows for more differentiation than on other grounds on account of States' sovereign right to control the entry and stay of foreigners on their territory.[63]

Despite this, it was noted in Section 4.4 of Chapter 1 that all migrants, regardless of their status in the host country, are entitled to, at a minimum, the right to emergency healthcare as well as healthcare that, if not granted, could expose the concerned person to a reasonably foreseeable risk that can result in loss of life; the right to an adequate standard of living, including shelter,

---

60 Chetail, V. (2014), p. 49.

61 In the European context, the Parliamentary Assembly of the Council of Europe explicitly recognised that irregular migrants are entitled to, at a minimum, the right to life, the right to be free from torture, protection from slavery and forced labour, the use of immigration detention as a last resort, the right to challenge detention, the right to asylum and non-refoulement, the right to challenge removal, protection against collective expulsion, the right to private and family life, the right to marry, the right to property and non-discrimination (Parliamentary Assembly (2006). Human rights of irregular migrants (Resolution 1509 (2006)). Council of Europe. Available at: https://pace.coe.int/en/files/17456/html).

62 In this regard, the UN special rapporteur on the human rights of migrants dedicated one of their reports to migrants' right to effective access to justice and the implications of this right, calling on States to establish firewalls between immigration enforcement and public services to ensure all migrants can enjoy it. See Report of the Special Rapporteur on the human rights of migrants (A/73/178/Rev.1) (2018). United Nations General Assembly.

63 Pijnenburg, A. (2021), p. 101.

food and water; education for children; and, when undesirable but unreturnable migrants engage in work (regardless of whether they work irregularly), they are entitled to just and favourable conditions, equal treatment and fair remuneration, and should also be able to benefit from social security contributions made or be reimbursed for such contributions if they leave the host country. Although all migrants are entitled to these rights, that section also noted that "(…) migrants, and especially irregular migrants, are in practice often prevented from effectively enjoying their rights by many legal and practical barriers."[64] Thus, as noted in Section 5.4 of Chapter 3, a lack of status may make the realisation of the rights that are owed to these migrants theoretical.[65]

Consequently, to ensure undesirable but unreturnable migrants can enjoy the rights they are entitled to, the solution proposed in this book prescribes the grant of status to all undesirable but unreturnable migrants, as will be explained below. Before outlining the proposed solution, however, it is worth recalling that undesirable but unreturnable migrants who are refugees are entitled to the rights prescribed in the Refugee Convention, described in Section 3.3 of Chapter 1.[66] As mentioned in that section, entitlement to these rights varies depending on the refugee's migration status in the host country. As some rights do not require lawful stay, even refugees who are not (or no longer) considered refugees under regional or national schemes but who still

---

64 Office of the High Commissioner for Human Rights (2014). The Economic, Social and Cultural Rights of Migrants in an Irregular Situation (HR/PUB/14/1). United Nations, p. 126.

65 Farcy, J.-B. (June 2019). Sécurité nationale et exclusion du statut de protection internationale: Vers une autonomie croissante du droit européen ? Cahiers de l'EDEM. Available at: https://cdn.uclouvain.be/groups/cms-editors-cedie/newsletter/Cahiers%20juin%202019.pdf.

66 As a reminder, the Convention refers to the prohibition of discrimination (article 3), freedom of religion (article 4), acquisition of movable and immovable property and other rights pertaining thereto (article 13), the protection of artistic rights and industrial property (article 14), rights of association and to form trade unions (article 15), free access to domestic courts (article 16(1)), access to legal assistance (article 16(2)); access to wage-earning employment (article 17), the right to engage in self-employment (article 18), the right to practice liberal professions (article 19), rationing (article 20), housing (article 21), primary education (article 22(1)), public relief (article 23), protection of labour legislation and social security (article 24), the right to freely move within the host territory (article 26), the delivery of identity papers (article 27), issuance of travel documents (article 28), fiscal equality (article 29), transfer of assets (article 30), the prohibition of penalties on account of illegal entry (article 31(1)), protection against refoulement (article 33(1)), and protection against expulsion (article 32).

qualify as refugees under the Refugee Convention are entitled to them. This was explicitly recognised by the Court of Justice of the European Union (hereafter CJEU) in a case,[67] discussed in Section 3.4 of Chapter 1, in which that Court found that those who meet the refugee definition (according to the Refugee Convention) would still be entitled to (some of) the rights prescribed in that instrument even if they did not (or no longer) qualify as refugees under the European asylum framework.

In Section 3.3 of Chapter 1, it was also mentioned that the level of protection offered by the Refugee Convention varies, with refugees enjoying some rights in the same way as nationals of the host country do, other rights being accorded to refugees in not less favourable manner than they are granted to migrants generally in the same circumstances, and, lastly, in certain cases, refugees should receive the most favourable treatment accorded to migrants in the same circumstances. In this regard, the Refugee Convention may, in some situations, grant access to a higher level of entitlement to refugees than to other migrants, as was shown in the CJEU case[68] presented in that section. In that case, the CJEU found that although social assistance could be limited to core benefits for beneficiaries of subsidiary protection, according to article 23 of the Refugee Convention (and article 29 of the Qualification Directive, as well as article 31 of the upcoming Qualification Regulation), refugees were entitled to the same social assistance provided to nationals.

In view of this, while the proposed solution includes granting status to all undesirable but unreturnable migrants, the exact status and entitlements granted may vary, taking into account the above analysis and the rights that are owed to the concerned migrant, who may or may not be a refugee, according to different international instruments.

As all undesirable but unreturnable migrants concerned by this book cannot be returned due to non-refoulement obligations, however, the main procedure to grant them status should be the international protection procedure, which is already the main procedure, in all three analysed countries, aimed at assessing non-refoulement claims. This procedure, however, would have to be reformed to include undesirable but unreturnable migrants as, under existing procedures, they are likely to be excluded from protection. The next subsections will thus be dedicated to explaining this reformed procedure and the different statuses that may arise from it.

67 Joined Cases C-391/16, C-77/17 and C-78/17 (Court of Justice of the European Union, 14 May 2019).

68 Case C-713/17 (Court of Justice of the European Union, 21 November 2018).

5.1 *Reformed International Protection Procedure*

5.1.1 Increasing the Reach of International Protection Procedures: Expanding the Application of Inclusion Clauses

As was noted in the previous chapters, States often expand the protection offered by the Refugee Convention by also granting protection to those who may not fit the refugee definition but whose return would still raise human rights concerns. This protection, commonly referred to as subsidiary or complementary protection, is based on State obligations stemming from international human rights treaties such as the ICCPR and the UN Convention against Torture.[69] This gradual evolution from refugee protection to a broader international protection, encompassing not only those covered by the Refugee Convention but also including those who are owed human rights non-refoulement obligations has in practice joined two different, yet often connected, assessments in one only procedure. This is why a request for international protection is the main procedure, in all three analysed countries, aimed at assessing non-refoulement claims, both in the refugee law and human rights law contexts. Thus, instead of creating a new procedure aimed specifically at undesirable but unreturnable migrants, the best way to provide status to those who cannot be returned due to human rights concerns is to reform current international protection procedures to embed the grant of status to those who may currently be excluded. The next paragraphs describe the proposed reformed procedure, further detailing the associated statuses, which may contain certain limitations for those who are undesirable.

As such a reformed procedure should ensure non-refoulement obligations are respected by the host country, no migrant who cannot access protection elsewhere at the moment they make an application should be barred from accessing it and thus any existing restriction in this regard[70] should be removed. To ensure compliance with both refugee law and human rights law non-refoulement, the reformed procedure would require States, as they already do, to extend international protection beyond refugee status to include human rights non-refoulement. It would also require that non-refoulement claims always be considered, as all those whose return would violate non-refoulement would be granted (some sort of) status. This would remove the possibility to exclude someone and consequently end the procedure without assessing non-refoulement. In practice, this already seems to be the favoured approach in Australia and Belgium. As noted in Section 3.1 above, the Australian administration has made significant efforts to enforce this. Belgium, in

69 Rikhof, J. (2023), p. 25.

70 Such as the ones in place in Australia and Canada mentioned in Section 3.1 above.

turn, seems to allow decision-makers to exclude someone without looking at their protection claim, but still requires that the compliance of their return with non-refoulement be assessed, thus already linking this analysis to the protection procedure in the country. Furthermore, to ensure respect for the absolute character of non-refoulement, States should refrain from adding provisions that limit the application of inclusion clauses in their national laws.[71]

In this proposed reformed procedure, when a non-refoulement assessment concludes that the concerned migrant would be at risk of harm upon return, they would be granted a status. This status would correspond to current existing protection statuses unless 1F clauses[72] or article 33(2) of the Refugee Convention apply.[73] In these latter two cases, certain conditions would be associated with the protection status granted. In view of the differences between these two exceptional clauses and especially considering that "(...) art 1F is therefore backwards looking (past conduct), whereas art 33(2) is forward looking (present and/or future threat to the host State),"[74] the conditions would be different whether 1F or 33(2) applies, as they aim to achieve different goals. This will be further elaborated below. Furthermore, it is worth noting that those who meet the inclusion clauses of the Refugee Convention yet fall under article 33(2) remain refugees under the Convention (as long as they are not excluded) and should thus be treated as such and enjoy the rights associated with this status. Before detailing the different statuses that may be granted to those falling under articles 1F and 33(2), some guidance on the application of these provisions is provided in the next subsection.

71 Such as the ones in place in Australia mentioned in Section 4.1 of Chapter 2.

72 While these clauses will continue to be referred to as exclusion clauses to keep the whole book consistent when referring to them, in the proposed reformed procedure, they would not serve to exclude someone from being granted status altogether, as everyone with a valid protection claim would be granted a protective status (although this would not be refugee status since those who fall under 1F are still excluded under the Refugee Convention). They would thus represent limiting clauses for a protective status instead, as their effect would be to limit the status granted to those who fall under one of them.

73 This chapter will refer to articles 1F and 33(2) of the Refugee Convention, however, in practice, it is likely that States would not apply the Convention directly, but instead the national provisions internalising these articles. The case studies showed, however, that the wording of the Convention in these articles is closely followed in their national equivalents.

74 Singer, S. (2018). National Security, Criminality and Exclusion from Refugee Protection under the EU Qualification Directive: Expanding the Grounds of Exclusion by the Back Door. Immigration, Asylum and Nationality Law, 32(3), 284–300, p. 286.

5.1.2 Increasing the Reach of International Protection Procedures: Restricted Application of Exceptions

When assessing 1F exclusion clauses, following the idea that exceptions should be interpreted restrictively as well as in line with the abovementioned efforts to reduce the pool of undesirable migrants, these should be applied in a narrow way. In this regard, a best practice identified in the national interpretation of the Refugee Convention is requiring more than membership alone for exclusion under 1F(a). Furthermore, as suggested by the Federal Court of Australia, possible defences applicable to the acts basing the exclusion should be taken into account.[75]

As for the application of 1F(b), the guidance of Canada's Federal Court, according to which a range of factors should be considered before excluding someone on this ground is also good practice to ensure this exclusion clause is applied in a restrictive manner. According to that Court, the factors to be considered include "(…) the elements of the crime, the mode of prosecution, the penalty prescribed, the facts and the mitigating and aggravating circumstances underlying the conviction"[76] as well as whether the crime would fall at the less serious end of a sentencing range. Similarly, the Federal Court of Australia's view that considerations of fair trial may also be taken into account when assessing foreign criminal procedures is welcomed.[77]

Regarding 1F(c), the only reference to this article identified in the cases analysed for this book was in relation to terrorist offences in Belgium. Indeed, Rikhof noted that, in general, 1F(c) was used scarcely and primarily in relation to human rights violations and terrorist activities.[78] Both Belgium and Canada seem to consider that, unlike for article 1F(a), membership in a terrorist group alone would suffice to consider someone excluded.[79] Considering the lack of clarification on the application of this exclusion clause, no particular best practice was identified.

75 See CMA19 v Minister for Home Affairs, [2020] FCA 736 (Federal Court of Australia, 29 May 2020). While this case does not concern a 1F exclusion clause, it relates to the consideration of whether the concerned migrant had committed or facilitated war crimes or crimes against humanity and thus the guidance is easily transferrable to exclusions under 1F(a). This also seems to be the case in Belgium (see Chapter 3, Section 3.1.1) and Canada (see Chapter 4, Section 3.1).

76 Jung v. Canada, 2015 FC 464 (Federal Court, 15 April 2015), para. 44.

77 ERY19 v Minister for Immigration, Citizenship, Migrant Services and Multicultural Affairs, [2020] FCA 569 (Federal Court of Australia, 4 May 2020). This also seems to be the understanding of the Canadian Federal Court. See Chapter 4, Section 3.2.3.

78 Rikhof, J. (2023), p. 651.

79 See Chapter 3, Section 3.1.3; and Chapter 4, Section 3.4.

Apart from the 1F exclusion clauses, which would lead to certain limitations to the status granted through the proposed reformed protection procedure (as will be explained below), article 33(2) of the Refugee Convention would be inserted in the procedure as a clause that may give rise to a different set of restrictions (as will also be explained below). The restrictions associated with article 33(2) would not relate to non-refoulement (as is the case in the Refugee Convention), since the reformed procedure should ensure non-refoulement (in the broad, human rights sense) is not violated. As it still presents an exception to a full protection status (given the fact that it is associated with certain restrictions), it should, as article 1F, be interpreted narrowly in national contexts. In this regard, a best practice would be to place the likelihood of (re)offending at the centre of the analysis, as the goal of the provision is to prevent a threat to the security of the community. In doing so, States should not, as the Canadian Federal Court advises, impose an unattainable standard on the concerned migrant, as it is never possible to guarantee that a person will not reoffend.[80] Similarly, as done in Australia and Belgium, all the elements surrounding the crime – including, for instance, the nature and seriousness of the offence, history of recidivism, applicable sentence – should be taken into account when determining whether someone would fall under the national provision reflecting article 33(2).[81]

When, however, migrants are deemed to fall under these provisions (namely, 1F and 33(2)), their protection status, as noted above, would be limited. Those who meet the inclusion clauses of the Refugee Convention, however, would still be granted refugee status if they fall under article 33(2) (provided that they are not excluded) and thus would still be entitled to all rights associated with such status. The next subsections thus serve to explain what the different statuses arising from the proposed reformed international protection procedure would look like.

5.1.3 Limited Status for Those Who Fall under 1F

As previously mentioned, in the proposed reformed procedure, articles 1F and 33(2) would not serve to exclude someone from being granted status altogether or from protection from refoulement, but, instead, would serve to limit the status received by migrants who are owed non-refoulement obligations. To maintain the integrity of the international protection regime, however, those who fall under 1F would not be granted refugee status as they cannot be recognised as refugees. As noted previously, since article 1F aims

80 See Chapter 4, Section 5.2.

81 See Chapter 2, Section 3.3; and Chapter 3, Section 3.2.1.

to exclude from protection those who are undeserving of it due to past acts (thus, backwards looking) and 33(2), in turn, has as its goal the protection of the host State's community and national security (thus, forward looking), the conditions associated with each article will differ, as they aim to address different issues.[82] Furthermore, those falling under 33(2) will still be considered refugees if they meet inclusion clauses and are not excluded.

In this proposed reformed protection procedure, those who are deemed to be owed non-refoulement obligations but who also fall under one of the situations prescribed in 1F would be granted (subsidiary or complementary) protection status (as they are excluded from being granted refugee status under the Refugee Convention).[83] This status should explicitly give them access to healthcare and social assistance to ensure their basic needs of housing, food and water. As noted above, while all migrants should be ensured these rights regardless of their status, they are not always able to enjoy them in practice due to their (lack of) status and so it is important to reinforce their entitlement. As undesirable but unreturnable migrants will be granted status through the reformed procedure, their entitlement may also go beyond the minimum rights owed to all migrants, including those in an irregular situation. In this regard, the level of rights afforded to other migrants in similar circumstances may further guide their entitlements at the national level. While "(…) there is no general, unqualified right for foreigners to seek or obtain work

82 The idea of having different restrictions apply to these articles is in line with what Cantor et al. noted in the introduction to the special edition on undesirable but unreturnable migrants of the Refugee Survey Quarterly. In that introduction, they said that: "(…) it is important to emphasise one point that comes across clearly from the contributions to this volume (and the RLI/CICJ project as a whole), i.e. that there are different profiles of "undesirability". This not only means that some aliens may be "more undesirable" than others from the point of view of public policy but, more importantly, that different kinds of policy responses may be appropriate depending on the specific profile. For instance, some are deemed "undeserving" of refugee protection because of alleged war crimes that may have occurred years ago in faraway countries, and may not pose an acute security threat to the receiving country. At the other end of the spectrum, others may be convicted terrorists who continue to pose a concrete threat to the host State's public order or public security. Recognising and delimiting the different profiles along this spectrum of "undesirability" thus represents a useful way for States to address the distinct sets of challenges that they pose." (James Cantor, D., van Wijk, J., Singer, S., & Bolhuis, M. (2017). The Emperor's New Clothing: National Responses to "Undesirable and Unreturnable" Aliens under Asylum and Immigration Law. Refugee Survey Quarterly, 36(1), 1–8, p. 7).

83 It should be noted that, in the European system (explained in Chapter 1, Section 3.4), they would also be excluded from subsidiary protection under European rules. Their status would thus be based on national law.

in another state,"[84] such status should allow migrants to engage in work as "[T]he right to work is essential for realizing other human rights and forms an inseparable and inherent part of human dignity."[85] In this regard, "[T]he right to work is closely related to other socio-economic rights, especially the right to an adequate standard of living, as earning money enables a person to pay for the provision of her basic needs."[86] Thus, allowing these migrants to work would ensure they can provide for themselves and are less dependent on government aid.[87] Furthermore, as the non-refoulement concerns that prevent the return of these migrants may be long lasting, obtaining permanent residence should be a possibility for them, as will be explained below. Consequently, as they are expected to spend a long time in the host country, allowing them to work is essential to ensure not only that they can provide for themselves but can also enjoy that right as part of their human dignity.[88] As mentioned above, they should also be entitled to all labour rights when they engage in work and also benefit from social security contributions. Lastly, as also noted above, in view of the principle of non-discrimination, undesirable but unreturnable migrants will also be entitled, as a general rule, to the civil and political rights prescribed in the ICCPR. In this regard, it is worth noting that, regarding the right to family and private life, in the European context, the European Court of Human Rights (ECtHR) found that, in some circumstances,

---

84 Pijnenburg, A. (2021), p. 135.

85 Committee on Economic, Social and Cultural Rights (2006). General comment No. 18: Article 6 of the International Covenant on Economic, Social and Cultural Rights (E/C.12/GC/18). United Nations Economic and Social Council, para. 1.

86 Pijnenburg, A. (2021), p. 135.

87 In this regard, the EU Agency for Fundamental Rights argued that EU member States may have more duties towards migrants who are not allowed to work when it said that "[W]hether the obligation to fulfil the right to adequate housing enshrined in international human rights law also includes the duty to provide adequate shelter to destitute migrants living in an irregular situation is controversial. (…) However, a strong case can be made that such a duty exists at least for those persons whose removal cannot be carried out through no fault of their own, particularly where they are not granted access to the labour market." European Union Agency for Fundamental Rights (2011). Fundamental rights of migrants in an irregular situation in the European Union, p. 69.

88 In this regard, Nansen, the Belgian Refugee Council, also suggested that, in case a new status is created for unreturnable migrants, they should be granted the right to work. See NANSEN (2021). CONTRIBUTION A LA RÉFLEXION 2021/2 – Pour un statut d'inéloignable. Available at: https://nansen-refugee.be/wp-content/uploads/2021/09/2.-Pour-un-statut-dinéloignable.pdf, p. 5.

this right may require States to allow family members of the concerned migrant to join them in the host country.[89]

Despite being granted status and enjoying the associated rights, as those who fall under 1F are considered undeserving of protection, they would have to make efforts to overcome their undeservingness to keep their status and become permanent residents. In this regard, prosecution can be an important step to show that the concerned migrant was held accountable for their acts and is thus on the path to redemption. Furthermore, as noted in Section 4.2 of Chapter 1, certain crimes require States to start investigations and, where appropriate, prosecute crimes that may give rise to 1F exclusions. Thus, when migration authorities are faced with a 1F crime that has not yet been prosecuted, the case should be referred to the concerned prosecutorial services for investigation. As also noted in Section 4.2 of Chapter 1, however, there are many challenges to prosecuting crimes committed abroad and so prosecution may not be feasible in practice. Furthermore, even when 1F crimes are successfully prosecuted, the concerned person remains excluded from refugee status and so, as mentioned earlier, prosecution alone is not a solution.

Thus, to ensure their status is not seen as a compensation for their actions or as a blank slate, their status would fall under the category of so-called 'earned regularisation'. In this regard:

> The idea behind these [earned regularisation] programmes is to provide migrants with a provisional, temporary living and working permit and to have them 'earn' the right to have the permit extended or become permanent through the fulfilment of various criteria, such as knowing the language of the host country, participating in community activities, having stable employment and paying taxes.[90]

---

89 While recognising State's right to control entry, residence and expulsion of non-nationals as well as State's wide margin of appreciation in deciding whether to impose a waiting period for family reunification requested by beneficiaries of subsidiary or temporary protection, the European Court of Human Rights noted that a State may, under certain circumstances, be required to allow the entry of an individual when it is a pre-condition for their exercise of the right to respect for family life. A number of elements should be considered to determine whether that is the case, including, among others, whether there were insurmountable or major obstacles in the way of the family living in the country of origin, which is likely to be the case for those in need of protection. See European Court of Human Rights (2025) Guide on the case-law of the European Convention on Human Rights: Immigration, paras. 6–9.

90 Regularisation programmes for irregular migrants (Doc. 11350) (2007). Council of Europe (Parliamentary Assembly), p. 9.

In practice, this would mean that those who are owed protection but who fall under 1F would be granted status for a limited duration of time and ordered to fulfil a certain number of conditions (exhaustively defined in law). These could include knowing the language of the host country, participating in community activities, having stable employment or engaging in educational activities, paying taxes,[91] as well not engaging in criminal activity. Furthermore, the concerned migrants should also be encouraged to, where available and relevant, engage in activities that could foster their integration and rehabilitation such as, for example, participating in transitional justice mechanisms.[92]

Renewal of status would then be dependent on fulfilment of the set conditions and, after a certain, fixed, number of renewals, unlimited permanent status would be granted to the concerned migrant, who should then be entitled to all rights granted to permanent residents in the host State under its national law. This is in line with the reasoning of the United Kingdom Court of Appeal, which has explicitly accepted that migrants who cannot be removed and who have been in the country for a long period should be given indefinite leave to remain.[93] Indeed, as noted in Chapter 3, Belgium provides in its legislation that the longer a person has regularly resided in the country, the higher the threshold that needs to be reached to withdraw their residence status.[94]

91 These conditions are similar to the social and economic integration requirements to obtain Belgian nationality, thus showing that these are considered by States as important factors that could lead to a permanent stay. See art. 12bis of the Belgian nationality code, (in original language: Code de la nationalité belge / Wetboek van de Belgische nationaliteit): https://www.ejustice.just.fgov.be/cgi_loi/change_lg.pl?language=fr&la=F&table_name=loi&cn=1984062835.

92 The author has argued, in another contribution, that transitional justice mechanisms can contribute to the reintegration of foreign fighters and their families in their country of origin. While foreign fighters are nationals of the country they are in, they are in a comparable situation to undesirable but unreturnable migrants as they committed crimes abroad that may put them in a position where they are no longer accepted by their host community. See Rigotti, C., & Zomignani Barboza, J. (2021). Unfolding the case of returnees: How the European Union and its member States are addressing the return of foreign fighters and their families. International Review of the Red Cross, 103(916–917), 681–703, pp. 701–703.

93 In this regard, the Court said: "[T]here may of course come a point where the appellant has been in the United Kingdom for so long and/or the prospect of his removal to Tunisia [where the applicant in that case was from] is so remote, that the only course reasonably open to the Secretary of State is to grant him indefinite leave to remain" (Kardi, R (On the Application Of) v Secretary of State for the Home Department, [2014] EWCA Civ 934 (United Kingdom: Court of Appeal (England and Wales) 10 July 2014), para. 32).

94 See Chapter 3, Section 3.2.2. This section also points to the practical limits of this protection. Settlement is also important in Australia and Canada, as in the former decision-makers must consider the strength, nature and duration of the person's ties to Australia

While the length of time necessary to grant permanent residence may be dependent on the national context, in Belgium, Nansen, the Belgian Refugee Council, suggested that, in case a new status is created for unreturnable migrants, they should be granted permanent residence after 5 years,[95] as is the case for most migrants in the country. Thus, following this suggestion, national practices can serve as a basis to determine the applicable timeframe.

5.1.4 Limited Status for Those Who Fall under 33(2)

As noted earlier, those falling under article 33(2) of the Refugee Convention are considered a danger to national security or to the community of the host State yet they are not excluded from refugee status (unless they fall under exclusion clauses as well) and thus, when they meet inclusion clauses, they remain refugees for the purposes of the Refugee Convention. The case studies showed that national security is a forward-looking assessment and that States place the risk of (re)offending at the centre of the analysis.[96] Consequently, those who are owed non-refoulement obligations yet fall under article 33(2) would be subjected to restrictions that would limit their chances of (re)offending and thus protect State interests of national security and public order. In this regard, this limited status would be similar to the temporary permits granted in Canada for those who cannot be returned. In view of the aforementioned potential downsides of the practical application of these permits, including possible strict long-term conditions migrants are subjected to in Canada, however, some safeguards would be in place to prevent them.

Firstly, a number of rights should be guaranteed to them. If they meet inclusion clauses of the Refugee Convention and are not excluded from that status, they will be considered refugees despite falling under article 33(2). They are thus entitled to all the rights prescribed in that Convention (outlined in Section 3.3 of Chapter 1), including the ones that require lawful stay, as they will be granted status to remain in the country. If, in turn, they do not meet inclusion clauses but, instead, are in need of subsidiary or complementary protection, they will not be considered refugees and thus will not be entitled

before deciding on their right to stay and in the latter they are called upon to take into account the longevity of a migrant's stay in Canada before finding them undesirable. Furthermore, a stronger protection is granted to permanent residents in Canada as they cannot, for example, be found inadmissible for reasons of criminality (only serious criminality). See Chapter 2, Section 3.6; and Chapter 4, Sections 3.2 and 3.6.

95 NANSEN (2021), p. 5.

96 See Chapter 2, Section 3.3, Chapter 3, Section 3.2.1; and Chapter 4, Section 5.1.

to the rights prescribed in the Refugee Convention. However, they should still be ensured, at a minimum, the rights outlined in Section 5.1.3 above, namely, access to healthcare, social assistance to ensure their basic needs, the right to work and associated labour rights, as well as the right to benefit from social security contributions and, as a general rule, the civil and political rights prescribed in the ICCPR. Following national practices, other rights afforded to migrants in similar circumstances may also be extended to them.

Secondly, regarding the conditions that may be associated with their status, they should be exhaustively prescribed in national law, similarly to what is done in Australia.[97] Measures applied in the countries under study[98] that could be applied to this status include periodic reporting requirements; the requirement to live in a specified address; the need to report any change of address; the requirement not to go to a certain place; the requirement to obtain permission before undertaking certain jobs (although prohibiting them from working regularly altogether should not be a possibility);[99] ban on any use, access or training with weapons; the requirement not to communicate with certain people or organisations (such as those considered terrorist); communications monitoring; and not engage in criminal activities.

In view of some of the detention practices noted in the case studies, it is worth noting here that detention would not be among the possible measures to be imposed against migrants benefitting from a limited status. This is because no migration link would exist to justify it, since undesirable but unre-

97 S 41 Migration Act. See also Australian Department for Home Affairs (website), Check visa details and conditions, visa conditions. Available at: https://immi.homeaffairs.gov.au/visas/already-have-a-visa/check-visa-details-and-conditions/conditions-list#.

98 See Chapter 2, Section 5.1; Chapter 3, Section 5.2; and Chapter 4, Section 5.5.

99 Restrictions of this type (that is, periodic reporting, communicating address changes and permission to undertake work) were considered acceptable restrictions in the context of the United Kingdom's Restricted Leave Policy, which applies to those who, due to their actions, are considered undeserving of protection status but who cannot be removed as their return would breach non-refoulement obligations. This policy grants such migrants a leave to remain in the United Kingdom that can be attached to a number of limitations. See Kardi, R (On the Application of) v Secretary of State for the Home Department, [2014] EWCA Civ 934, paras. 36–39. See also: United Kingdom Home Office (2023). Restricted Leave (version 8.0). Available at: https://assets.publishing.service.gov.uk/media/6538ef3280884d000df71a90/Restricted+leave.pdf; Singer, S. (2017). "Undesirable and Unreturnable" in the United Kingdom. Refugee Survey Quarterly, 36(1), 9–34.

turnable migrants benefitting from limited status would have the right to remain in the country.[100]

Regarding the practical application of the conditions, it should be noted that they would not all apply at once. Instead, decision-makers would have to assess the danger posed by the concerned migrant and identify the measures that most suitably and in the least intrusive way mitigate the identified threat.[101] For example, a person who is considered a danger to children for

---

100 Indeed, as the case studies showed, detention presupposes that return is being envisaged and, when there is no real prospect of return (as would be the case for migrants who were granted the right to stay), detention can no longer continue. This migration link (that is, the possibility of return) was explicitly required to justify detention in Belgium (see Chapter 3, Section 5.2) and Canada (see Chapter 4, Section 5.4). In Australia, not having the right to enter or stay in the country was long considered enough to justify detention and thus no real possibility of return was required. However, the High Court's decision of 2023 changed that, as in that case, the Court ruled that as there was "(…) no real prospect of the removal of the plaintiff from Australia becoming practicable in the reasonably foreseeable future," detention could no longer be validly authorised according to the Migration Act (NZYQ v Minister for Immigration, Citizenship and Multicultural Affairs [2023] HCA 37 (High Court of Australia, 28 November 2023), para. 70). When the reason preventing removal is the concerned migrant's voluntary lack of cooperation in removal procedures, however, detention can continue, as was decided in ASF17 v Commonwealth of Australia [2024] HCA 19 (High Court of Australia, 10 May 2024). See Chapter 2, Section 5.5. In this regard, it is also worth noting that, in the European context, the ECtHR stated that "Article 5 § 1 (f) [of the European Convention on Human Rights, authorising "the lawful arrest or detention of a person to prevent his effecting an unauthorised entry into the country or of a person against whom action is being taken with a view to deportation or extradition"] does not demand that detention be reasonably considered necessary, for example to prevent the individual from committing an offence or fleeing. Any deprivation of liberty under the second limb of Article 5 § 1 (f) will be justified, however, only for as long as deportation or extradition proceedings are in progress. If such proceedings are not prosecuted with due diligence, the detention will cease to be permissible under Article 5 § 1 (f)" (A. and Others v. the United Kingdom, 3455/05 (European Court of Human Rights, 19 February 2009), para. 164). See also: Al Husin v. Bosnia and Herzegovina, 10112/16 (European Court of Human Rights, 25 June 2019); and European Court of Human Rights (2025) Guide on the case-law of the European Convention on Human Rights: Immigration, para. 104. Lutz further noted that pre-removal detention for reasons of security is incompatible with the EU Return Directive when he wrote that "[T]he possibility of maintaining or extending pre-removal detention for public order reasons is not covered by the text of the Return Directive and Member States are not allowed to use immigration detention for the purposes of removal as a form of 'light imprisonment' for public order reasons. This was made crystal clear by the ECJ [European Court of Justice] in its first judgment on the Return Directive, Kadzoev" (Lutz, F. (2018), p. 38).

101 As noted in Chapter 4, in Canada, similar guidance is provided with regard to conditions of release from detention, which establish that such conditions should be linked to the

having committed sexual offences against minors may be ordered not to go to certain places such as playgrounds where children are always expected to be present. Similarly, in this case, the concerned migrant may be obliged to ask for authorisation for taking up a job that would involve direct contact with children. The identification of the danger and suitability of the applied measures must be spelled out in the decision setting the restrictions, to allow the concerned migrant to understand the decision as well as to make a judicial review of the decision possible.

To ensure the continued proportionality of the measures in place, their application must be revised periodically. Following the Belgian example, it can be provided that measures can be revised every six months.[102] Thus, looking at the example above, should the concerned migrant who is considered a threat to children complete treatments and be considered to have possible underlying sexual disorders under control, the limitations on freedom of movement and employment imposed can be relaxed or completely removed during a revision. Furthermore, a maximum duration for restrictions must be set in national law, after which all restrictions must be lifted.

As the limited status proposed for those who fall under 1F, these statuses (refugee or not) would also be granted for a limited duration initially, renewable upon compliance with the set restrictions, and, after a certain, fixed, number of renewals (for example, after the maximum duration for restrictions is reached), unlimited permanent residence should be granted to concerned migrants. The same reasoning behind the grant of a permanent status and the timelapse required to reach that moment mentioned in the previous subsection apply here.

As renewal of limited statuses, both based on 1F and on 33(2), is conditional on compliance with the applicable measures, a renewal may sometimes not be granted. The next subsection thus assesses this situation.

5.1.5 Non-compliance with Limited Status Conditions

To ensure compliance with the conditions of the abovementioned limited statuses and to protect States' interests of national security and public order as well as maintain the integrity of the international protection regime, re-

---

risk factors, that each condition must be justified in view of the circumstances of the case and that the principle of proportionality should be followed. Immigration and Refugee Board of Canada, Chairperson Guideline 2: Detention. Available at: https://irb.gc.ca/en/legal-policy/policies/Pages/GuideDir02.aspx#s3, para. 3.1.2. See also Canada v. Hamdan, 2019 FC 1129 (Federal Court, 3 September 2019), para. 67.

102 See Chapter 3, Section 5.4.

newal of the temporary status (and conversion into a permanent one, when the number of years required is reached) would be dependent on migrants respecting the imposed limitations. Thus, at each renewal, the concerned migrant would have to show that the conditions were respected. Where the measures imposed were not complied with, concerned migrants should be given the opportunity to provide explanations of why that was the case. This follows the abovementioned logic, applied in all countries under study, that migrants who may have a right to stay withdrawn should first have the opportunity to present the reasons why their right to stay should, instead, continue. Should the decision-maker find that the reasons provided justify the continuation of stay, the limited status should be renewed. When the assessment does not favour the continuation of stay, however, the renewal is denied. In such cases, the concerned migrants may find themselves in an irregular situation. As noted above, however, even in an irregular situation, they are still entitled to certain rights and, those who are considered refugees, are also entitled to the rights prescribed in the Refugee Convention that do not require lawful stay.

As also noted above, since the proposed reformed procedure should ensure non-refoulement obligations are respected, no migrant who cannot access protection elsewhere should be barred from accessing it. Thus, even those who did not have their status renewed should be allowed to re-apply for international protection. In a new application, non-refoulement will again be assessed and, should it be found that the situation in the country of origin has changed and that the concerned migrant would no longer be at risk there, no status will be granted and non-refoulement will no longer prevent their return.

Should, however, non-refoulement obligations still be owed by the host State to the concerned migrant, they will be granted (most likely limited) status. The fact that such migrants would obtain status despite having disrespected conditions before may lead some to argue that this re-granting of status would reward 'lawbreakers' and encourage further migration to the host country of migrants in a similar situation (such as having a criminal background).[103] However, it is important to note that the re-granting of status would have important consequences for the concerned migrants. Mainly, as it is a new status and not the renewal of an old one, the time period required to obtain permanent residence would re-start, putting these migrants further

---

103 Regularisation programmes for irregular migrants (Doc. 11350) (2007), p. 20.

away from a more stable situation and from accessing possible rights that may only be granted to permanent residents.

This reformed procedure is particularly relevant for new arrivals who are undesirable yet are in need of protection and who immediately request it upon arriving in the host country. At the same time, however, by removing bars to accessing it, it also provides a safety net for undesirables who may have lost an existing status but are in need of protection and thus cannot be returned. Considering the particularities that may apply to long settlers (mentioned above), however, the proposed reformed procedure must be complemented by specific safeguards to these migrants, which will be explained in the next subsection.

5.2 *The Situation of Undesirable but Unreturnable Long Settlers*

As was shown throughout this book, undesirable but unreturnable migrants do not constitute a homogenous group. While being unreturnable due to human rights concerns may mean that they are more likely to go through an international protection procedure (and could thus benefit from the statuses proposed above, should such procedure be reformed), this is not necessarily the case. Furthermore, even when they do ask for protection, this may happen many years after arrival in the host country. For example, AJL20 arrived in Australia holding a child visa and first asked for protection after nine years living in Australia, when his initial visa was cancelled.[104] Consequently, while the abovementioned reformed international protection procedure and associated statuses provide an important safety net to ensure all undesirable but unreturnable migrants obtain status and have their human rights respected, alone, they are not sufficient to respond to the challenge of regulating the situation of these migrants as they do not properly address the situation of all undesirable but unreturnable migrants, particularly that of long settlers. Thus, such procedure and associated statuses should be complemented by the enaction of safeguards aimed specifically at this last group of undesirable but unreturnable migrants.

In this regard, the case studies showed that, at the national level, all three analysed States offer greater protection against loss of status for those who have strong ties to the country. This is demonstrated by the higher threshold needed for a long settler to be considered undesirable (as is the case in Belgium and Canada) and by the need to take private and family life as well as the

---

104 See Chapter 2, Section 5.4.

ties to the host country into account when deciding to withdraw a migrant's right to stay (the first best practice identified above).

While these practices are welcome developments that may serve to reduce the pool of undesirables, the case studies also showed some of their current weaknesses. For example, in Belgium, it has been said that the different thresholds established according to the level of settlement to determine who is undesirable (that is, reasons of public order and national security, serious reasons of public order or national security and compelling reasons of national security) cannot be determined precisely and thus leave too much discretion to decision-makers to decide the seriousness requirements.[105] In Canada, in turn, the serious criminality threshold (instead of simply criminality) required to consider a permanent resident inadmissible is clear yet it sets a very low threshold (a conviction to a term of imprisonment of at least six months),[106] which may in practice undermine this stronger protection granted to permanent residents. Lastly, when it comes to the discretion given to decision-makers when deciding who is undesirable, this does not guarantee that a human rights-based approach will always be taken.

In view of this and building on the first best practice identified above, to ensure long settlers are afforded greater protection and to effectively reduce the pool of undesirables, States should revise their national laws to establish clear thresholds to consider a migrant undesirable, according to their level of settlement. For example, when it comes to the commission of crimes, those authorised to stay on a temporary basis could be considered undesirable when they are convicted to a minimum term of imprisonment (which seems to be one of the lowest thresholds applied in Australia and Canada). Permanent residents, in turn, could only be found undesirable and risk losing their right to stay in case they were convicted to a (higher) minimum term of imprisonment for the commission of specific serious or violent crimes,[107] which must be exhaustively prescribed in national law (instead of just setting a minimum term of imprisonment for them, as Canada does, or unclear thresholds, as is the case in Belgium). Permanent residents who have lived in the host country for a certain number of years (for example, Belgium affords greater pro-

105 See Chapter 3, Section 3.2.2.

106 See Chapter 4, Section 3.2.

107 These would have to be defined according to the national context. Examples from the case studies include people smuggling, human trafficking and sexual crimes against children, which are singled out in Australia (see Chapter 2, Section 3.2) as well as organised criminality, which is singled out in both Australia (see Chapter 2, Section 3.2) and Canada (see Chapter 4, Section 3.5).

tection to those who live in the country for over 10 years), in turn, may only be considered undesirable and risk losing their existing status in case of recidivism of serious or violent crimes or the commission of the most serious crimes,[108] which must also be exhaustively prescribed in national law. Lastly, these thresholds should not be applied automatically but, instead, some discretion should still be granted to decision-makers to assess whether, in the specific case at hand, the concerned migrant should keep their existing status. When exercising such discretion, decision-makers should take into account the longevity of the concerned migrant's stay and their ties to the host country. Should such ties be so strong as to consider the host country the concerned migrant's own country, this should favour continued stay, as even if they lose their right to stay it is unlikely that they could be returned without violating human rights.

In this regard, the Human Rights Committee's jurisprudence on return of undesirable migrants indicates that there may come a point in an undesirable migrant's life in which their links to the host country are so strong that they should be allowed to stay in that country regardless of the criminal acts they may have been involved in. In some of its cases, the Committee goes as far as finding that the concerned migrant's ties to the host country are so strong that the host country should be considered the migrant's own country for the purpose of the application of article 12(4) ICCPR,[109] which establishes that "[N]o one shall be arbitrarily deprived of the right to enter his own country." Similarly, in the European context, the ECtHR also requires that decision-makers consider undesirable migrants' private and family life before deciding on returning them and affords greater protection against return to migrants who were born in the host country or moved there at a young age.[110]

---

108 Again, these would have to be defined according to the national context and could likely include international crimes giving rise to exclusion from protection statuses, which are also singled out as crimes that could lead to the rejection or withdrawal of the right to enter or stay of migrants outside international protection procedures in Australia (see Chapter 2, Section 3.1) and Canada (see Chapter 4, Section 3.1) as well as terrorism, which is considered contrary to the principles and purposes of the UN (see Chapter 2, Section 3.2; Chapter 3, Section 3.1.3; and Chapter 4, Sections 3.3 and 3.4).

109 See e.g. Communication No. 2264/2013, CCPR/C/122/D/2264/2013 (Human Rights Committee, 6 April 2018); Communication No. 1959/2010, CCPR/C/102/D/1959/2010 (Human Rights Committee, 21 July 2011); Communication No. 1557/2007, CCPR/C/102/D/1557/2007 (Human Rights Committee, 18 July 2011).

110 See European Court of Human Rights (2025) Guide on the case-law of the European Convention on Human Rights: Immigration, paras. 93–94; see also Thym, D. (2014). Residence as De Facto Citizenship? Protection of Long-term Residence under Article 8 ECHR. In R. Rubio Marín, Human rights and immigration (pp. 106–144). Oxford Univer-

Based on existing practices in the countries under study in this book, other elements to consider could include the migrant's ties to their country of origin, their likelihood of reoffending, the consequences of loss of status to their family members and whether the concerned migrant would be at risk upon return.[111] This last element is particularly relevant for undesirable but unreturnable migrants as they are in need of international protection. Even though they may still apply for protection and obtain status under the proposed reformed international protection procedure (as explained above), this status is likely to be different than their existing one. For example, if they are currently permanent residents, they are likely to be entitled to more rights, according to the host State's national laws, than they would be entitled to with a (limited) protection status.[112] Consequently, it is important to ensure decision-makers consider their non-refoulement claims before withdrawing their right to stay. Lastly, migrants should have a chance to show they are rehabilitated, as is the case in Canada.[113]

Establishing clearer and progressively higher thresholds should work to reduce the pool of undesirables and give greater protection to long settlers in practice. For those whose acts meet these thresholds and who, after assess-

sity Press, pp. 124–125; Thym, D. (2008). Respect for Private and Family Life Under Article 8 ECHR in Immigration Cases: A Human Right to Regularize Illegal Stay? International and Comparative Law Quarterly, 57(1), 87–112, pp. 93–94.

111 See Chapter 2, Section 3.6; Chapter 3, Section 3.2.1; and Chapter 4, Section 3.6. Despite these factors already being considered, as noted above, decision-makers discretion currently plays a central role in such decisions, which is why setting clearer and progressively higher thresholds for considering someone undesirable is important to provide greater protection against loss of status to long settlers.

112 Indeed, this was one of issues noted by the primary judge of the Federal Court of Australia when deciding the Omar case (see Chapter 2, Sections 4.2 and 4.3). In that case, when assessing the differences between considering non-refoulement in a visa cancellation procedure and in a protection visa application, the judge noted that the question before the decision-maker when deciding on a visa cancellation "(…) is whether or not to revoke the cancellation of a particular visa: a previously existing visa, which entitled the person to remain in the Australian community, on a particular basis, with the particular status and benefits that accompany that visa. Thus, the question for the Assistant Minister [the decision-maker] was whether to restore that particular visa to the applicant. In determining whether or not to exercise that power, if the person makes representations that she or he is a person to whom Australia has non-refoulement obligations, and sets out a serious and substantive basis in fact and in law for that representation, part of the statutory task involves consideration of that representation, just as it does any other serious and substantive representation advanced by that person." Omar v Minister for Home Affairs, [2019] FCA 279 (Federal Court of Australia, 7 March 2019), para. 82.

113 See Chapter 4, Sections 3.2.3 and 3.6.

ment of their situation, do lose their existing status, the reformed international protection procedure proposed above provides a safety net to ensure that those who are in need of protection obtain (limited) refugee or subsidiary or complementary protection status. In case the migrants applying for protection under the proposed reformed international protection procedure are long settlers, however, their settlement and previous presence in the host country should be taken into account when determining which conditions may be associated with their status.[114] For example, long settlers falling under article 1F are likely to already meet certain integration requirements such as knowing the language of the host country and thus such conditions need not be applied to their protection status. Long settlers who fall under article 33(2), in turn, are likely to be considered dangerous due to actions they committed in the host country, as opposed to actions committed abroad (which is likely to be the case for new arrivals). They can thus be subjected to national measures to protect national security and public order that apply to all and not just migrants, including the national criminal justice system. For example, they may have to follow mandatory psychological treatment as a condition to be released from prison and may have reporting obligations to judicial authorities as a parole condition, which would not be the case had the acts been committed abroad. In this case, requiring them to comply with extra security measures just because they are migrants may constitute unlawful discrimination.[115] Thus, instead of attaching extra conditions to their migration status, the only conditions that should be applied to them are to comply with court-imposed obligations and not engage in criminal activity.

6 Conclusions

The previous chapters took an in depth look at how three States, located in different continents and following different legal systems, regulate the situa-

114 This is the case for both those who apply for international protection after an existing permit or visa was cancelled and those whose initial protection status was not renewed due to the unfulfillment of established conditions.

115 For example, when the United Kingdom extended its powers to detain foreign nationals in the context of the fight against terrorism, the ECtHR found that "(…) the impugned powers were not to be seen as immigration measures, where a distinction between nationals and non-nationals would be legitimate, but instead as concerned with national security" (A. and others v. The United Kingdom, para. 186), concluding that "(…) the derogating measures were disproportionate in that they discriminated unjustifiably between nationals and non-nationals" (ibid., para. 190).

tion of undesirable but unreturnable migrants. The first sections of this chapter thus presented the main similarities between the analysed States' legal framework regarding: who is undesirable (Section 2), the procedures in place for migrants to have their non-refoulment claims assessed (Section 3) and the solutions applied to undesirable but unreturnable migrants (Section 4).

This analysis makes it clear that, while the three countries under study provide that a balancing between a migrant's undesirability and the factors favouring their stay in the country should be done before denying or ending their stay, other long-term solutions are rarely available for migrants who are not favoured by such assessment. Consequently, these migrants often have their fundamental rights disrespected. At the same time, all three States have long-term solutions for unreturnable migrants, which, however, are not extended to those who are also undesirable.

In view of this and recognising that a coherent solution and guidance on how to regulate the situation of undesirable but unreturnable migrants is currently lacking,[116] the current chapter, based on existing measures applied in the analysed States, fills this gap by proposing that different limited statuses be granted to such migrants. These statuses would imply measures to maintain the integrity of the international protection regime as well as to protect the community of a State from any possible danger but would also, in the long-term, provide a more stable and thus sustainable solution for undesirable but unreturnable migrants as a human rights compliant alternative to existing practices.

Section 5 showed that such statuses should be embedded in international protection procedures, which are already the main procedure in place to assess unreturnability linked to non-refoulement. It also provided an overview of the minimum rights that should be granted to undesirable but unreturnable migrants under these statuses, including the rights that undesirable but unreturnable migrants who are refugees are entitled to. Thus, the proposed solution would turn articles 1F and 33(2) of the Refugee Convention into limiting clauses for both refugee and subsidiary or complementary protection statuses, instead of *de facto* exclusion clauses to the grant of national statuses, as they currently are. Considering the differences between both articles (mainly the fact that 1F is backward looking while 33(2) is forward looking as well as the fact that those who fall under 33(2) but meet inclusion clauses of the Refugee Convention are still refugees), the rights and conditions associated with these statuses would be different according to which article applies. Conditions as-

116 Refugee Law Initiative, Arts & Humanities Research Council and Center for International Criminal Justice (2016), p. 3.

sociated with 1F would be focused on integration aspects while conditions associated with 33(2) would aim to limit the chances of the concerned migrant (re)offending. To protect migrants against possible disproportionate measures, applicable restrictions must be prescribed in law, applied in proportionality to the danger they pose, revised periodically and decisions regarding them subject to judicial review. Furthermore, these statuses would be associated with a number of rights, including, in some cases, the rights prescribed by Refugee Convention, which undesirable but unreturnable migrants who are refugees are entitled to. Renewal of temporary limited statuses would be dependent on compliance with the imposed conditions and, after a certain, predefined, number of renewals, migrants would receive unrestricted permanent status. This proposed reformed protection procedure would provide a human rights compliant and long-term solution for new arrivals while at the same time addressing possible danger concerns or undeservingness they may present.

Considering the particularities associated with the situation of long settlers, however, it was noted that the proposed reformed international protection procedure and its associated statuses alone are not enough to regulate the situation of undesirable but unreturnable migrants, as they do not sufficiently address the situation of undesirable but unreturnable long settlers. Thus, the proposed reform of the international protection procedure should be accompanied by a set of provisions to safeguard long settlers. These include establishing clear thresholds to determine who is considered undesirable. These thresholds should be progressively higher according to the level of settlement in the host country. Even when such thresholds are met, migrants should not automatically lose their current status but, instead, different aspects should be taken into account to determine whether loss of status is warranted. Furthermore, when a long settler loses an existing status and applies for protection under the reformed international protection procedure, the conditions that are associated with their protection statuses should take into account their settlement and previous presence in the host country. In particular, the fact that they may already meet integration requirements and that they most likely can be held accountable for their acts by the national criminal justice system need to be properly reflected in the (lack of) conditions imposed.

CHAPTER 6

Concluding Remarks on the Challenges Associated with Regulating the Situation of Undesirable but Unreturnable Migrants in Compliance with Human Rights

Undesirable but unreturnable migrants are migrants who, due to their involvement in criminal acts or due to being seen as a threat to national security or public order, are usually denied the right to enter or stay in their host country but who, at the same time, would suffer irreparable harm if returned to their country of origin. Regulating the situation of these migrants is a challenge to States, which in recent years have pushed forward stricter migration policies aiming to keep undesirable migrants out of their territories, even if that meant disrespecting the concerned migrants' rights and thus putting States in violation of their human rights obligations.

Against this background, this book set out to analyse different solutions to regulate the situation of these migrants in literature and to study in practice how three States, namely Australia, Belgium and Canada, located in different continents and following different legal systems regulate the situation of undesirable but unreturnable migrants. When looking at who is considered an undesirable migrant in these countries, it was shown that while Australia and Canada have multiple provisions in their legislations listing the different situations that would lead to a migrant being considered undesirable, Belgian law limits itself to considering undesirable those who violate public order and national security. Public order and national security, however, are not defined in Belgian law, which limits migrant's possibilities of adapting their behaviour to ensure they are not seen as undesirable. This is somewhat remedied in Australia and Canada, as the laws in these States specify situations that would lead to a migrant being deemed undesirable. These include, for example, a criminal conviction of a certain duration as well as convictions for certain specified crimes. At the same time, however, Australia and Canada also contain provisions referring to national security, which, as in Belgium, carry a higher level of uncertainty.

Even in circumstances where the law prescribes a clear situation that would lead to a migrant being considered undesirable (such as a conviction of a certain duration), in all three States, decision-makers are asked not to con-

 | DOI:10.1163/9789004719910_008

sider a migrant undesirable in an automated way. This is because all three analysed States provide (either in law, jurisprudence or through government guidelines) that the undesirability of migrants needs to be balanced with other aspects that may favour their stay in the country. These aspects include, among others, the situation surrounding the commission of the crime and the migrant's settlement in the host country. As States' default response to undesirable migrants is return, this discretion given to decision-makers allows them to evaluate whether return would violate the concerned migrant's human rights and, if so, remediate this situation by not finding them undesirable (although this remains a discretionary power that will not always weigh in favour of the concerned migrant or guarantee a rights-based assessment).

Even when such discretion does not favour the continued stay of the concerned migrants, return may still be halted by human rights law. This is because the rights to life and to be free from torture are non-derogable rights that are associated with an obligation (known as non-refoulement) not to return someone to a place where these rights may be violated. Thus, these rights, when implicated, are likely to create an absolute bar to return. While under human rights law these rights will only prevent return, in refugee law, those who may suffer persecution upon return may have a right to be granted protection in the host country, including by obtaining a legal migration status. Refugee law, however, offers a more limited protection than human rights law in some ways as, first, it only protects those subjected to persecution for specific reasons; second, it provides an exception to the non-refoulement principle when a refugee is considered a threat to security; and, third, it excludes from refugee status those considered undeserving of it due to past (criminal) actions. At the same time, however, the Refugee Convention grants certain rights to those who are considered refugees, which may go beyond human rights obligations States have towards migrants.

Efforts to reconcile the different protections offered by refugee law and human rights law can be found at the regional and national levels. In the European Union (hereafter EU) context, protective status is granted not only to those who fall within the refugee definition in accordance with the Refugee Convention, but also to those who risk harm upon return due to human rights concerns that are not covered by that international instrument. This latter protective status, based on human rights non-refoulement obligations, is known as subsidiary protection in the EU. At the same time, the EU framework excludes those who are excluded from refugee status (in accordance with the Refugee Convention) from being granted subsidiary protection. Furthermore, in the EU framework, the exception to non-refoulement (provided in article 21 of the Qualification Directive) has lost most of its power when a decision of the Court of Justice of the European Union (hereafter CJEU) stated that, where returning a refugee would expose them to the risk of their fundamental rights being infringed, the EU member State concerned may not derogate from the principle of non-refoulement under Article 33(2) of the Geneva [Refugee] Convention.[1] Indeed, the upcoming Qualification Regulation, which will replace the current Directive, has removed such an exception from its text. At the same time, however, the EU framework allows EU member States to use the refugee law non-refoulement exception as an extra exclusion ground to deny refugee and subsidiary protection status. When asked whether this extra exclusion ground would make the EU framework incompatible with the Refugee Convention, the CJEU concluded that this was not the case, as the EU framework still grants greater protection than the Refugee Convention, since it does not allow EU member States to return someone in violation of (human rights) non-refoulement. In this regard, even though migrants falling under the EU framework exclusion clauses would not be granted protective status in EU member States, they would still be protected against return to harm. Implementation of this protection against (human rights) non-refoulement is overseen by the CJEU, as noted above, and by the European Court of Human Rights. The CJEU also noted that those who may be excluded from refugee status under the EU framework may still be considered refugees according to the Refugee Convention and thus may be entitled to the rights prescribed in that instrument.

At the national level, Belgium, as an EU member State, follows the above-mentioned EU framework. Australia and Canada, however, also extend (subsidiary or complementary) protection to those whose rights to life and to be free from torture would be at risk upon return. Despite this expansion of protection, all three analysed States also exclude from subsidiary or complementary protection those who are excluded from refugee protection. Furthermore, Belgium, following the EU framework, frames the refugee law non-refoulement exception as an extra exclusion clause for both refugee and subsidiary or complementary protection, and so does Australia. Thus, migrants may find themselves in a situation in which they are not entitled to a protection status, but also cannot be returned.

Some of the solutions that have been proposed to address this situation include obtaining diplomatic assurances to allow the safe return of these migrants despite initial human rights concerns; prosecuting migrants for crimes

1 Joined Cases C-391/16, C-77/17 and C-78/17 (Court of Justice of the European Union, 14 May 2019), para. 95.

committed before their arrival in the host country (for example, through universal jurisdiction); immigration detention; and limbo.

In practice, Chapters 2, 3 and 4 presented the solutions in place in Australia, Belgium and Canada. Surprisingly, despite the absolute character of the non-refoulement obligation, this analysis showed that all three States will return some undesirables to harm. Canada does so in accordance with national law, as its legislation includes a non-human rights compliant exception to non-refoulement. Australia and Belgium, in turn, do not allow a violation of non-refoulement in their legal framework but may do it in practice – Australia by putting undesirable but unreturnable migrants in a position in which they have to choose between indefinite detention and return to harm and Belgium by not properly assessing claims of harm.

When it comes to immigration detention, all three States make use of it, although to very different degrees. Belgium is the only State that puts a cap on the time a migrant can spend in detention and also considers detention to be without legal base when the concerned migrant cannot be returned due to human rights concerns. Australia and Canada, in turn, do not prescribe a maximum period of detention and may, in practice, keep migrants in indefinite detention, which is by default arbitrary.

Limbo is the most likely fate of undesirable but unreturnable migrants in Belgium, since they are unlikely to be granted a residence permit, but will also (in most cases) not be returned in violation of human rights. Limbo leaves migrants in a precarious situation as they do not have access to the rights that could ensure their livelihoods such as the right to work or to housing. Even though migrants in limbo are still entitled to certain rights that should ensure they have an adequate standard of living, in practice, they may not be able to enjoy them due to legal or practical barriers associated with their lack of status.

Lastly, all three analysed States allow the exceptional grant of visas or permits to unreturnable migrants. Members of government often have a discretionary power over the grant of such visas or permits, which usually limits their availability for undesirable migrants. In Canada, however, temporary permits can be granted to undesirable migrants although the practical application of such permits (presented in Chapter 4) showed some of the shortcomings of this measure.

Based on the lessons learned from the study of these three States, this book proposed a solution for States to regulate the situation of undesirable but unreturnable migrants in compliance with international human rights obligations. This proposed solution is the grant of limited residence statuses for these migrants through a reformed international protection procedure. In this reformed procedure, to ensure that all migrants who cannot be returned due to human rights concerns are allowed to remain in the host country, currently existing exclusion clauses could no longer serve to exclude undesirable but unreturnable migrants from being granted a protection status. Instead, exclusion clauses would act as limiting clauses, in that, instead of serving to deny status to undesirable migrants, they would serve to limit the status they get. In this regard, those who committed heinous acts in the past, but who no longer pose a threat to the host State would be subjected to integration measures that would allow them to overcome their undeservingness of a protection status. Those who are still considered to be at a high risk of offending, in turn, may have their freedoms restricted to limit their chances of engaging in criminal conduct. Despite the conditions imposed, migrants being granted status under such a reformed procedure would be entitled to certain rights, including, at a minimum, access to healthcare, social assistance to ensure their basic needs, the right to work and associated labour rights, as well as the right to benefit from social security contributions and, as a general rule, the civil and political rights prescribed in the International Covenant on Civil and Political Rights. Those who are considered dangerous but who still qualify as refugees in accordance with the Refugee Convention should be recognised as such and also be entitled to the rights prescribed in that instrument.

After a certain time and upon compliance with the imposed restrictions, undesirable but unreturnable migrants would have the conditions lifted and would be able to benefit from permanent status in their host country. This possibility seeks to prevent situations in which undesirable but unreturnable migrants spend several years under temporary permits with great restrictions attached to it, which may constitute a disproportionate interference with their rights, as may be the case of Mohamed Harkat in Canada.

While this reformed international protection procedure and associated statuses provide an important safety net to ensure all undesirable but unreturnable migrants obtain status and have their human rights respected, they do not address the situation of all undesirable but unreturnable migrants, particularly that of long settlers. Thus, it was also proposed in this book that such procedures and associated statuses be complemented by the enaction of safeguards aimed specifically at this last group of undesirable but unreturnable migrants. These include establishing clear thresholds to determine who is considered undesirable. These thresholds should be progressively higher according to the level of settlement in the host country. Even when such thresholds are met, migrants should not automatically lose their current status but, instead, different aspects should be taken into account to determine whether the loss of status is warranted. Furthermore, when a long settler loses an existing status and applies for protection under the reformed international protection procedure, the conditions associated with their protection statuses should take into account their settlement and previous presence in the host country.

As shown throughout this book, the fate of undesirable but unreturnable migrants is currently greatly dependent on decision-makers' discretion. This is because decision-makers are given discretion to decide who is undesirable (although the elements to be taken into account in such analysis may be set in law, jurisprudence or other binding guidance) and also to decide on whether undesirable but unreturnable migrants should be granted the right to stay in the host State's territory. As decision-makers are usually members of the government, these discretions may be influenced by politics and anti-migration discourse.

This is problematic as not only it creates great uncertainty for undesirable but unreturnable migrants but may also, in some cases, lead to a violation of their rights. This is because when these discretions do not favour them, they may either be sent back to harm, be kept in indefinite detention, left in a precarious limbo situation, or be subjected to great restrictions without a secure status.

The proposal of this book to grant all unreturnable migrants residence status is innovative in that it addresses some of these concerns. First of all, it removes some of the discretion given to decision-makers to decide on the fate of undesirable but unreturnable migrants as it obliges them to grant status to all those who cannot be returned due to non-refoulement. This gives migrants more certainty about their future in the host country and also prevents human rights violations. From a State's perspective, not violating a migrant's human rights is also in the State's interest in view of their international obligations. Furthermore, the limitations that can be imposed to the status given to such migrants can help mitigate any possible risk they may represent to the host country's society as well as ensure their status is not seen as a reward to 'lawbreakers'. Economically, it is also likely that allowing migrants to participate in society is more advantageous than keeping them in detention or limbo.[2]

2 For example, the Platform for International Cooperation on Undocumented Migrants (PICUM) noted, regarding regularisations, that "Governments and wider society benefit as inequality and social exclusion are reduced because people are better able to participate in all the economic, social, and cultural facets of the society they live in. Stronger and more durable connections between people and the government are built as people engage more with entities, organisations and bodies become more representative, and labour relation-

The enaction of safeguards to long settlers, in turn, limits the discretion given to decision-makers when deciding who is undesirable by establishing clearer and progressively higher thresholds that need to be followed to withdraw someone's right to stay, thus reducing the pool of undesirables in any given country.

---

ships are regularised. Countries' finances also benefit as people can start paying taxes" (Van der Vennet, L. (2022) Regularisation mechanisms and programmes: Why they matter and how to design them. PICUM, p. 6). Regarding detention, it was noted that, in Australia, "(...) mandatory detention costing on average $346,000 per person per year, compared to $10,221 per person per year for those living in the Australian community on bridging visas." (Asylum Seeker Resource Centre, Save the Children, Get up (2019) At what cost? The human and economic cost of Australia's offshore detention policies 2019, p. 8).

Bibliography

Legislation

International Treaties

UN General Assembly, Convention on the Prevention and Punishment of the Crime of Genocide, 9 December 1948, United Nations, Treaty Series, vol. 78, p. 277.

UN General Assembly, Convention Relating to the Status of Refugees, 28 July 1951, United Nations, Treaty Series, vol. 189, p. 137.

UN General Assembly, International Covenant on Civil and Political Rights, 16 December 1966, United Nations, Treaty Series, vol. 999, p. 171

UN General Assembly, International Covenant on Economic, Social and Cultural Rights, 16 December 1966, United Nations, Treaty Series, vol. 993, p. 3.

UN General Assembly, Convention Against Torture and Other Cruel, Inhuman or Degrading Treatment or Punishment, 10 December 1984, United Nations, Treaty Series, vol. 1465, p. 85.

European Union and Council of Europe Legislation

European Convention on Human Rights (1950)

European Social Charter (1961)

Charter of Fundamental Rights of the European Union (2000).

Council Directive 2001/55/EC of 20 July 2001 on minimum standards for giving temporary protection in the event of a mass influx of displaced persons and on measures promoting a balance of efforts between Member States in receiving such persons and bearing the consequences thereof.Council Directive 2004/83/EC of 29 April 2004 on minimum standards for the qualification and status of third country nationals or stateless persons as refugees or as persons who otherwise need international protection and the content of the protection granted.

Directive 2008/115/EC of the European Parliament and of the Council of 16 December 2008 on common standards and procedures in Member States for returning illegally staying third-country nationals.

Directive 2009/52/EC of the European Parliament and of the Council of 18 June 2009 providing for minimum standards on sanctions and measures against employers of illegally staying third-country nationals.

Directive 2011/95/EU of the European Parliament and of the Council of 13 December 2011 on standards for the qualification of third-country nationals or stateless persons as beneficiaries of international protection, for a uniform status for refugees or for persons eligible for subsidiary protection, and for the content of the protection granted.

Directive 2013/32/EU of the European Parliament and of the Council of 26 June 2013 on common procedures for granting and withdrawing international protection.

Consolidated versions of the Treaty on European Union and the Treaty on the Functioning of the European Union (2012).

Regulation (EU) 2016/399 of the European Parliament and of the Council of 9 March 2016 on a Union Code on the rules governing the movement of persons across borders (Schengen Borders Code).

Regulation (EU) 2024/1347 of the European Parliament and of the Council of 14 May 2024 on standards for the qualification of third-country nationals or stateless persons as beneficiaries of international protection, for a uniform status for refugees or for persons eligible for subsidiary protection and for the content of the protection granted, amending Council Directive 2003/109/EC and repealing Directive 2011/95/EU of the European Parliament and of the Council.

Regulation (EU) 2024/1348 of the European Parliament and of the Council of 14 May 2024 establishing a common procedure for international protection in the Union and repealing Directive 2013/32/EU

Australia

Migration Act 1958: https://www.legislation.gov.au/C1958A00062/latest/text.

Federal Court of Australia Act 1976: https://www.legislation.gov.au/C2004A01586/latest/text.

Migration and Maritime Powers Legislation Amendment (Resolving the Asylum Legacy Caseload) Act 2014: https://www.legislation.gov.au/C2014A00135/latest/text.

Migration Amendment (Clarifying International Obligations for Removal) Regulations 2021: https://www.legislation.gov.au/Details/F2021L01078.

Migration Amendment (Bridging Visa Conditions) Act 2023: https://www.legislation.gov.au/Details/C2023A00093.

Belgium

Lois coordonées du 12 janvier 1973 sur le Conseil d'État / Gecoördineerde wetten van 12 januari 1973 op de Raad van State: https://www.ejustice.just.fgov.be/cgi_loi/change_lg_2.pl?language=fr&nm=1973011250&la=F.

Loi organique du 8 juillet 1976 des centres publics d'action sociale: https://www.ejustice.just.fgov.be/cgi_loi/change_lg.pl?language=fr&la=F&cn=1976070837&table_name=loi.

Loi du 15 décembre 1980 sur l'accès au territoire, le séjour, l'établissement et l'éloignement des étrangers / Wet van 15 december 1980 betreffende de toegang tot het grondgebied, het verblijf, de vestiging en de verwijdering van vreemdelingen: https://www.ejustice.just.fgov.be/eli/loi/1980/12/15/1980121550/justel#LNK0005.

Arrêté royal du 8 octobre 1981 sur l'accès au territoire, le séjour, l'établissement et l'éloignement des étrangers / Koninklijk besluit van 8 oktober 1981 betreffende de toegang tot het grondgebied, het verblijf, de vestiging en de verwijdering van vreemdelingen: https://www.ejustice.just.fgov.be/cgi_loi/change_lg.pl?language=fr&la=F&cn=1981100831&table_name=loi.

Code de la nationalité belge / Wetboek van de Belgische nationaliteit (1984): https://www.ejustice.just.fgov.be/cgi_loi/change_lg.pl?language=fr&la=F&table_name=loi&cn=1984062835.

Loi du 22 décembre 1999 relative à la régularisation de séjour de certaines catégories d'étrangers séjournant sur le territoire du Royaume / Wet van 22 december 1999 betreffende de regularisatie van het verblijf van bepaalde categorieën van vreemdelingen verblijvend op het grondgebied van het Rijk: https://www.ejustice.just.fgov.be/cgi/article_body.pl?language=fr&caller=summary&pub_date=00-01-10&numac=1999000985.

Loi du 15 septembre 2006 modifiant la loi du 15 décembre 1980 sur l'accès au territoire, le séjour, l'établissement et l'éloignement des étrangers / Wet van 15 september 2006 tot wijziging van de wet van 15 december 1980 betreffende de toegang tot het grondgebied, het verblijf, de vestiging en de verwijdering van vreemdelingen: https://www.ejustice.just.fgov.be/cgi/article_body.pl?language=fr&caller=summary&pub_date=06-10-06&numac=2006000703.

Code pénal social / Sociaal Strafwetboek (2010): https://www.ejustice.just.fgov.be/cgi_loi/change_lg.pl?language=fr&la=F&cn=2010060607&table_name=loi.

Loi prévoyant des sanctions et des mesures à l'encontre des employeurs de ressortissants de pays tiers en séjour illegal / Wet tot vaststelling van sancties en maatregelen voor werkgevers van illegaal verblijvende onderdanen van derde landen (2013): https://www.ejustice.just.fgov.be/cgi_loi/change_lg.pl?language=fr&la=F&table_name=loi&cn=2013021113.

Loi du 24 février 2017 modifiant la loi du 15 décembre 1980 sur l'accès au territoire, le séjour, l'établissement et l'éloignement des étrangers afin de renforcer la protection de l'ordre public et de la sécurité nationale / Wet van 24 februari 2017 tot wijziging van de wet van 15 december 1980 betreffende de toegang tot het grondgebied, het verblijf, de vestiging en de verwijdering van vreemdelingen, met het doel de bescherming van de openbare orde en de nationale veiligheid te versterken: https://www.ejustice.just.fgov.be/cgi/article_body.pl?language=fr&caller=summary&pub_date=17-04-19&numac=2017011464.

Canada

Criminal Code (R.S.C., 1985, c. C-46): https://laws-lois.justice.gc.ca/eng/acts/c-46/index.html.

Supreme Court Act (R.S.C., 1985, c. s-26): https://laws-lois.justice.gc.ca/eng/acts/s-26/index.html.

Department of Citizenship and Immigration Act (S.C. 1994, c. 31): https://laws-lois.justice.gc.ca/eng/acts/C-29.4/page-1.html.

Immigration and Refugee Protection Act of 2001: https://laws.justice.gc.ca/eng/acts/i-2.5/.

Immigration and Refugee Protection Regulations (SOR/2002-227): https://laws-lois.justice.gc.ca/eng/regulations/sor-2002-227/.

Case Law (Organised Chronologically)

International Court of Justice

Questions relating to the obligation to prosecute or extradite (Belgium v. Senegal) (International Court of Justice, 20 July 2012)

European Court of Human Rights

Chahal v. United Kingdom, 22414/93 (European Court of Human Right, 15 November 1996).

Teshome Goraga Bonger v. the Netherlands, 10154/04 (European Court of Human Rights, 15 September 2005).

A. and others v. The United Kingdom, 3455/05 (European Court of Human Rights 19 February 2009).

M.S. v. Belgium, 50012/08 (European Court of Human Rights, 31 January 2012).

Ouabour v. Belgium, 26417/10 (European Court of Human Rights, 2 September 2015).

Paposhvili v. Belgium, 41738/10 (European Court of Human Rights, 13 December 2016).

Al Husin v. Bosnia and Herzegovina, 10112/16 (European Court of Human Rights, 25 June 2019).

Court of Justice of the European Union

Case C-146/14 (Court of Justice of the European Union, 5 June 2014).

Case C-562/13 (Court of Justice of the European Union, 18 December 2014).

Case C-373/13 (Court of Justice of the European Union, 24 June 2015).

Case C-713/17 (Court of Justice of the European Union, 21 November 2018).

Joined Cases C-391/16, C-77/17 and C-78/17 (Court of Justice of the European Union, 14 May 2019).

European Committee of Social Rights

International Federation of Human Rights Leagues (FIDH) v. France, Complaint No. 14/2003 (European Committee of Social Rights, 8 September 2004).

Defence for Children International (DCI) v. the Netherlands, Complaint No. 47/2008 (European Committee of Social Rights, 20 October 2009).

Defence for Children International (DCI) v. Belgium, Complaint No. 69/2011 (European Committee of Social Rights, 23 October 2012).

Conference of European Churches (CEC) v. the Netherlands, Complaint No. 90/2013 (European Committee of Social Rights, 1 July 2014).

Australia

Minister for Immigration and ethnic Affairs v Ah Hin Teoh, [1995] 183 CLR 273, (High Court of Australia, 7 April 1995).

Ayoub v Minister for Immigration and Border Protection, [2015] FCAFC 83 (Federal Court of Australia, 12 June 2015).

BCR16 v Minister for Immigration and Border Protection, [2016] FCA 965 (Federal Court of Australia, 17 August 2016).

Minister for Immigration and Border Protection v Le, [2016] FCAFC 120 (Federal Court of Australia, 9 September 2016).

DMH16 v Minister for Immigration and Border Protection, [2017] FCA 448 (Federal Court of Australia, 3 May 2017).

ALN17 v Minister for Immigration and Border Protection, [2017] FCA 726 (Federal Court of Australia, 5 June 2017).

BCR16 v Minister for Immigration and Border Protection, [2017] FCAFC 96 (Federal Court of Australia, 13 June 2017).

Steyn v Minister for Immigration and Border Protection, [2017] FCA 1131 (Federal Court of Australia, 25 September 2017).

BHA17 v Minister for Immigration and Border Protection, [2017] FCA 1288 (Federal Court of Australia, 7 November 2017).

Suleiman v Minister for Immigration and Border Protection, [2018] FCA 594 (Federal Court of Australia, 2 May 2018).

Minister for Immigration and Border Protection v BHA17, [2018] FCAFC 68 (Federal Court of Australia, 4 May 2018).

Ali v Minister for Immigration and Border Protection, [2018] FCA 650 (Federal Court of Australia, 10 May 2018).

Greene v Assistant Minister for Home Affairs, [2018] FCA 919 (Federal Court of Australia, 31 May 2018).

aqm18 v Minister for Immigration and Border Protection, [2018] FCA 944 (Federal Court of Australia, 21 June 2018).

Turay v Assistant Minister for Home Affairs, [2018] FCA 1487 (Federal Court of Australia, 3 October 2018).

DOB18 v Minister for Home Affairs, [2018] FCA 1523 (Federal Court of Australia, 17 October 2018).

FKP18 v Minister for Immigration and Border Protection, [2018] FCA 1555 (Federal Court of Australia, 18 October 2018).

Ibrahim v Minister for Home Affairs, [2018] FCA 1592 (Federal Court of Australia, 24 October 2018).

BKS18 v Minister for Home Affairs, [2018] FCA 1731 (Federal Court of Australia, 13 November 2018).

Sowa v Minister for Home Affairs, [2018] FCA 1999 (Federal Court of Australia, 14 December 2018).

AQM18 v Minister for Immigration and Border Protection, [2019] FCAFC 27 (Federal Court of Australia, 22 February 2019).

Ezegbe v Minister for Immigration and Border Protection, [2019] FCA 216 (Federal Court of Australia, 27 February 2019).

Hamidy v Minister for Immigration and Border Protection, [2019] FCA 221 (Federal Court of Australia, 27 February 2019).

Omar v Minister for Home Affairs, [2019] FCA 279 (Federal Court of Australia, 7 March 2019).

DOB18 v Minister for Home Affairs, [2019] FCAFC 63 (Federal Court of Australia, 18 April 2019).

Sowa v Minister for Home Affairs, [2019] FCAFC 111 (Federal Court of Australia, 28 June 2019).

Flores v Minister for Home Affairs, [2019] FCA 1043 (Federal Court of Australia, 5 July 2019).

GBV18 v Minister for Home Affairs, [2019] FCA 1132 (Federal Court of Australia, 29 July 2019).

FQM18 v Minister for Home Affairs, [2019] FCA 1263, (Federal Court of Australia, 14 August 2019).

CHJK v Minister for Home Affairs, [2019] FCA 1330 (Federal Court of Australia, 23 August 2019).

RZSN v Minister for Home Affairs, [2019] FCA 1731 (Federal Court of Australia, 24 October 2019).

Minister for Home Affairs v Omar, [2019] FCAFC 188 (Federal Court of Australia, 29 October 2019).

CWGF v Minister for Home Affairs, [2019] FCA 1802 (Federal Court of Australia, 7 November 2019).

EKC19 v Minister for Home Affairs, [2019] FCA 1823 (Federal Court of Australia, 8 November 2019).

DGI19 v Minister for Home Affairs, [2019] FCA 1867 (Federal Court of Australia, 14 November 2019).

FBW18 v Minister for Home Affairs, [2019] FCA 1878 (Federal Court of Australia, 15 November 2019).

Ali v Minister for Home Affairs, [2019] FCA 1900 (Federal Court of Australia, 18 November 2019).

DYY18 v Minister for Home Affairs, [2019] FCA 1901 (Federal Court of Australia, 18 November 2019).

CTB19 v Minister for Immigration, Citizenship, Migrant Services and Multicultural Affairs, [2019] FCA 2128 (Federal Court of Australia, 18 December 2019).

BAL19 v Minister for Home Affairs, [2019] FCA 2189 (Federal Court of Australia, 24 December 2019).

Hernandez v Minister for Home Affairs, [2020] FCA 415 (Federal Court of Australia, 31 March 2020).

Ahmed v Minister for Immigration, Citizenship and Multicultural Affairs, [2020] FCA 557 (Federal Court of Australia, 29 April 2020).

BFW20 by his Litigation Representative BFW20A v Minister for Immigration, Citizenship, Migrant Services and Multicultural Affairs, [2020] FCA 562 (Federal Court of Australia, 30 April 2020).

ERY19 v Minister for Immigration, Citizenship, Migrant Services and Multicultural Affairs, [2020] FCA 569 (Federal Court of Australia, 4 May 2020).

AEM20 v Minister for Home Affairs, [2020] FCA 623 (Federal Court of Australia, 12 May 2020).

CCF20 v Minister for Home Affairs, [2020] FCA 676 (Federal Court of Australia, 20 May 2020).

GCRM v Minister for Immigration, Citizenship, Migrant Services and Multicultural Affairs, [2020] FCA 678 (Federal Court of Australia, 20 May 2020).

BRO18 v Minister for Home Affairs, [2020] FCA 688 (Federal Court of Australia, 22 May 2020).

CMA19 v Minister for Home Affairs, [2020] FCA 736 (Federal Court of Australia, 29 May 2020).

DFTD v Minister for Home Affairs, [2020] FCA 859 (Federal Court of Australia, 23 June 2020).

KDSP v Minister for Immigration, Citizenship, Migrant Services and Multicultural Affairs, [2020] FCAFC 108 (Federal Court of Australia, 23 June 2020).

Ali v Minister for Home Affairs, [2020] FCAFC 109 (Federal Court of Australia, 29 June 2020).

MNLR v Minister of Home Affairs, [2020] FCA 948 (Federal Court of Australia, 8 July 2020).

DGP20 v Minister for Home Affairs, [2020] FCA 1055 (Federal Court of Australia, 24 July 2020).

WGKS v Minister for Immigration, Citizenship, Migrant Services and Multicultural Affairs, [2020] FCA 1060, (Federal Court of Australia, 24 July 2020).

KYMM v Minister for Immigration, Citizenship, Migrant Services and Multicultural Affairs, [2020] FCA 1069 (Federal Court of Australia, 28 July 2020).

FAK19 v Minister for Immigration, Citizenship, Migrant Services and Multicultural Affairs, [2020] FCA 1124 (Federal Court of Australia, 7 August 2020).

WKMZ v Minister for Home Affairs, [2020] FCA 1127, (Federal Court of Australia, 7 August 2020).

Uolilo v Minister for Home Affairs, [2020] FCA 1135 (Federal Court of Australia, 7 August 2020).

BPL20 v Minister for Home Affairs, [2020] FCA 1207 (Federal Court of Australia, 20 August 2020).

Guclukol v Minister for Home Affairs, [2020] FCAFC 148 (Federal Court of Australia, 4 September 2020).

AJL20 v Commonwealth of Australia, [2020] FCA 1305 (Federal Court of Australia, 11 September 2020).

CZW20 v Minister for Immigration, Citizenship, Migrant Services and Multicultural Affairs, [2020] FCA 1380 (Federal Court of Australia, 24 September 2020).

Minister for Immigration, Citizenship, Migrant Services and Multicultural Affairs v CTB19, [2020] FCAFC 166 (Federal Court of Australia, 1 October 2020).

DGPZ v Minister for Immigration, Citizenship, Migrant Services and Multicultural Affairs, [2020] FCA 1569 (Federal Court of Australia, 30 October 2020).

DFTD v Minister for Home Affairs, [2020] FCAFC 207 (Federal Court of Australia, 26 November 2020).

Commonwealth of Australia v AJL20, [2021] HCA 21 (High Court of Australia, 23 June 2021).

NZYQ v Minister for Immigration, Citizenship and Multicultural Affairs & Anor [2023] HCA Trans 154 (High Court of Australia, 8 November 2023) (hearing transcripts).

NZYQ v Minister for Immigration, Citizenship and Multicultural Affairs [2023] HCA 37 (High Court of Australia, 28 November 2023) (Court's reasons).

ASF17 v Commonwealth of Australia [2024] HCA 19 (High Court of Australia, 10 May 2024).

Belgium

Ordonnance° 10.993, (Conseil d'État, 5 January 2015).

Ordonnance n° 11.084, (Conseil d'État, 9 February 2015).

Arrêt n° 230.503, (Conseil d'État, 12 March 2015).

Arrêt n° 230.956, (Conseil d'État, 23 April 2015).

Ordonnance n° 11.515, (Conseil d'État, 3 September 2015).

Arrêt n 152 020, (Conseil du Contentieux des Etrangers, 9 September 2015).

Arrêt n 152 940, (Conseil du Contentieux des Etrangers, 21 September 2015).

Arrêt n 153 269, (Conseil du Contentieux des Etrangers, 24 September 2015).

Arrêt n° 232.397, (Conseil d'État, 1 October 2015).
Arrêt n 154 705, (Conseil du Contentieux des Etrangers, 16 October 2015).
Arrêt n° 232.858, (Conseil d'État, 10 November 2015).
Arrêt n° 232.859, (Conseil d'État, 10 November 2015).
Arrêt n 156 593, (Conseil du Contentieux des Etrangers, 18 November 2015).
Arrêt n° 232.949, (Conseil d'État, 19 November 2015).
Arrêt n 157 475, (Conseil du Contentieux des Etrangers, 30 November 2015).
Ordonnance n° 11.681, (Conseil d'État, 21 December 2015).
Arrêt n 159 074, (Conseil du Contentieux des Etrangers, 21 December 2015).
Arrêt n 159 138, (Conseil du Contentieux des Etrangers, 22 December 2015).
Arrêt n 159 147, (Conseil du Contentieux des Etrangers, 22 December 2015).
Arrêt n 159 164, (Conseil du Contentieux des Etrangers, 22 December 2015).
Arrêt n 159 337, (Conseil du Contentieux des Etrangers, 23 December 2015).
Ordonnance n° 11.805, (Conseil d'État, 17 February 2016).
Ordonnance n° 11.929, (Conseil d'État, 26 April 2016).
Arrêt n 173 880, (Conseil du Contentieux des Etrangers, 1 September 2016).
Arrêt n 174 351, (Conseil du Contentieux des Etrangers, 8 September 2016).
Arrêt n 174 380, (Conseil du Contentieux des Etrangers, 8 September 2016).
Arrêt n 176 498, (Conseil du Contentieux des Etrangers, 18 October 2016).
Arrêt n 176 961, (Conseil du Contentieux des Etrangers, 27 October 2016).
Arrêt n 177.002, (Conseil du Contentieux des Etrangers, 28 October 2016).
Arrêt n 177 215, (Conseil du Contentieux des Etrangers, 31 October 2016).
Arrêt n 177 216, (Conseil du Contentieux des Etrangers 31 October 2016).
Arrêt n 177 338, (Conseil du Contentieux des Etrangers, 4 November 2016).
Ordonnance n° 12.204, (Conseil d'État, 17 November 2016).
Arrêt n 178 845, (Conseil du Contentieux des Etrangers, 1 December 2016).
Arrêt n 178 846, (Conseil du Contentieux des Etrangers, 1 December 2016).
Arrêt n 178 953, (Conseil du Contentieux des Etrangers, 5 December 2016).
Arrêt n 179 112, (Conseil du Contentieux des Etrangers 9 December 2016).
Ordonnance n° 12.254, (Conseil d'État, 22 December 2016).
Ordonnance n° 12.333, (Conseil d'État, 3 March 2017).
Arrêt n° 238.210, (Conseil d'État, 16 May 2017).
Arrêt n 190 701, (Conseil du Contentieux des Etrangers, 18 August 2017).
Arrêt n 190 991, (Conseil du Contentieux des Etrangers, 29 August 2017).
Arrêt n° 239.259, (Conseil d'État, 28 September 2017).
Arrêt n 193 479, (Conseil du Contentieux des Etrangers, 12 October 2017).
Arrêt n 193 687, (Conseil du Contentieux des Etrangers, 13 October 2017).
Arrêt n 194 086, (Conseil du Contentieux des Etrangers, 24 October 2017).
Arrêt n 194 142, (Conseil du Contentieux des Etrangers, 24 October 2017).
Arrêt n 194 542, (Conseil du Contentieux des Etrangers, 30 October 2017).

Arrêt n 195 544, (Conseil du Contentieux des Etrangers, 24 November 2017).
Arrêt n 196 044, (Conseil du Contentieux des Etrangers, 1 December 2017).
Arrêt n 196 353 (Conseil du Contentieux des Étrangers, 8 December 2017).
Arrêt n 196 682, (Conseil du Contentieux des Etrangers, 15 December 2017).
Arrêt n 196 685, (Conseil du Contentieux des Etrangers, 15 December 2017).
Arrêt n 196 796, (Conseil du Contentieux des Etrangers, 18 December 2017).
Arrêt n 197 240, (Conseil du Contentieux des Etrangers, 22 December 2017).
Arrêt n 197 241, (Conseil du Contentieux des Etrangers, 22 December 2017).
Arrêt n 197 242, (Conseil du Contentieux des Etrangers, 22 December 2017).
Arrêt n 197 401, (Conseil du Contentieux des Etrangers, 30 December 2017).
Arrêt n 197 404, (Conseil du Contentieux des Etrangers, 30 December 2017).
Ordonnance n° 12.683, (Conseil d'État, 23 January 2018).
Arrêt n° 240.691, (Conseil d'État, 8 February 2018).
Arrêt n° 240.734, (Conseil d'État, 16 February 2018).
Arrêt n° 240.760, (Conseil d'État, 20 February 2018).
Arrêt n 204 589, (Conseil du Contentieux des Etrangers, 4 April 2018).
Arrêt n 203 271, (Conseil du Contentieux des Etrangers, 27 April 2018).
Arrêt n 204 346, (Conseil du Contentieux des Etrangers, 24 May 2018).
Arrêt n° 241.632, (Conseil d'État, 29 May 2018).
Arrêt n 204 588, (Conseil du Contentieux des Etrangers, 29 May 2018).
Arrêt n 204 605, (Conseil du Contentieux des Etrangers, 30 May 2018).
Arrêt n 204 797, (Conseil du Contentieux des Etrangers, 1 June 2018).
Ordonnance n° 12.882, p. 3 (Conseil d'État, 5 June 2018).
Arrêt n 204 918, (Conseil du Contentieux des Etrangers, 6 June 2018).
Arrêt n 204 919, (Conseil du Contentieux des Etrangers, 6 June 2018).
Arrêt n 205 094, (Conseil du Contentieux des Etrangers, 8 June 2018).
Arrêt n 205 280 (Conseil du Contentieux des Etrangers, 13 June 2018).
Arrêt n 205 297, (Conseil du Contentieux des Etrangers, 13 June 2018).
Arrêt n 204 798, (Conseil du Contentieux des Etrangers, 18 June 2018).
Arrêt n 205 434, (Conseil du Contentieux des Etrangers, 18 June 2018).
Arrêt n 205 737, (Conseil du Contentieux des Etrangers, 21 June 2018).
Ordonnance n° 12.926, (Conseil d'État, 12 July 2018).
Ordonnance n° 12.927, (Conseil d'État, 12 July 2018).
Arrêt n 207 579, (Conseil du Contentieux des Etrangers, 8 August 2018).
Arrêt n 207 878, (Conseil du Contentieux des Etranger, 20 August 2018).
Arrêt n 208 222, (Conseil du Contentieux des Etrangers, 27 August 2018).
Arrêt n 210 425, (Conseil du Contentieux des Etrangers, 2 October 2018).
Arrêt n° 242.627, (Conseil d'État, 11 October 2018).
Arrêt n 211 193, (Conseil du Contentieux des Etrangers, 18 October 2018).
Arrêt n 211 232, (Conseil du Contentieux des Etrangers, 18 October 2018).

Arrêt n 212 351, (Conseil du Contentieux des Etrangers, 15 November 2018).
Arrêt n 213 120 (Conseil du Contentieux des Etrangers, 29 November 2018).
Arrêt n 213 188, (Conseil du Contentieux des Etrangers, 29 November 2018).
Ordonnance nº 13.078, (Conseil d'État, 29 November 2018).
Arrêt n 213 378, (Conseil du Contentieux des Etrangers, 3 December 2018).
Arrêt n 243.152 (Conseil d'État, 6 December 2018).
Arrêt n 213 507, (Conseil du Contentieux des Etrangers, 6 December 2018).
Arrêt n 213 511, (Conseil du Contentieux des Etrangers, 6 December 2018).
Arrêt n 213 616, (Conseil du Contentieux des Etrangers, 6 December 2018).
Arrêt n 213 699, (Conseil du Contentieux des Etrangers, 10 December 2018).
Arrêt n 213 807, (Conseil du Contentieux des Etrangers, 13 December 2018).
Arrêt n 214 067, (Conseil du Contentieux des Etrangers, 14 December 2018).
Arrêt n 214 615, (Conseil du Contentieux des Etrangers, 24 December 2018).
Arrêt n 214 622, (Conseil du Contentieux des Etrangers, 26 December 2018).
Arrêt n 243.788, (Conseil d'État, 22 February 2019).
Arrêt n 222 085, (Conseil du Contentieux des Etrangers, 28 May 2019).
Arrêt n 222 108, (Conseil du Contentieux des Etrangers, 28 May 2019).
Arrêt n 222 419, (Conseil du Contentieux des Etrangers, 7 June 2019).
Arrêt n 222 425, (Conseil du Contentieux des Etrangers, 7 June 2019).
Arrêt n 222 630, (Conseil du Contentieux des Etrangers, 14 June 2019).
Arrêt n 223 833, (Conseil du Contentieux des Etrangers, 9 July 2019).
Arrêt n 223 863, (Conseil du Contentieux des Etrangers, 10 July 2019).
Arrêt n 223 931, (Conseil du Contentieux des Etrangers, 12 July 2019).
Arrêt n 224 331, (Conseil du Contentieux des Etrangers, 26 July 2019).
Arrêt n 224 927, (Conseil du Contentieux des Etrangers, 13 August 2019).
Arrêt n 226 101, (Conseil du Contentieux des Etrangers, 13 September 2019).
Arrêt n 228 708, (Conseil du Contentieux des Etrangers, 13 November 2019).
Arrêt n 229 831, (Conseil du Contentieux des Etrangers, 5 December 2019).
Arrêt n 229 938, (Conseil du Contentieux des Etrangers, 9 December 2019).
Arrêt n 230 558, (Conseil du Contentieux des Etrangers, 19 December 2019).
Arrêt n 230 778, (Conseil du Contentieux des Etrangers, 23 December 2019).
Arrêt n 233 525, (Conseil du Contentieux des Etrangers, 3 March 2020).
Arrêt n 245 068, (Conseil du Contentieux des Etrangers, 30 November 2020).
Arrêt n 246 394, (Conseil du Contentieux des Etrangers, 17 December 2020).

Canada

Aazamyar v. Canada, 2015 FC 99 (Federal Court, 26 January 2015).
Kanagendren v. Canada, 2015 FCA 86 (Federal Court of Appeal, 7 April 2015).
Jung v. Canada, 2015 FC 464 (Federal Court, 15 April 2015).
Torre v. Canada, 2015 FC 591 (Federal Court, 6 May 2015).

Balazuntharam v. Canada, 2015 FC 607 (Federal Court, 8 May 2015).
Go v. Canada, 2015 FC 635 (Federal Court, 14 May 2015).
Tabagua v. Canada, 2015 FC 709 (Federal Court, 4 June 2015).
Ahmed v. Canada, 2015 FC 876 (Federal Court, 17 July 2015).
Nguesso v. Canada, 2015 FC 879 (Federal Court, 17 July 2015).
Mohamed v. Canada, 2015 FC 1006 (Federal Court, 25 August 2015).
Ahmed v. Canada, 2015 FC 1024 (Federal Court, 28 August 2015).
Wafa v. Canada, 2015 FC 1153 (Federal Court, 9 October 2015).
Canada v. Tran, 2015 FCA 237 (Federal Court of Appeal, 30 October 2015).
B010 v. Canada, 2015 SCC 58 (Supreme Court of Canada, 27 November 2015).
Habibi v. Canada, 2016 FC 253 (Federal Court, 26 February 2016).
Mirza v. Canada, 2016 FC 510 (Federal Court, 6 May 2016).
Reynosa v. Canada, 2016 FC 1058 (Federal Court, 20 September 2016).
Bajraktari v. Canada, 2016 FC 1136 (Federal Court, 12 October 2016).
Canada v. Lunyamila, 2016 FC 1199 (Federal Court 27 October 2016).
Horvath v. Canada, 2016 FC 1261 (Federal Court, 14 November 2016).
A. B. v. Canada, 2016 FC 1385 (Federal Court, 16 December 2016).
Sharma v. Canada, 2016 FCA 319 (Federal Court of Appeal, 21 December 2016).
Suresh v. Canada, 2017 FC 28 (Federal Court, 10 January 2017).
Al Khayyat v. Canada, 2017 FC 175 (Federal Court, 13 February 2017).
Ali v. Canada, 2017 FC 182 (Federal Court, 14 February 2017).
S.A. v. Canada, 2017 FC 494 (Federal Court, 12 May 2017).
Ezici v. Canada, 2017 FC 512 (Federal Court, 18 May 2017).
Ramanathan v. Canada, 2017 FC 834 (Federal Court, 22 September 2017).
Oladele v. Canada, 2017 FC 851 (Federal Court, 25 September 2017).
Revell v. Canada, 2017 FC 905 (Federal Court, 12 October 2017).
Abdi v. Canada, 2017 FC 950 (Federal Court, 26 October 2017).
Odosashvili v. Canada, 2017 FC 958 (Federal Court, 26 October 2017).
Halilaj v. Canada, 2017 FC 1062 (Federal Court, 23 November 2017).
Barre v. Canada, 2017 FC 1091 (Federal Court, 1 December 2017).
Sivalingam v. Canada, 2017 FC 1185 (Federal Court, 21 December 2017).
Lunyamila v. Canada, 2018 FCA 22 (Federal Court of Appeal, 19 January 2018).
Harkat (Re), 2018 FC 62 (Federal Court, 23 January 2018).
Mansouri v. Canada, 2018 FC 144 (Federal Court, 7 February 2018).
Canada v. Lunyamila, 2018 FC 211 (Federal Court, 23 February 2018).
Ma v. Canada, 2018 FC 252 (Federal Court, 6 March 2018).
Nwobi v. Canada, 2018 FC 317 (Federal Court, 20 March 2018).
Sarwary v. Canada, 2018 FC 437 (Federal Court, 24 April 2018).
Ahmed v. Canada, 2018 FC 471 (Federal Court, 2 May 2018).
Canada v. Ali, 2018 FC 552 (Federal Court, 29 May 2018).

Murugamoorthy v. Canada, 2018 FC 650 (Federal Court, 21 June 2018).
Gurbuz v. Canada, 2018 FC 684 (Federal Court, 6 July 2018).
Baladie v. Canada, 2018 FC 706 (Federal Court, 9 July 2018).
Abdi v. Canada, 2018 FC 733 (Federal Court, 13 July 2018).
Shababy v. Canada, 2018 FC 810 (Federal Court, 1 August 2018).
Magsanoc v. Canada, 2018 FC 821 (Federal Court, 9 August 2018).
Ching v. Canada, 2018 FC 839 (Federal Court, 16 August 2018).
Alam v. Canada, 2018 FC 922 (Federal Court, 17 September 2018).
Bellevue v. Canada, 2018 FC 926 (Federal Court, 19 September 2018).
Aghayere v. Canada, 2018 FC 869 (Federal Court, 29 August 2018).
Revell v. Canada, 2019 FCA 262 (Federal Court of Appeal, 18 October 2019).
Rana v. Canada, 2018 FC 1080 (Federal Court, 29 October 2018).
Canada v. Aly, 2018 FC 1140 (Federal Court, 13 November 2018).
Tahhan v. Canada, 2018 FC 1279 (Federal Court, 18 December 2018).
Abbas v. Canada, 2019 FC 12 (Federal Court, 7 January 2019).
Yousif v. Canada, 2019 FC 128 (Federal Court, 30 January 2019).
Saleheen v. Canada, 2019 FC 145 (Federal Court, 5 February 2019).
Solmaz v. Canada, 2019 FC 736 (Federal Court, 24 May 2019).
Tapambwa v. Canada, 2019 FCA 34 (Federal Court of Appeal, 31 May 2019).
Ghirme v. Canada, 2019 FC 805 (Federal Court, 12 June 2019).
Kooner v. Canada, 2019 FC 806 (Federal Court, 12 June 2019).
Niyungeko v. Canada, 2019 FC 820 (Federal Court, 17 June 2019).
Makomena v. Canada, 2019 FC 894 (Federal Court, 5 July 2019).
Canada v. Hamdan, 2019 FC 1129 (Federal Court, 3 September 2019).
Canada v. Arook, 2019 FC 1130 (Federal Court, 3 September 2019).
Mason v. Canada, 2019 FC 1251 (Federal Court, 2 October 2019).
Canada v. Smith, 2019 FC 1454 (Federal Court, 19 November 2019).
A.B. v. Canada, 2020 FC 203 (Federal Court, 5 February 2020).
Hashi v. Canada, 2020 FC 309 (Federal Court, 26 February 2020).
Canada v. Taino, 2020 FC 427 (Federal Court, 25 March 2020).
Ahmed v. Canada, 2020 FC 507 (Federal Court, 9 April 2020).
Bellevue v. Canada, 2020 FC 560 (Federal Court, 28 April 2020).
McLeish v. Canada, 2020 FC 705 (Federal Court, 18 June 2020).
Harkat (Re), 2020 FC 715 (Federal Court, 19 June 2020).
Pascal v. Canada, 2020 FC 751 (Federal Court, 9 July 2020).
Brown v. Canada, 2020 FCA 130 (Federal Court of Appeal, 7 August 2020).
Randhawa v. Canada, 2020 FC 905 (Federal Court, 17 September 2020).
Zhang v. Canada, 2020 FC 927 (Federal Court, 24 September 2020).
Khudeish v. Canada, 2020 FC 1124 (Federal Court, 8 December 2020).

United Kingdom

Kardi, R (On the Application Of) v Secretary of State for the Home Department, [2014] EWCA Civ 934 (United Kingdom: Court of Appeal (England and Wales) 10 July 2014).

R (on the application of MS) v Secretary of State for the Home Department (excluded persons: Restrictive Leave policy) (IJR), [2015] UKUT 539 (Upper Tribunal – Immigration and Asylum Chamber, 22 September 2015).

UN Case Law (Organised Chronologically)

Communication No. 327/2007, CAT/C/47/D/327/2007 (Committee against Torture, 1 July 1996).

Communication No 39/1996, CAT/C/18/D/39/1996 (Committee Against Torture, 28 April 1997).

Communication No. 829/1998, CCPR/C/78/D/829/1998 (Human Rights Committee, 5 August 2002).

Communication No. 900/1999, CCPR/C/76/D/900/1999 (Human Rights Committee, 28 October 2002).

Communication No. 1051/2002, CCPR/C/80/D/1051/2002 (Human Rights Committee, 29 March 2004).

Communication No. 1011/2001, CCPR/C/81/D/1011/2001 (Human Rights Committee, 26 July 2004).

Communication No. 1222/2003, CCPR/C/82/D/1222/2003 (Human Rights Committee, 1 November 2004).

Communication No. 258/2004, CAT/C/35/D/258/2004 (Committee against Torture, 23 November 2005).

Communication No. 297/2006, CAT/C/39/D/297/2006 (Committee against Torture, 16 November 2007).

Communications Nos. 1461/2006, 1462/2006, 1476/2006 and 1477/2006, CCPR/C/93/D/1461,1462,1476 & 1477/2006 (Human Rights Committee, 16 July 2008).

Communication No. 1792/2008, CCPR/C/96/D/1792/2008 (Human Rights Committee, 28 July 2009).

Communication No. 1544/2007, CCPR/C/98/D/1544/2007 (Human Rights Committee, 18 March 2010).

Communication No. 1557/2007, CCPR/C/102/D/1557/2007 (Human Rights Committee, 18 July 2011).

Communication No. 1959/2010, CCPR/C/102/D/1959/2010 (Human Rights Committee, 21 July 2011).

Communication No. 2024/2011, CCPR/C/103/D/2024/2011 (Human Rights Committee, 31 October 2011).

Communication No. 343/2008, CAT/C/48/D/343/2008 (Committee against Torture, 18 May 2012).
Communication No. 370/2009, CAT/C/48/D/370/2009 (Committee against Torture, 21 May 2012).
Communication No. 2136/2012, CCPR/C/108/D/2136/2012 (Human Rights Committee, 25 July 2013).
Communication No. 2094/2011, CCPR/C/108/D/2094/2011 (Human Rights Committee, 26 July 2013).
Communication No. 2243/2013, CCPR/C/112/D/2243/2013 (Human Rights Committee, 24 October 2014).
Communication No. 1875/2009, CCPR/C/113/D/1875/2009 (Human Rights Committee, 26 March 2015).
Communication No. 1937/2010, CCPR/C/113/D/1937/2010 (Human Rights Committee, 26 March 2015).
Opinion No. 8/2015 concerning Sayed Abdellatif, Ms. A and their six children, whose names are known to the Working Group on Arbitrary Detention, A/HRC/WGAD/2015/8 (Working Group on Arbitrary Detention, 24 April 2015).
Communication No. 2060/2011, CCPR/C/116/D/2060/2011 (Human Rights Committee, 11 March 2016).
Communication No. 2233/2013, CCPR/C/116/D/2233/2013 (Human Rights Committee, 22 March 2016).
Communication No. 2229/2012, CCPR/C/116/D/2229/2012 (Human Rights Committee, 29 March 2016).
Communication No. 2387/2014, CCPR/C/117/D/2387/2014 (Human Rights Committee, 15 July 2016).
Opinion No. 28/2017 concerning Abdalrahman Hussein, A/HRC/WGAD/2017/28 (Working Group on Arbitrary Detention, 25 April 2017).
Opinion No. 42/2017 concerning Mohammad Naim Amiri, A/HRC/WGAD/2017/42 (Working Group on Arbitrary Detention, 21 August 2017).
Opinion No. 71/2017 concerning Said Imasi, A/HRC/WGAD/2017/71 (Working Group on Arbitrary Detention, 21 November 2017).
Communication No. 2264/2013, CCPR/C/122/D/2264/2013 (Human Rights Committee, 6 April 2018).
Opinion No. 21/2018 concerning Ghasem Hamedani, A/HRC/WGAD/2018/21 (Working Group on Arbitrary Detention, 20 April 2018).
Opinion No. 20/2018 concerning William Yekrop, A/HRC/WGAD/2018/20 (Working Group on Arbitrary Detention, 20 April 2018).
Communication No. 488/2012, CAT/C/63/D/488/2012 (Committee against Torture, 11 May 2018).

Communication No. 2371/2014, CCPR/C/123/D/2371/2014 (Human Rights Committee, 17 July 2018).

Communication No. 2348/2014, CCPR/C/123/D/2348/2014 (Human Rights Committee, 24 July 2018).

Opinion No. 50/2018 concerning Edris Cheraghi, A/HRC/WGAD/2018/50 (Working Group on Arbitrary Detention, 22 August 2018).

Communication No. 3041/2017, CCPR/C/125/D/3041/2017 (Human Rights Committee, 19 March 2019).

Opinion No. 7/2019 concerning Ebrahim Toure, A/HRC/WGAD/2019/7 (Working Group on Arbitrary Detention, 25 April 2019).

UN Documents (Organised Chronologically)

Human Rights Committee (1982). General comment No. 6: Article 6 (Right to life). Office of the High Commissioner for Human Rights.

Human Rights Committee (1988). General Comment No. 16: Article 17 (The right to respect of privacy, family, home and correspondence, and protection of honour and reputation). Office of the High Commissioner for Human Rights.

Human Rights Committee (1990). General comment No. 19: Article 23 (The family). Office of the High Commissioner for Human Rights.

Committee on Economic, Social and Cultural Rights (1990). General comment No. 3: The nature of States parties' obligations (art. 2, para. 1, of the Covenant). United Nations Economic and Social Council.

Committee on Economic, Social and Cultural Rights (1991). General comment No. 4: The right to adequate housing (art. 11 (1) of the Covenant) (E/1992/23). United Nations Economic and Social Council.

Human Rights Committee (1992). CCPR General Comment No. 20: Article 7 (Prohibition of Torture, or Other Cruel, Inhuman or Degrading Treatment or Punishment).

Committee on Economic, Social and Cultural Rights (2000). General Comment No. 14 (2000): The right to the highest attainable standard of health (article 12 of the International Covenant on Economic, Social and Cultural Rights) [E/C.12/2000/4].

UNHRC (2003). Guidelines on International Protection: "Internal Flight or Relocation Alternative" within the Context of Article 1A(2) of the 1951 Convention and/or 1967 Protocol relating to the Status of Refugees (HCR/GIP/03/04).

Human Rights Committee (2004). General Comment No. 31 [80] The Nature of the General Legal Obligation Imposed on States Parties to the Covenant (CCPR/C/21/Rev.1/Add. 13). Office of the High Commissioner for Human Rights.

Model Law on Extradition (2004), Chapter 2, Section 6: Torture, cruel, inhuman or degrading treatment or punishment. United Nations Office on Drugs and Crime.

Committee Against Torture (2005). Summary Record of the Public Part of the 652nd Meeting (CAT/C/SR.652).

Commission on Human Rights (2005). Protection of human rights and fundamental freedoms while countering terrorism (Human Rights Resolution 2005/80).

Committee Against Torture (2006). Consideration of Reports Submitted by States Parties under Article 19 of the Convention (CAT/C/FRA/CO/3).

Human Rights Committee (2006). Consideration of Reports Submitted by States Parties under Article 40 of the Covenant (CCPR/C/CAN/CO/5).

Committee on Economic, Social and Cultural Rights (2006). General comment No. 18: Article 6 of the International Covenant on Economic, Social and Cultural Rights (E/C.12/GC/18). United Nations Economic and Social Council.

UNHCR, Note on Diplomatic Assurances and International Refugee Protection (August 2006).

Committee Against Torture (2007). Consideration of Reports Submitted by States Parties under Article 19 of the Convention (CAT/C/NPL/CO/2).

International Law Commission (2013). Report of the working group on the obligation to extradite or prosecute (aut dedere aut judicare) (No. A/CN.4/L.829). United Nations.

Human Rights Committee (2014). General comment No. 35: Article 9 (Liberty and security of person) (CCPR/C/GC/35). Office of the High Commissioner for Human Rights.

Office of the High Commissioner for Human Rights (2014). The Economic, Social and Cultural Rights of Migrants in an Irregular Situation (HR/PUB/14/1). United Nations.

Human Rights Committee (2015). Concluding observations on the sixth periodic report of Canada (CCPR/C/CAN/CO/6). United Nations.

Emmerson, B. (2016). Report of the Special Rapporteur on the promotion and protection of human rights and fundamental freedoms while countering terrorism (No. A/71/384). United Nations.

Committee on Economic, Social and Cultural Rights (2016). General comment No. 23 (2016) on the right to just and favourable conditions of work (article 7 of the International Covenant on Economic, Social and Cultural Rights) [E/C.12/GC/23]. United Nations Economic and Social Council.

Human Rights Committee (2017). Concluding observations on the sixth periodic report of Australia (CCPR/C/AUS/CO/6). United Nations.

Committee on Economic, Social and Cultural Rights (2017). Duties of States towards refugees and migrants under the International Covenant on Economic, Social and Cultural Rights (E/C.12/2017/1). United Nations Economic and Social Council.

Committee against Torture (2018). General comment No. 4 (2017) on the implementation of article 3 of the Convention in the context of article 22 (CAT/C/GC/4). United Nations.

Human Rights Committee (2018). General comment No. 36 (2018) on article 6 of the International Covenant on Civil and Political Rights, on the right to life (CCPR/C/GC/36). Office of the High Commissioner for Human Rights.

UN Special Procedures (2018). Joint communication of Special Procedures ahead of the informal summit of EU heads of State or government in Salzburg (No. OL OTH 64/2018).

Committee against Torture (2018). Concluding observations on the seventh periodic report of Canada (CAT/C/CAN/CO/7). United Nations.

Human Rights Council (2018). Report of the Special Rapporteur on the human rights of migrants (A/HRC/38/41). United Nations

Human Rights Council (2018). Report of the Special Rapporteur on torture and other cruel, inhuman or degrading treatment or punishment (A/HRC/37/50). United Nations.

Report of the Special Rapporteur on the human rights of migrants (A/73/178/Rev.1) (2018). United Nations General Assembly.

Human Rights Committee (2019). Concluding observations on the sixth periodic report of Belgium (CCPR/C/BEL/CO6). United Nations.

UNHCR (2019). Handbook on Procedures and Criteria for Determining Refugee Status under the 1951 Convention and the 1967 Protocol relating to the Status of Refugees (HCR/1P/4/ENG/REV. 4).

Committee on Economic, Social and Cultural Rights (2020). Concluding observations on the fifth periodic report of Belgium (E/C.12/BEL/CO/5). United Nations Economic and Social Council.

Committee against Torture (2021). Observations finales concernant le quatrième rapport périodique de la Belgique (CAT/C/BEL/CO/4). United Nations.

EU Documents

Carrera, S., Vosyliute, L., Allsopp, J., Smialowski, S., & Sanchez, G. (2018). Fit for purpose? The Facilitation Directive and the criminalisation of humanitarian assistance to irregular migrants: 2018 update. European Parliament.

Council implementing decision (EU) 2022/382 of 4 March 2022 establishing the existence of a mass influx of displaced persons from Ukraine within the meaning of Article 5 of Directive 2001/55/EC, and having the effect of introducing temporary protection.

Return Handbook (Commission Recommendation (EU) 2017/2338). (2017). European Commission.

Academic Monographs

d'Appollonia, A. C. (2015). Migrant Mobilization and Securitization in the US and Europe – How Does It Feel to Be a Threat? Palgrave Macmillan.

Gosme, C. (2014). Limbo spaces between illegal and legal stay: Resulting from EU management of non-removable third country nationals (PhD thesis, Sciences Po).

Hathaway, J. C. (2021). The Rights of Refugees under International Law (2nd ed.). Cambridge University Press.

Pijnenburg, A. (2021). At the Frontiers of State Responsibility: Socio-economic Rights and Cooperation on Migration (1st ed.). Intersentia.

Rikhof, J. (2023). Exclusion and Refoulement: Criminality in International and Domestic Refugee Law. Irwin Law Inc.

Zago de Moraes, A. L. (2015). Crimigração: A Relação Entre Política Migratória e Polítical Criminal no Brasil (PhD Thesis, Pontifícia Universidade Católica – RS).

Chapters in Edited Volumes/Edited Volumes

Chetail, V. (2014). Are Refugee Rights Human Rights? An Unorthodox Questioning of the Relations between Refugee Law and Human Rights Law. In R. Rubio Marín, Human rights and immigration (pp. 19–72). Oxford University Press.

Chetail, V. (2021). Moving Towards an Integrated Approach of Refugee Law and Human Rights Law. In C. Costello, M. Foster, & J. McAdam (Eds.), The Oxford Handbook of International Refugee Law (1st ed., pp. 202–C11.P64). Oxford University Press.

Di Pascale, A. (2014). Italy and Unauthorized Migration: Between State Sovereignty and Human Rights Obligations. In R. Rubio Marín, Human rights and immigration (pp. 278–310). Oxford University Press.

Farcy, J.-B. (2020). Unremovability under the Return Directive: An Empty Protection? In M. Moraru, G. Cornelisse, & P. De Bruycker, Law and Judicial Dialogue on the Return of Irregular Migrants from the European Union (pp. 437–453). Hart Publishing

Gilbert, G. (2014). Exclusion under Article 1F since 2001: Two steps backwards, one step forward. In V. Chetail & C. Bauloz (Eds.), Research Handbook on International Law and Migration (pp. 519–540). Edward Elgar Publishing.

Hoecke, M. van (Ed.). (2011). Methodologies of legal research: which kind of method for what kind of discipline? Oxford; Portland, Or.

Mitsilegas, V. (2017). The Security Union as a paradigm of preventive justice: Challenges for citizenship, fundamental rights and the rule of law. In S. Carrera & V. Mitsilegas (Eds.), Constitutionalising the Security Union: Effectiveness, rule of law and rights in countering terrorism and crime (pp. 5–20). Centre for European Policy Studies (CEPS).

Perkowska, M. (2018). The Impact of the Migration Crisis on Polish Immigration and Criminal Law. In E. Kuzelewska, A. Weatherburn, & D. Kloza (Eds.), Irregular Migration as a Challenge for Democracy (Vol. 5, pp. 165–177). Intersentia.

Thym, D. (2014). Residence as De Facto Citizenship? Protection of Long-term Residence under Article 8 ECHR. In R. Rubio Marín, Human rights and immigration (pp. 106–144). Oxford University Press.

Top, S. (2018). The Collapse of the Political Offence Exemption in EU Extradition Law: The End of Political Asylum? In E. Kuzelewska, A. Weatherburn, & D. Kloza (Eds.), Irregular Migration as a Challenge for Democracy (Vol. 5, pp. 165–177). Intersentia.

van Ert, G. (2019). The Domestic Application of International Law in Canada. In C. A. Bradley (ed.), The Oxford Handbook of Comparative Foreign Relations Law (pp. 501–518). Oxford University Press.

Academic Articles

Alexy, R. (2003). Constitutional Rights, Balancing, and Rationality. Ratio Juris, 16(2), 131–140.

Baker, C. (2022). No Refuge for the Sick: How the EU's Health-Based Non-Refoulement Standard Compounds the Exclusionary Nature of International Refugee Law. Washington International Law Journal, 31(2), 251–291.

Bigo, D. (1998). Sécurité et immigration: Vers une gouvernementalité par linquiétude ? Cultures & conflits, 31–32, 1–19.

Bond, J. (2017). Unwanted but Unremovable: Canada's Treatment of "Criminal" Migrants Who Cannot be Removed. Refugee Survey Quarterly, 36(1), 168–186.

Bribosia, E., & Weyembergh, A. (1997). Extradition et asile: Vers un espace judiciaire européen ?. Revue belge de droit international, 1, 69–98.

Cantor, D. J., van Wijk, J., Singer, S., & Bolhuis, M. (2017). The Emperor's New Clothing: National Responses to "Undesirable and Unreturnable" Aliens under Asylum and Immigration Law. Refugee Survey Quarterly, 36(1), 1–8.

Chlebny, J. (2018). Public Order, National Security and the Rights of Third-Country Nationals in Immigration Cases. European Journal of Migration and Law, 20(2), 115–134.

Eckert, G. (2021). Caught in Limbo: The Precarious (legal) Situation of Non-removable Migrants Stranded in Europe. Journal of Immigration, Asylum and Nationality Law, 35(3), 252–277.

Farmer, A. (2008). Non-Refoulement and Jus Cogens: Limiting Anti-Terror Measures that Threaten Refugee Protection. Georgetown Immigration Law Journal, 23(1).

Gilbert, G. (2003). The protection of refugees in international law post September 11 2001. Yearbook of International Humanitarian Law, (6), 389–408.

Gilbert, G. (2017). Undesirable but Unreturnable Extradition and Other Forms of Rendition. Journal of International Criminal Justice, 15(1), 55–74.

Golder, B., & Williams, G. (2006). Balancing national security and human rights: Assessing the legal response of common law nations to the threat of terrorism. Journal of Comparative Policy Analysis: Research and Practice, 8(1), 43–62.

Hastie, B., & Crépeau, F. (2015). The Case for 'Firewall' Protections for Irregular Migrants: Safeguarding Fundamental Rights. European Journal of Migration and Law, 17(2–3), 157–183.

Hert, P. D. (2005). Balancing security and liberty within the European human rights framework. A critical reading of the Court's case law in the light of surveillance and criminal law enforcement strategies after 9/11. Utrecht Law Review, 1(1), 68–96.

Hiemstra, N. (2016). Deportation and detention: Interdisciplinary perspectives, multi-scalar approaches, and new methodological tools. Migration Studies, 4(3), 433–446.

Jasmontaite-Zaniewicz, L., & Zomignani Barboza, J. (2021). Disproportionate Surveillance: Technology-Assisted and Automated Decisions in Asylum Applications in the EU? International Journal of Refugee Law, 33(1), 89–110.

Juss, S. S. (2017). Detention and Delusion in Australia's Kafkaesque Refugee Law. Refugee Survey Quarterly, 36(1), 146-167.

Kelly, M. J. (2004). Aut Dedere Aut Judicare and the Death Penalty Extradition Prohibition. International Legal Theory, 10, 53–82.

Kidane, W. (2009). The Terrorism Bar to Asylum in Australia, Canada, the United Kingdom, and the United States: Transporting Best Practices. Fordham International Law Journal, 33(2), 300–371.

Klaassen, M. (2019). Between facts and norms: Testing compliance with Article 8 ECHR in immigration cases. Netherlands Quarterly of Human Rights, 37(2), 157–177.

Kodiyath, S. P., & Padathu Veettil, S. (2017). Invisible People: Suspected LTTE Members in the Special Refugee Camps of Tamil Nadu. Refugee Survey Quarterly, 36(1), 126–145.

Kraler, A. (2019). Regularization of Irregular Migrants and Social Policies: Comparative Perspectives. Journal of Immigrant & Refugee Studies, 17(1), 94–113.

Laidey, N. M. (2015). Privacy vs. National Security: Where Do We Draw the Line? International Journal of Social, Behavioral, Educational, Economic, Business and Industrial Engineering, 9(6), 2235–2238.

Lutz, F. (2018). Non-removable Returnees under Union Law: Status Quo and Possible Developments. European Journal of Migration and Law, 20(1), 28–52.

Macq, C. (2018). Le point sur le retrait du droit au séjour et l'éloignement pour motifs d'ordre public des étrangers en séjour legal. Revue du droit des étrangers, 198, 179–219.

McHarg, A. (1999). Reconciling Human Rights and the Public Interest: Conceptual Problems and Doctrinal Uncertainty in the Jurisprudence of the European Court of Human Rights. Modern Law Review, 62(5), 671–696.

Michaelsen, C. (2006). Balancing Civil Liberties against National Security – A Critique of Counterterrorism Rhetoric. UNSW Law Journal, 29(2), 1–21.

Moyo, M. P. (2015). Final Report on the Obligation to Extradite or Prosecute (Aut Dedere Aut Judicare). International Legal Materials, 54(4), 758–779.

Peers, S. (2015). Irregular Migrants: Can Humane Treatment be Balanced against Efficient Removal? European Journal of Migration and Law, 17(4), 289–304.

Peyronnet, C. (2017). Undesirable and Unreturnable Migrants under French Law: Between Legal Uncertainty and Legal Limbo. Refugee Survey Quarterly, 36(1), 35–60.

Rigotti, C., & Zomignani Barboza, J. (2021). Unfolding the case of returnees: How the European Union and its member States are addressing the return of foreign fighters and their families. International Review of the Red Cross, 103(916–917), 681–703.

Rikhof, J. (2017). Prosecuting Asylum Seekers Who cannot be Removed. Journal of International Criminal Justice, 15(1), 97–113.

Rimmer, S. H. (2009). Is Asio a Good Judge of Character? Alternative Law Journal, 34(2), 102–123.

Saad-Diniz, E. (2018). Crimmigration Law. International Journal of Refugee Law, 30(2), 401–403.

Salerno, M. E. (2017). Can diplomatic assurances, in their practical application, provide effective protection against the risk of torture and ill treatment? A focus on the evolution of the pragmatic approach of the European Court of Human Rights in removal cases of suspected terrorists. New Journal of European Criminal Law, 8(4), 453–475.

Simeon, J. C. (2015). The Application and Interpretation of International Humanitarian Law and International Criminal Law in the Exclusion of those Refugee Claimants who have Committed War Crimes and/or Crimes Against Humanity in Canada. International Journal of Refugee Law, 27(1), 75–106.

Singer, S. (2017). "Undesirable and Unreturnable" in the United Kingdom. Refugee Survey Quarterly, 36(1), 9–34.

Singer, S. (2018). National Security, Criminality and Exclusion from Refugee Protection under the EU Qualification Directive: Expanding the Grounds of Exclusion by the Back Door. Immigration, Asylum and Nationality Law, 32(3), 284–300.

Tsakyrakis, S. (2009). Proportionality: An assault on human rights? International Journal of Constitutional Law, 7(3), 468–493.
Thym, D. (2008). Respect for Private and Family Life Under Article 8 ECHR in Immigration Cases: A Human Right to Regularize Illegal Stay? International and Comparative Law Quarterly, 57(1), 87–112.
UNHCR (2018). Persons in need of international protection. International Journal of Refugee Law, 30(1), 134–139.
van der Sloot, B. (2016). The Practical and Theoretical Problems with 'Balancing': Delfi, Coty and the Redundancy of the Human Rights Framework. Maastricht Journal of European and Comparative Law, 23(3), 439–459.
Vavoula, N. (2021). Artificial Intelligence (AI) at Schengen Borders: Automated Processing, Algorithmic Profiling and Facial Recognition in the Era of Techno-Solutionism. European Journal of Migration and Law, 23(4), 457–484.

Reports, Working Papers, Guidelines and Policy Briefs

Administrative Appeals Tribunal, Guide to Refugee Law in Australia (2020), Chapter 1: Protection Visas.
Amnesty International (April 2017). Diplomatic Assurances Against Torture – Inherently Wrong, Inherently Unreliable.
Asylum Seeker Resource Centre, Save the Children, Get up (2019) At what cost? The human and economic cost of Australia's offshore detention policies 2019.
Australian Department of Home Affairs (2020), 2019 – 20 Migration Program Report: Program year to 30 June 2020.
Australian Department of Home Affairs and Australian Border Force (2020), Immigration Detention and Community Statistics Summary – 30 June 2020.
Australian Department of Home Affairs (2021), 2020 – 21 Migration Program Report: Program year to 30 June 2021.
Australian Department of Home Affairs and Australian Border Force (2021), Immigration Detention and Community Statistics Summary – 30 June 2021.
Australian Human Rights Commission (2013). Tell Me About: Refugees with Adverse Security Assessments.
Australian Human Rights Commission (2017). Asylum seekers, refugees and human rights – Snapshot report (2nd edition).
Australian Human Rights Commission (2020). Inspections of Australia's immigration detention facilities 2019 – Report – December 2020.
European Court of Human Rights (2025). Guide on Article 2 of the European Convention on Human Rights – Right to life.

European Court of Human Rights (2025) Guide on the case-law of the European Convention on Human Rights: Immigration.

European Union Agency for Fundamental Rights (2011). Fundamental rights of migrants in an irregular situation in the European Union.

Federal Institute for the protection and promotion of Human Rights (15 July 2021). Garantir les droits humains des personnes sans papiers.

Giuffré, M. (2015). Expelling Undesirable Foreigners: The Challenge of Human Rights. Centre of International Criminal Justice, Free University Amsterdam.

Hennessy, A. (9 November 2023) Landmark Australian Ruling Rejects Indefinite Immigration Detention: Longstanding Practice to Deter Asylum Seekers Found Unlawful. Human Rights Watch.

Larsaeus, N. (2006). The Use of Diplomatic Assurances in the Prevention of Prohibited Treatment. Refugee Studies Centre Working Paper No. 32. University of Oxford.

Levinson, A. (2005). The Regularisation of Unauthorized Migrants: Literature Survey and Country Case Studies. University of Oxford's Centre on Migration, Policy and Society (COMPAS).

Manieri, M. G., & LeVoy, M. (2015). PICUM Position Paper on the EU Return Directive.

Myria. (2020). Avis de Myria, le Centre fédéral Migration, sur la proposition de loi modifiant la loi du 15 décembre 1980 sur l'accès au territoire, le séjour, l'établissement et l'éloignement des étrangers, en vue d'y insérer des critères clairs, justes et précis de régularisation pour les personnes en situation de séjour irrégulier sur le territoire du Royaume et instituant une Commission indépendante de régularisation (DOC 55 1415/001).

Parliament of Australia, Chapter 6 – The Assessment Process.

Refugee Law Initiative, Arts & Humanities Research Council and Center for International Criminal Justice (2016). Undesirable and Unreturnable? Policy challenges around excluded asylum seekers and other migrants suspected of serious criminality who cannot be removed (Policy brief).

Reichel, D., Kraler, A., Dzhengozova, M., Wöger, A., Bonjour, S., Ruspini, P., Baldwin-Edwards, M., & Targonskiene, V. (2009). REGINE – Regularisations in Europe: Study on practices in the area of regularisation of illegally staying third- country nationals in the Member States of the EU (Ref. JLS/B4/2007/05). International Centre for Migration Policy Development.

Van der Vennet, L. (2022) Regularisation mechanisms and programmes: Why they matter and how to design them. Picum.

Newspaper Articles

Arratibel, A. J. (28 May 2023). Récit. "Les États-Unis sont ma patrie": ces vétérans de l'armée américaine renvoyés au Mexique. Courrier International. Available at: https://www.courrierinternational.com/long-format/recit-les-etats-unis-sont-ma-patrie-ces-veterans-de-l-armee-americaine-renvoyes-au-mexique.

BBC News (22 March 2016) Brussels attacks: Zaventem and Maelbeek bombs kill many. Available at: https://www.bbc.com/news/world-europe-35869254.

Doran, M. (22 November 2023) Emergency powers regarding people released from immigration facing High Court challenge, less than a week after passing parliament. ABC News. Available at: https://www.abc.net.au/news/2023-11-22/emergency-powers-immigration-detention-high-court-challenge/103139022.

Doran, M. (1 February 2024) Immigration detainees drop High Court challenges after ankle monitoring bracelets removed. ABC News. Available at: https://www.abc.net.au/news/2024-02-01/immigration-detainee-challenges-dropped-ankle-monitoring-lifted/103409080.

Karp, P. (8 November 2023) Indefinite immigration detention ruled unlawful in landmark Australian high court decision. The Guardian. Available at: https://www.theguardian.com/australia-news/2023/nov/08/australia-high-court-indefinite-detention-ruling-government.

Knaus, C. and Karp, P. (12 November 2023) Malaysian hitman released from Australian immigration detention after high court ruling. The Guardian. Available at: https://www.theguardian.com/australia-news/2023/nov/12/malaysian-hitman-released-from-australian-immigration-detention-after-high-court-ruling?CMP=Share_AndroidApp_Other.

Blogs and Other Online Sources

Adanan, A. (16 May 2019). Symposium on the Genocide Convention: Reflecting on the Genocide Convention at 70: How genocide became a crime subject to universal jurisdiction. EJIL: Talk! Available at: https://www.ejiltalk.org/symposium-on-the-genocide-convention-reflecting-on-the-genocide-convention-at-70-how-genocide-became-a-crime-subject-to-universal-jurisdiction/.

Andrew & Renata Kaldor Centre for International Refugee Law, Complementary protection decision. Available at: https://www.kaldorcentre.unsw.edu.au/publication/complementary-protection-decisions.

Australian Department of Home Affairs, Visa statistics, Visa cancellation. Available at: https://www.homeaffairs.gov.au/research-and-statistics/statistics/visa-statistics/visa-cancellation.

Australian Department of Home Affairs, Immigration and Citizenship, Status Resolution Service, Unique or exceptional circumstances. Available at: https://immi.homeaffairs.gov.au/what-we-do/status-resolution-service/ministerial-intervention.

Australian Department for Home Affairs, Check visa details and conditions, visa conditions. Available at: https://immi.homeaffairs.gov.au/visas/already-have-a-visa/check-visa-details-and-conditions/conditions-list.

Australian Human Rights Commission (24 April 2023), Immigration detention and human rights. Available at: https://humanrights.gov.au/our-work/asylum-seekers-and-refugees/projects/immigration-detention-and-human-rights.

Australian visa categories. Available at: https://immi.homeaffairs.gov.au/visas/getting-a-visa/visa-listing.

Canada Border Services Agency, ENF 5 Writing 44(1) Reports. Available at: https://www.canada.ca/content/dam/ircc/migration/ircc/english/resources/manuals/enf/enf05-eng.pdf.

Canada Border Services Agency, ENF 6 – Review of reports under subsection A44(2). Available at: https://www.canada.ca/content/dam/ircc/migration/ircc/english/resources/manuals/enf/enf06-eng.pdf.

European Commission against Racism and Intolerance (ECRI), ECRI Conclusions on the Implementation of the Recommendations in Respect of Belgium – Subject to Interim Follow-Up (2022). Available at: https://rm.coe.int/ecri-conclusions-on-the-implementation-of-the-recommendations-in-respe/1680a807d0.

Farcy, J.-B. (June 2019). Sécurité nationale et exclusion du statut de protection internationale: Vers une autonomie croissante du droit européen? Cahiers de l'EDEM Available at: https://cdn.uclouvain.be/groups/cms-editors-cedie/newsletter/Cahiers%20juin%202019.pdf.

Federal Court of Australia, Migration Guide: Migration Matters in the Federal Court. Available at: https://www.fedcourt.gov.au/law-and-practice/guides/migration.

Government of Canada, Pre-removal risk assessment: Who can apply. Available at: https://www.canada.ca/en/immigration-refugees-citizenship/services/refugees/protection/refusal-options/pre-removal-risk-assessment/eligibility.html.

Gregoire, P. (9 January 2021). Australia: The indefinite detention Achilles Heel: An interview with Human Rights for All director principal Alison Battisson. Mondaq. Available at: https://www.mondaq.com/australia/human-rights/1023966/the-indefinite-detention-achilles-heel-an-interview-with-human-rights-for-all-director-principal-alison-battisson.

Honnery, C. (29 April 2020). The confused construction of 'non-refoulement' in the Ministerial Directions for visa cancellations. AUSPUBLAW. Available at: https://

auspublaw.org/2020/04/the-confused-construction-of-non-refoulement-in-the-ministerial-directions-for-visa-cancellations/.

Human Rights for All, Our Stories. Available at: https://www.hr4a.com.au/services-4.

Human Rights Law Centre (17 November 2023), Summary: Migration Amendment (Bridging Visa Conditions) Bill 2023. Available at: https://www.hrlc.org.au/reports-news-commentary/2023/11/17/summary-migration-amendment-bridging-visa-conditions-bill-2023.

Human Rights Law Centre (10 May 2024) Explainer: High Court's decision in ASF17 v Commonwealth. Available at: https://www.hrlc.org.au/reports-news-commentary/2024/05/10/asf17-high-court.

Immigration and Refugee Board of Canada, Chairperson Guideline 2: Detention. Available at: https://irb.gc.ca/en/legal-policy/policies/Pages/GuideDir02.aspx.

Immigration, Refugees and Citizenship Canada, ENF 28 – Ministerial opinions on danger to the public, nature and severity of the acts committed and danger to the security of Canada. Available at: https://www.canada.ca/content/dam/ircc/migration/ircc/english/resources/manuals/enf/enf28-eng.pdf.

Inter-American Commission on Human Rights, Follow-up of the recommendations of the IACHR Report on asylum seekers in Canada (2000) (hearing), 7 September 2017. Available at: https://www.oas.org/en/iachr/sessions/hearings.asp?Country=CAN&Topic=0&Year=2017.

NANSEN (2021). CONTRIBUTION A LA RÉFLEXION 2021/2 – Pour un statut d'inéloignable. Available at: https://nansen-refugee.be/wp-content/uploads/2021/09/2.-Pour-un-statut-dinéloignable.pdf

Parliament of Australia (2021), Migration Amendment (Clarifying International Obligations for Removal) Bill 2021 – Revised Explanatory Memorandum. Available at: https://parlinfo.aph.gov.au/parlInfo/download/legislation/ems/r6696_ems_b5bd7c14-8a16-4782-8418-21f2a0c27b3d/upload_pdf/21040rem.pdf;fileType=application%2Fpdf#search=%22legislation/ems/r6696_ems_b5bd7c14-8a16-4782-8418-21f2a0c27b3d%22.

Parliamentary Assembly (2006). Human rights of irregular migrants (Resolution 1509 (2006)). Council of Europe. Available at: https://pace.coe.int/en/files/17456/html.

Pillai, S. (8 August 2021). AJL20 v Commonwealth: Non-refoulement, indefinite detention and the 'totally screwed.' Australian Public Law. Available at: https://auspublaw.org/2021/09/ajl20-v-commonwealth-non-refoulement-indefinite-detention-and-the-totally-screwed/.

Regularisation programmes for irregular migrants (Doc. 11350) (2007). Council of Europe (Parliamentary Assembly).

Right to Know, International Treaty Obligations Assessment (ITOA). Available at: https://www.righttoknow.org.au/request/international_treaty_obligations.

Singer, S. (14 March 2023). Undesirable but Unreturnable? Policy implications of the UK's Illegal Migration Bill. RLI Blog on Refugee Law and Forced Migration. Available at: https://rli.blogs.sas.ac.uk/2023/03/14/undesirable-but-unreturnable-policy-implications-of-the-uks-illegal-migration-bill/?utm_source=Refugee+Law+Initiative&utm_campaign=102cd30e2d-EMAIL_CAMPAIGN_2017_10_03_COPY_01&utm_medium=email&utm_term=0_304c0b75a9-102cd30e2d-581036941.

United Kingdom Home Office (2023). Restricted Leave (version 8.0). Available at: https://assets.publishing.service.gov.uk/government/uploads/system/uploads/attachment_data/file/1174252/Restricted_leave.pdf.

United Kingdom Home Office, Restricted leave: caseworker guidance. Available at: https://www.gov.uk/government/publications/restricted-leave-asylum-casework-instruction.

Wessels, J. (17 March 2023). Planned destitution as a policy tool to control migration in the EU: Socio-economic deprivation and international human rights law. EU Immigration and Asylum Law and Policy. Available at: https://eumigrationlawblog.eu/planned-destitution-as-a-policy-tool-to-control-migration-in-the-eu-socio-economic-deprivation-and-international-human-rights-law/.

Index

www.ingramcontent.com/pod-product-compliance
Lightning Source LLC
Chambersburg PA
CBHW051358240926
51852CB00001B/60
9789004719903